DIGITAL TRANSFORMATION SUCCESS

ACHIEVING ALIGNMENT AND DELIVERING RESULTS WITH THE PROCESS INVENTORY FRAMEWORK

Michael Schank

Digital Transformation Success: Achieving Alignment and Delivering Results with the Process Inventory Framework

Michael Schank
Cary, NC, USA

ISBN-13 (pbk): 978-1-4842-9815-2   ISBN-13 (electronic): 978-1-4842-9816-9
https://doi.org/10.1007/978-1-4842-9816-9

Managing Director, Apress Media LLC: Welmoed Spahr
Acquisitions Editor: James Robinson-Prior
Development Editor: James Markham
Coordinating Editor: Gryffin Winkler
Technical Reviewer: Brandon O'Grady

Cover designed by eStudioCalamar

Cover image by Isaac Soler at eStudioCalamar

Distributed to the book trade worldwide by Apress Media, LLC, 1 New York Plaza, New York, NY 10004, U.S.A. Phone 1-800-SPRINGER, fax (201) 348-4505, e-mail orders-ny@springer-sbm.com, or visit www.springeronline.com. Apress Media, LLC is a California LLC and the sole member (owner) is Springer Science + Business Media Finance Inc (SSBM Finance Inc). SSBM Finance Inc is a **Delaware** corporation.

For information on translations, please e-mail booktranslations@springernature.com; for reprint, paperback, or audio rights, please e-mail bookpermissions@springernature.com.

Apress titles may be purchased in bulk for academic, corporate, or promotional use. eBook versions and licenses are also available for most titles. For more information, reference our Print and eBook Bulk Sales web page at http://www.apress.com/bulk-sales.

Any source code or other supplementary material referenced by the author in this book is available to readers on GitHub (https://github.com/Apress). For more detailed information, please visit https://www.apress.com/gp/services/source-code.

Paper in this product is recyclable

This book is dedicated to the motivated, critically thinking, solution-oriented leaders who are at the forefront of transforming organizations. Your commitment to innovation and your relentless pursuit of excellence is an inspiration. You're no stranger to how well-designed transformation programs can be undermined by the complexities and competing agendas within your organization. You are not satisfied with the status quo, regularly challenge assumptions, and have a strong desire to deliver meaningful and long-term change that your organization needs. I hope you find this book valuable in your ongoing quest.

Contents

About the Author

Michael Schank is a founder and Managing Director at Process Inventory Advisors LLC. He has over 25 years of experience in the financial services industry, mainly as a management consultant advising clients on a range of topics, including technology, process, risk, and large-scale business and digital transformations. He has also held leadership roles with prominent banks.

After earning a BS degree in operations management and information systems at Northern Illinois University, he spent 13 years of his career at Accenture, focusing on technology and system integration programs. After a technology leadership role at Bank of America, he joined EY and shifted his focus to developing and applying process-driven frameworks to a large range of his financial services clients' transformation challenges. At EY, he established the first US Financial Services Process Excellence practice and has personally driven over $100 million in Process Excellence–related services and led delivery teams on many large and complex transformation programs. He subsequently joined Citi as the Head of Process Excellence for the US Personal Bank and instituted the Process Inventory framework as part of the program they set up in response to their 2020 Consent Order.

Beyond his professional achievements, Michael loves spending time with his teenage children and is an avid reader, runner, and traveler.

Introduction

Organizations face numerous challenges in the digital age and find themselves navigating a sea of frameworks and methodologies, each promising to address specific challenges. From Agile for driving change to Lean Six Sigma for process improvement and ITIL for managing IT operations, these approaches have merits and have been successful within their respective domains. However, as leaders in transformation well know, none of them are solutions to an enterprise-wide effort needed to transform an organization to maximize the business value of digital technologies and drive operational excellence.

The digital technology landscape is evolving at an unprecedented pace, a force that challenges established organizations to either adapt or face obsolescence. Adapting to this ever-shifting landscape often requires radical transformations in business models, customer engagement strategies, and core operational practices. The struggle becomes even more apparent for organizations that have grown complex and bureaucratic over time. This complexity hinders an organization's ability to adapt.

This urgency for change is driving the need for an approach that ensures all parts of an organization align seamlessly and work in harmony, delivering the efficiency necessary for organizational agility.

It is my belief that achieving thorough mastery of an organization's processes—by building and maintaining a comprehensive inventory of all processes—is the key to success in digital transformation efforts.

My journey, which spans over 25 years as a consultant and within large financial services organizations, has been one of continuous learning and discovery. Alongside incredibly talented colleagues and clients, I have encountered a diverse array of challenges across domains such as large-scale transformation, technology, risk, and business operations. Being naturally curious, I studied each deeply to understand the root challenges and to improve on the standard solutions that were generally accepted.

What became clear was the disconnect that exists across teams, frameworks, and deliverables. Knowledge in one domain was often underutilized or entirely isolated from other domains. For example, strategies conceived at the C-suite level remained disconnected from the realities of what teams were delivering on the ground level, the needs of customers became disconnected from the solutions that technology built, and risk management operated without a detailed understanding of how the business truly operated. These disconnections led to inefficiencies, giving rise to organizational silos, redundancies, exorbitant expenses, and other impediments to achieving organizational agility.

The disconnects and inefficiencies I observed motivated me to develop and test the Process Inventory framework across numerous financial services organizations. This framework acts as the connective tissue, bridging and addressing virtually all challenges an organization encounters. It serves as an index of organizational knowledge, empowering individuals to understand how their efforts directly support the business's goals.

In this book, I aim to educate you on why the Process Inventory framework is the key to transformational success and how to deliver transformational value from it. I cover the high-level vision for organization-wide transformation as well as low-level implementation details. It will delve into the following crucial aspects:

- **Frameworks and Models:** A comprehensive description of the Process Inventory framework and its constituent models, complete with detailed definitions and construction guidelines.

- **Best Practices:** Numerous best practices, spanning from building modeling standards to maintaining models effectively, engaging stakeholders, and maximizing the value derived from the models.

- **Methods:** Detailed methods for creating and maintaining Process Inventory and process models, alongside insights into leveraging the Process Inventory framework to transform how an organization operates.

- **Tooling and Data Infrastructure:** An exploration of the necessary tools and data infrastructure required to effectively manage and maintain the framework, including insights into leading platforms, key features, and data management routines.

- **Accountability Model:** A detailed operating model outlining the role played by a centralized process organization, known as the Process Center of Excellence (Process COE). Additionally, the model details the accountabilities of diverse stakeholders across various domains throughout the organization.

- **Case Studies:** A collection of case studies that serve as real-world evidence of the transformative power unlocked through the implementation of these methods.

This book is tailored for leaders who are driving organizational transformations, including those with titles such as chief transformation officer, chief operating officer, chief information officer, or any leader possessing the motivation and authority to shape their organization's approach to transformation. The success of this framework hinges on the presence of a senior-level champion who can drive its adoption.

Additionally, this book is an invaluable resource for teams tasked with implementing the framework, providing essential insights for members of a Process COE team and practitioners from various domains poised to leverage these models for their specific use cases.

The book has three parts, each building upon the preceding section:

Part 1—Foundations for Success

- **Chapter 1—The Key to Digital Transformation Success:** A deep dive into why understanding processes is the cornerstone of transformational success.

- **Chapter 2—Overview of the Process Inventory Framework:** Details of the Process Inventory framework, which integrates models with metadata to provide an exhaustive description of the operating environment.

- **Chapter 3—Defining the Digital Transformation Program:** A comprehensive guide to defining a digital transformation program, including key digital trends to consider when crafting a digital strategy.

Part 2—Applying Process Inventory to Transform Ways of Working

- **Chapter 4—Driving Operational Excellence:** An exploration of operational excellence—a broad term encompassing enterprise-wide efficiency across diverse domains and key operating metrics.

- **Chapter 5—Transforming the Change Process:** A demonstration of how the Process Inventory framework promotes tight alignment and effectiveness in driving change.

- **Chapter 6—The Technology Path to Digitization:** A spotlight on how this framework fosters a technical environment closely aligned with the business strategy and conducive to the adoption of digital technologies.

- **Chapter 7—Strengthening Risk Management:** An in-depth examination of how this framework enhances risk management and ensures compliance with laws and regulations.

Part 3—Implementing the Process Inventory Framework

- **Chapter 8—The Process Inventory Accountability Model:** An outline of the operating model and accountability framework essential for creating and maintaining the framework, along with insights into leveraging it to drive business value.

- **Chapter 9—Process Methods and Modeling Rules:** Detailed methods for creating Process Inventory and associated process models that adhere to high-quality standards.

- **Chapter 10—Modeling Platform and Data Infrastructure:** A comprehensive coverage of the platforms required to manage the models and metadata. This section covers select vendor platforms and their key features.

Join me on this journey as we dive into the potential of the Process Inventory framework, and I will empower you with the knowledge and tools needed to guide your organization toward lasting success in the digital era of constant change.

Foundations for Success

The Key to Digital Transformation Success

In the age of digitization, businesses face a critical imperative: to adapt and embrace innovation or risk being left behind in a rapidly evolving world.

The concept of creative destruction, which is the process where innovation and technology advancements are reshaping industries and business models, is the driving force behind digital transformations. In this chapter, you'll explore what digital transformation is and the state of digital transformation programs where unfortunately there is a high failure rate. Learn about the challenges of digital transformation and the key role strategic alignment plays in its success. Discover how process serves as a common language, aligning organizations vertically and horizontally, and explore the Process Inventory

© Michael Schank 2023
M. Schank, *Digital Transformation Success*,
https://doi.org/10.1007/978-1-4842-9816-9_1

framework's role in identifying, managing, and aligning processes. By the end of this chapter, you'll be equipped with an understanding of how Process Inventory not only enables digital transformation's success but also has the power to transform how the organization integrates technical capabilities, leads to operational excellence, streamlines the management of change, and enhances risk management capabilities.

Nokia's Mobile Phone Business

Founded in 1865 in Finland, Nokia initially focused on various industries, including pulp and paper, rubber, and electronics [1]. In the 1990s, Nokia made a strategic decision to shift its focus toward mobile phones. The company overtook Motorola in October 1998 to become the best-selling mobile phone brand in the world. Their net operating profits went from $1 billion in 1995 to almost $4 billion by 1999. A major reason for their success was catering to a youthful consumer market and fashion-oriented consumers with colorful and replaceable back covers. They were also innovators, introducing the first camera phone to the market in 2002 and pioneering mobile gaming with a preloaded version of Snake.

In 2007, Apple introduced the iPhone. By Q4 2007, half of all smartphones sold in the world were Nokias, while the iPhone market share was 5% [2].

The iPhone revolutionized the mobile industry with its touchscreen interface and robust app ecosystem. Nokia underestimated the impact of smartphones and the changing preferences of consumers. They continued to rely on their traditional strengths, such as hardware design and the Symbian operating system, while underestimating the importance of software and user experience. The Symbian platform quickly became outdated and posed difficulties for developers after the advent of iOS and Android. Nokia's market share dropped by 90%, and in 2013, their mobile phone business was acquired by Microsoft.

A study named "Distributed Attention and Shared Emotions in the Innovation Process: How Nokia Lost the Smartphone Battle" [3] was conducted, interviewing 76 of Nokia's top and middle managers, engineers, and external experts to determine the root causes. The study found that the downfall can be attributed to a lack of organizational alignment. It highlighted several factors, including a culture of fear, intimidated middle managers, a lack of technical competence among top managers, and a short-term focus on market demands. The internal politics and shared fear created a climate of mistrust that hindered innovation.

Creative Destruction in the Age of Digitization

The concept of creative destruction, introduced by Austrian American economist Joseph Schumpeter in 1942 [4], has impacted various companies, such as Nokia, Blockbuster Video, Kodak, Blackberry, and Toys 'R' Us to name a few. Creative destruction describes the process whereby innovation and technological advancements disrupt established industries and business models.

According to Schumpeter's theory, it is inherent in human nature to be creative and strive for an improved standard of living. Additionally, the pursuit of profit incentives drives constant innovation and technological advancements [5]. In a competitive environment, producers generate ideas that advance technologies, redesign existing products and processes, and introduce new products. This competition results in improved products at lower costs, ultimately benefiting consumers.

This continuous process of innovation and economic competition contributes to overall economic growth and enhances the standard of living for consumers. However, it also poses a significant risk to incumbent organizations that fail to adapt as they can be displaced or even eliminated by more innovative competitors. This is driving the urgency in many organizations to invest in their own digital transformation program.

Digital Transformation Defined

Digital transformation is the application of digital capabilities to processes, products, and assets to improve efficiency, enhance customer value, manage risk, and uncover new monetization opportunities [6]. There are many digital capabilities driving this, such as artificial intelligence, cloud computing, Internet of Things (IoT), big data analytics, blockchain, and more. This goes beyond simply acquiring these new technologies and teaching your staff to use them.

Digital transformation must be framed in a business context, which is why the preceding definition includes "uncover new monetization opportunities." Monetization opportunities may mean new product revenue streams, deepening customer relationships, expanding to new ones, or reducing the cost of doing business. The implications of maximizing these capabilities for an organization can be far-reaching and may fundamentally change core business models.

The essence of digital transformation lies in becoming a customer-centric, data-driven, and agile organization. It entails ensuring that key decisions, actions, and processes are guided by data-driven insights rather than just human intuition [7].

The challenge, and opportunity, is that the capabilities of these technologies are advancing at a rapid rate, making it hard to accurately predict how they will impact businesses in the next five years or beyond. The external environment must also be factored in, such as changes to the competitive landscape, customer preferences, globalization, and regulatory environment.

This means that digital transformation must be viewed as a continuous journey, requiring a strong digital strategy and adaptive execution to respond to changes through iterations and continuous learning. A crucial factor in being adaptive is achieving operational excellence, which involves optimizing and maximizing efficiency across all resources leveraged to operate your business. By embracing operational excellence, organizations ensure their flexibility and responsiveness in the face of advancing digital capabilities and evolving external environments.

State of Digital Transformation

According to a study, digital companies achieve 1.8 times higher [8] earnings growth. Technology advancements mean that digital companies have greater productivity improvements, better customer experiences, and stronger innovation. The global digital transformation market is projected to grow from $695.5 billion in 2023 to over $3.14 trillion by 2030, at a compound annual growth rate (CAGR) of 24.1% during this period [9]. About 89% [10] of enterprises are planning to adopt or have already adopted a digital business strategy.

Shockingly, 70% of such initiatives have been found to fail to reach their goals [8]. This represents a massive investment with a very high failure rate. The implication is more than just lost investment; it also means frustrated stakeholders, lost ground to competitors, unsatisfied customers, and in some cases, costs such as high regulatory penalties.

Why Digital Transformations Fail

According to McKinsey [11], the reasons transformations fail are as follows:

- **Lack of Aspiration**: The CEO fails to set a sufficiently high aspiration. People throughout the organization do not buy in, and they lack the motivation to invest extra energy in making the change happen.

- **Lack of a Shared Vision**: During the early stages of the transformation, the CEO does not build conviction within the team about the importance of the change or craft a change narrative that convinces people they need to drive the transformation.

- **Lack of Engagement**: People throughout the organization do not buy in, resulting in a lack of willingness to invest the extra energy required to drive the transformation.

- **Low Investment in Capability Building**: The leadership team neglects to address skill gaps within the organization or fails to free up key resources from their other day-to-day responsibilities.

- **Insufficient Structure of the Transformation Team**: The organization fails to establish the right change management structure and cadence for leadership and transformation management oversight.

For many medium and large organizations, these can be challenging hurdles to overcome due to their complexity. With organizations that have tens or hundreds of thousands of employees, it becomes an immense challenge to align and coordinate all those resources, especially when the transformation goals are ambitious. However, complexity alone cannot be solely blamed as there are many digitally successful organizations that effectively manage complexity.

The underlying root cause of these challenges is a lack of **strategic alignment**. Strategic alignment means that all elements of a business, including market strategy and the way the company is organized, are arranged in such a way as to best support the fulfillment of its long-term purpose [12]. This means aligning the purpose, vision, and mission statements, which articulate why the organization exists and the future they are driving toward, with strategy, which is how the business will achieve that purpose. Strategy defines which products and services to offer, which markets to serve, and in this context, how they will adopt digital technology to further support the purpose of the organization. Strategy needs to be aligned with the capabilities of the organization, which are all resources including people, processes, technology, data, vendors, etc. that support the organization. An example is an organization that is looking to achieve superior customer service must translate that into a high level of excellence when frontline staff are engaging with customers directly.

There are two important aspects of strategic alignment: vertical alignment and horizontal alignment. Vertical alignment refers to aligning strategies, goals, and performance metrics hierarchically from the CEO through middle management down to the single contributors. Horizontal alignment means that business units and functional areas such as technology, finance, and risk collaborate strongly across these areas and avoid siloed operating models, which bring a great number of inefficiencies. Achieving strategic alignment facilitates unification across resources which not only enables an organization to meet their digital transformation goals but enables organizational agility.

But how do organizations achieve strategic alignment? After all, this is not a new concept, yet it exists in so few organizations. I believe the answer lies in language. Everyone in these organizations is focused on their responsibilities, and they develop their perspectives based on their work. This often results in lower-level contributors not fully understanding the strategic messages coming from the CEO. As a result, they may fail to invest their energies in contributing to the transformational ambitions of leadership. When a person from a business unit conveys requirements to a technology professional, they may struggle to accurately communicate what they are looking for, leading to poor requirements, or delivered software that misses the mark. This lack of understanding and effective collaboration contributes to the formation of redundancies within organizations, where different functional units create processes that others already perform.

A common language should create a shared understanding vertically and horizontally. It would align objectives, facilitate better communications, bridge cultural differences, and enable conflict resolution. What are the requirements of this common language? First, since it must support the purpose of the organization, it has to be oriented in the language of the business. This eliminates, for instance, technical terminology, you wouldn't want to state as a strategy that you're going to implement artificial intelligence unless you could convey how it supports your customers, generates revenues, or furthers the mission. But it does have to be a bridge to cross-functional topics such as technology, risk, data, and regulators. Lastly, it needs to connect a high-level view that senior leadership would understand to a low-level view that a single contributor would understand.

Process Is the Common Language

The only candidate that meets those requirements is process. I'll illustrate this in a story that highlights how organizations evolve with process at its core.

Let's say that you are talking to a couple of friends about starting a business. That conversation begins with the actions or processes that must occur. The conversation would go something like this: "We can create great designs, print them on t-shirts, and sell them at concerts." The purpose of the company will be to make money or get a message out, but in that statement, the business processes have been identified:

- Create designs
- Print design on T-shirts
- Sell at concerts

Let's say that this company has success. Then they realize that they will have to file taxes, but none of them have the skill set or the time, so they hire someone for that purpose and have now added the process of

- Calculate tax liabilities
- File taxes
- Pay tax liabilities

This means that they've now expanded the organization chart to support the need to do taxes. Then they purchase tax software for them which is the beginning of their technology portfolio. The business is doing so well that you seek out investors, but investors will want financial reports that are based on solid accounting standards, which leads to them hire an accountant to perform the following processes:

- Close books
- Create financial report

This accountant will require accounting software. Now they've started a finance functional unit which has tax and accounting processes, an organization chart, and a technology portfolio.

I can go on, but what you can see is that the needs of the organization to support its purpose drive the need for processes. Process is core to organizational capabilities as people are hired, technology is purchased or built, and risk is incurred, all to support the processes of the business. Plus, a hierarchy of processes evolves as processes get more complex and lower-level resources are hired to perform more detailed tasks.

The Process Inventory Framework

The Process Inventory is a framework for capturing every process within an organization and a methodology for managing this information sustainably over time. One of the guiding principles for Process Inventory is that it must be a complete representation of processes for the organization in scope. To accomplish this, interviews must be conducted following the organizational chart since that represents a complete inventory of people in the organization.

These interviews start at the top of the organizational chart, working down from business units or functional levels to the team or individual contributor level. Stakeholders are requested to provide formal attestations to ensure completeness and accuracy in the inventory, including any process inventories collected by their teams.

Starting from the top of the organizational chart enables vertical alignment, allowing for a direct trace of process ownership from the CEO to individual contributors at all levels.

Organizations often have multiple sources of information that describe various aspects of their operations, such as application repositories, risk repositories, product, and channel repositories, and more. However, this data is usually managed in silos and lacks concrete associations across topics, hindering horizontal alignment.

The Process Inventory framework establishes a taxonomy that classifies all processes executed to support the organization's purpose. This taxonomy serves as an index for aligning different aspects of the organization through a single business-oriented language. A modeling team can extract information from these repositories and create associations, at the process name level or through creating process models, where operational information intersects with processes.

This achieves horizontal alignment in three ways. Firstly, it enables functional teams to precisely identify how their concepts intersect with processes. For example, by examining the intersection of applications in an application repository with processes, it becomes possible to determine which applications support specific processes and even drill down to the level of identifying which APIs within those applications support specific steps in a process. This is valuable in identifying the scope and requirements for change management initiatives. Secondly, it provides transparency to all stakeholders regarding the activities of each business unit and functional team. This transparency helps break down silos and facilitates better coordination. Lastly, it promotes a culture of accountability by identifying points of ownership and fostering strong collaboration across organizational units where necessary.

This framework is analogous to Google Maps, where you can view Earth from space, but then you can zoom in to see details of your house and the signs on your street. Google's initiative called Ground Truth [13] marries numerous data sets about our world, such as traffic patterns, restaurant ratings, and street view images to physical locations. This has revolutionized not only navigation but also how we interact in the world and how advertisers reach us.

The Digital Transformation Journey

In a digital transformation, this common language enables the leadership team to articulate their aspirations for a digital future, and the transformation teams can identify specific processes that need to change or processes to be added. The shared vision can be cascaded throughout the organization, clearly defining responsibilities and performance metrics to drive the transformation. This culture of accountability will foster engagement as everyone will understand how their work directly contributes to the bigger picture. Essentially, this enables solutions to the typical failures encountered in digital transformations.

In this book, I will extensively detail the constructs of this framework, including the operating model and the methods to create and maintain the process inventory and associated metadata sourced from various repositories.

I will cover the method of defining a digital strategy and how to set up the transformation program for success. The core of this process involves defining the digital transformation strategy in the context of how it supports the organization's purpose and aligns with operational capabilities. This encompasses defining the business areas and use cases that need improvement, along with the ways of working. I provide details on how the Process Inventory framework can transform these use cases.

A significant aspect of adapting to the digital age is integrating new **technology** capabilities. Technology is typically one of the largest investments an organization makes and can be a source of pain, especially when the technical architecture becomes rigid. I will detail how this framework can lead to much better IT architecture documentation, creating alignment between IT assets and the processes they serve. This visibility can help rationalize complexity by eliminating redundant systems and increasing reuse, which is key to flexibility and efficiency. Additionally, I will demonstrate how this directly supports the design and implementation of digital technologies such as intelligent process automation, the adoption of artificial intelligence and machine learning at scale, and how to build a business-led modular architecture design, which is crucial for an agile architecture.

Operational excellence is achieved with this level of transparency at your fingertips. You can precisely identify all the resources that support a business or process area, enabling the identification of inefficiencies or opportunities to streamline operations. Continuous improvement will be promoted by a framework that enables better monitoring of business processes and the collection of key performance indicators.

Workforces will be transformed by having greater training and development programs to equip staff members with skills and knowledge, not only in their domain but also with a broader understanding. This will foster a culture of innovation by unlocking knowledge that was held by so few and encouraging everyone to identify better ways of doing things.

Change management is a significant challenge for many organizations, particularly in large change efforts. This framework has the potential to greatly transform the entire process. The alignment of strategic priorities can be mapped to the impacted processes. This clarity brings more objectivity to the change portfolio investment process, resulting in stronger effectiveness in the allocation of discretionary funds to projects with the greatest strategic needs.

Project scope can be stated in terms of the business processes involved. This approach ensures certainty of impacts across all resources leveraged by the business process, including people, processes, controls, data, and technology. The result is enhanced cost and timeline estimates and better resource alignment.

The change process would undergo significant changes by anchoring it to this framework. Framing the contents of SDLC, Agile, and organizational change management deliverables, such as business requirements, agile user stories, technology designs, control designs, testing scripts, and user training, using the Process Inventory taxonomy as the structure will increase coordination across teams and enhance traceability for those responsible for project management in these efforts. This also has the benefit of generating better change status reports by communicating the progress and readiness of individual processes as the numerator for percent complete reporting.

The efficiencies provided by this framework will enable faster change implementation with reduced investment needs, thereby freeing up resources to concentrate on enhancing customer experience and driving product innovations.

Risk management is strengthened by giving risk professionals a comprehensive inventory of processes, which will enable them to perform better risk assessments and create a more accurate inventory of risks across all risk types. This allows them, in conjunction with their business partners, to prioritize and design effective controls and ensure regulatory compliance. The risk operating model will be empowered across all three lines of defense for stronger effectiveness and coordination such as arming internal audit with information needed to effectively test controls. This will give senior leaders and boards confidence that they are getting accurate risk information to make their strategic decisions.

Framework Implementation Considerations

This may seem overwhelming, but I assure you it's not. I have dedicated 12 years of my career to developing and testing this framework in various scenarios. I have successfully implemented it at multiple large financial institutions, tailoring it to their specific needs. I have refined the methods to be efficient with limited resources and to ensure the quality of the models, which forms the basis for all the benefits I have presented.

The framework is designed to be incremental and scalable according to your requirements as defined by your transformation strategy. It can be applied at the enterprise level or selectively to specific business units or functions. You have the flexibility to implement only the use cases that are relevant to your organization.

Indeed, adopting this framework requires an investment of time and resources. However, it's important to recognize that organizations pay a price for misalignment. You have a choice: invest upfront to avoid inefficiencies, costly penalties, or losing market share to more digitally adept competitors, or bear the consequences later.

Key Takeaways

- **Creative destruction** is driving the digital age through innovation and technological advancements which are reshaping business models and industries.

- **Digital transformation** is the application of digital capabilities to processes, products, and assets to improve efficiency, enhance customer value, manage risk, and uncover new monetization opportunities.

- **High failure rate** as 70% of such initiatives fail to reach their goals, which means lost investment, frustrated stakeholders, lost ground to competitors, unsatisfied customers, and potentially high regulatory penalties.

- **Lack of strategic alignment** is the underlying root cause of failure which hinders collaboration and organizational focus toward strategic goals.

- **A common language** is needed to facilitate alignment. Process, as captured by the Process Inventory framework, provides the common language.

- **Process Inventory** enables digital transformation success and transforms how the organization operates which leads to operational excellence.

In the next chapter, we will describe the Process Inventory framework, which includes models, modeling characteristics, metadata, and conceptual architecture.

Overview of the Process Inventory Framework

In this chapter, you will explore the components of the Process Inventory framework. Delve into the significance of this framework in establishing an ontology to organize organizational knowledge. Understand the methods for constructing and maintaining a Process Inventory, and explore the conceptual architecture used to integrate metadata from diverse authoritative sources. Additionally, you'll gain insights into related models, such as process models, customer journeys, and value streams. The framework, with all its associated components, is critical for structuring and utilizing knowledge effectively within an organization to deliver transformational value.

© Michael Schank 2023
M. Schank, *Digital Transformation Success*,
https://doi.org/10.1007/978-1-4842-9816-9_2

The Origins of the Process Inventory Framework

I started my career in 1996 at Andersen Consulting, which later became Accenture. My college degree had a focus on information systems, so I began in a technology practice. My first engagement was with a large bank in Charlotte that was developing a direct banking platform, an emerging concept at that time.

I initially joined a production support team where we handled issues with middleware code. Middleware is an application pattern for distributing messages to appropriate platforms. My role involved triaging issues, identifying root causes within the application code, and developing and testing fixes.

During the first 15 years of my career, I primarily focused on technology. I worked as a C++ and Java developer and a solution architect and led large teams in software delivery.

I transitioned from retail banking to commercial banking without having a strong understanding of these businesses. While I knew about retail banks since I was a customer with a checking account, commercial banking was completely foreign to me. My focus was on delivering quality software on time and supporting production to minimize customer impact. Most of my interactions were with other technologists; I was curious about what the business did, but I didn't have a clear path to explore it.

In 2011, I joined EY, which introduced me to a new world. At that time, EY had limited software development engagement, and their clients were typically senior leaders across various business areas such as risk, technology, and more. The work involved helping these leaders develop solutions to enhance their organizations' effectiveness. It was a refreshing shift from my technology-centric mindset.

One of my early engagements at EY was with a large retail bank. They had surplus budgeted funds that needed to be spent; otherwise, the funds would be lost the following year. One of their requirements was to build a business capability model for their retail banking business. While not an exhaustive exercise, we interviewed key individuals in their businesses and created a model with three levels of depth. It was a moment of epiphany for me. The entire business's activities were encapsulated in a single model, exactly what I had been seeking during my technology days to understand what the business did. I was enthused about the potential of this concept to bring diverse perspectives together and what this could mean for delivery on a wide range of topics. From that point on, I positioned myself as a business architect, eager to delve deeper into this concept, and using this branding helped me connect with clients implementing similar approaches.

BUSINESS ARCHITECTURE

Business architecture emerged as a concept in the 1980s. British management consultant Edwin E. Tozier was one of the first to mention the concept in an article he wrote titled "Developing Strategies for Management Information Systems" [1]. In this article, he distinguished between information architecture and business architecture, stating his theory that each business function may be supported by one or more information systems and that information systems need to be adaptable to organizational strategies.

Business architecture has evolved significantly since then. Several standard-setting organizations such as TOGAF (The Open Group Architecture Framework), OMG (Object Management Group), the Business Architecture Guild, and others have been advancing the concepts and practices, although a common definition remains elusive.

The definition that has resonated the most with me is from OMG, which states that business architecture is "a blueprint of the enterprise that provides a common understanding of the organization and is used to align strategic objectives and tactical demands" [1]. This definition always made intuitive sense to me as changes to a physical building wouldn't be made without such a blueprint, but many organizations will spend significant amounts of money without any similar concept.

The core deliverable in business architecture is the business capability model. A business capability model represents the required capabilities that an organization must deliver for its purpose. They are largely independent of specific organizational structures, reporting relationships, political agendas, cultural aspects of individual business leaders, current initiatives, and projects [2]. Business capability models have been used for various purposes, such as strategic planning, where a heatmap may be created to highlight the capabilities in most need of improvement and investment. They are also used to map assets, such as IT systems, which enables better communication with teams involved in implementing strategies. Generally, however, business architecture and business capability models do not model specific processes as their aim is to be high level and agnostic to organizational structure.

Shortly after that, I was brought in to assist a client in the mortgage industry. As a mitigation strategy following the 2008 financial crisis, they had decided to outsource several critical business functions to a third-party provider. However, the project was in deep trouble, with status reports showing red on most measures despite a significant investment made in terms of dollars and resources. The requirements team lacked structure and was not making progress toward delivering a complete and high-quality product. Additionally, the business architecture team they had in place was struggling to add value. Recognizing the need for a strategic pause to recalibrate the approach, the senior client stakeholders gave us a three-week timeframe.

The business architecture team was implementing an approach I had not encountered before. They utilized a sophisticated modeling platform and connected their business capability model to detailed process models. During the pause, I collaborated with the leadership of the business architecture team to develop a comprehensive plan. This plan included a stakeholder engagement model, a rigorous approach to work product creation, developing standards, a quality assurance process, and even an estimating model for more precise delivery date projections. When the work resumed, we essentially created a Process Inventory, although that was not the name used at that time. We conducted interviews with functional areas to capture every process they performed and then created process models to detail how those processes were executed. These inventories and process models underwent a stringent quality assurance review to ensure compliance with standards before the identified process owner attested to their accuracy. This structure enabled the requirements team to measure their progress toward completion, gain a detailed understanding of the process operations, and obtain sign-off on final requirements from named process owners. By establishing this factory-like model with clear activity sequences and accountabilities, the project transformed from red to bright green. This experience taught me valuable lessons, particularly the anchoring power of this concept in large-scale transformation programs. I also recognized the importance of connecting business processes, maintaining high standards, and prioritizing quality as critical success factors.

From that point on, I sought to refine this methodology and test it in diverse scenarios, including an insurance spin-off, a bank merger, strategic architecture design for a wealth management firm, business continuity planning for a capital markets firm, and risk management for a global financial utility.

My focus shifted to selling this concept within the financial services industry, which put me in front of numerous clients with complex problems to solve. While many of these clients acknowledged the significance of process within their solutions, they struggled to articulate how it would play a role. For others, I seamlessly integrated it into proposals, knowing it would be beneficial. Regardless, I achieved success in selling the approach as its intuitive appeal resonated with everyone.

This chapter delves into the framework's details, encompassing various models and their interconnectedness, providing a solid foundation for transformation initiatives.

The Process Inventory Framework

In Chapter 1, I described how Process Inventory is a common language that facilitates strategic alignment, which is critical for transforming an organization into the digital age and operating with excellence. This is certainly true, but I'd like to go a bit deeper to describe what it represents.

The Process Inventory framework represents an ontology for an organization. The word "ontology" gained usage with ancient philosophers like Plato and Aristotle. "Ontology" comes from the Greek words "ontos," meaning "being," and "logos," meaning "study" or "discourse" [3]. As they defined the term, ontology was the study of what exists and how the things that exist relate to each other, providing answers to fundamental questions about existence.

In modern times, ontologies are used in many fields such as information sciences, Semantic Web, bioinformatics, healthcare, natural language processing, artificial intelligence, and more. Today, the concept is defined as a formal representation of knowledge that encompasses a set of concepts, their properties, and the relationships between them within a specific domain. It provides a shared understanding of the structure and semantics of a domain, enabling effective knowledge organization, reasoning, and information integration [4]. To put this in layman's terms for an organization, it maps out how all the resources and concepts intersect to support the mission of the organization.

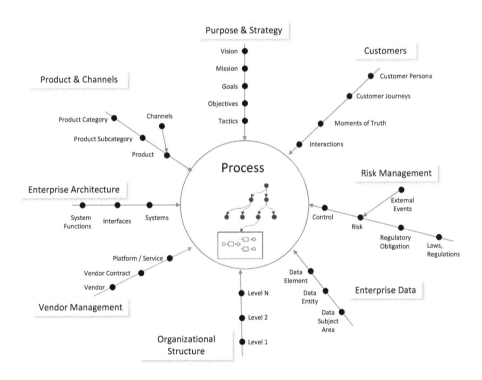

Figure 2-1. Organizational Ontology

Figure 2-1 is a visual representation of this ontology. As you can see, and this is not an exhaustive representation, there are numerous concepts that must come together to support an organization. Organizing knowledge in a specific domain is typically done through a taxonomy. Taxonomies are classification systems in which entities in domains are placed in hierarchical categories that are exclusive and exhaustive. Exhaustive means that every possible category, especially at the top of the hierarchy, is represented, and exclusive means that every entity belongs to only one category. To illustrate this, I'll use the classic example of the animal kingdom taxonomy. At the top level of the hierarchy, each animal is classified as vertebrate or invertebrate. A level below vertebrates are reptiles, birds, fish, mammals, and amphibians. The levels go deeper, but this taxonomy is exhaustive as there are no other high-level categories. It's exclusive in that any animal can exist in one and only one category.

As represented in Figure 2-1, each of the concepts that support an organization is its own taxonomy, which makes the ontology for an organization a polycategorical ontology, meaning knowledge is to be understood in how multiple taxonomies intersect. In polycategorical ontologies, entities are distinguished by how fundamental they are to the ontology, meaning how dependent their existence is relative to other entities. I discussed in Chapter 1 that the organization's purpose and strategy are the most fundamental to the existence of everything, but after that, the process is fundamental to all capabilities of the organization. For instance, an accounting system wouldn't be needed without the need for accounting processes.

The earlier ontology definition includes understanding the relationships between concepts within a specific domain; in this case, the domain is the organization. So, a consistent approach for mapping the concepts between these taxonomies is needed to have a coherent representation of knowledge. Since process is the most fundamental to the capabilities of the organization, it must be the top-level concept, meaning the entities in other taxonomies need to be mapped to how they support processes in the Process Inventory taxonomy. That is how process becomes the common language of the organization within this ontology.

Since organizational units are constructed to support the need of processes, this ontology explicitly maps disparate concepts to the Process Inventory taxonomy, providing horizontal alignment of knowledge and information.

For the remainder of this book, I will refer to the integration of these concepts as **process metadata**, which is information about the process. There are two broad categories of metadata. The first is operational information metadata, which provides information on the process's existence. This includes the products it supports, the legal entity it belongs to, or who owns the process, or the business capabilities it represents. The second is resource metadata, which details the resources leveraged in the execution of the process. This includes systems, data, channels, organizational units, third-party vendors, etc. The implication for modeling is that operational information metadata can be designated at the taxonomy or process definition level, while resource metadata can be further detailed through process models.

Figure 2-2 shows the same model but framed hierarchically. Since Process Inventory is constructed following the organizational structure, then it provides views that are relevant from the CEO through a low-level individual contributor, which is key to vertical alignment.

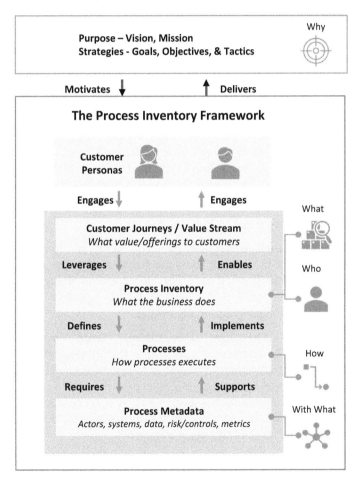

Figure 2-2. The Process Inventory Framework

This framework clearly delineates aspects of the 5W (and 1 H) model, which are crucial for understanding the motivational system of the organization. This provides a tool that helps organizations connect the "Why" in terms of their purpose and strategies to the "What" processes they execute to achieve their goals, the "Who" responsible for the results, and the "How" those processes are performed, as well as "With What" resources are leveraged.

The framing in Figure 2-2 will be leveraged in the rest of this chapter to describe various parts of this framework.

Process Inventory

Definition

Merriam-Webster defines a process as "a series of actions or operations conducing to an end." I point out this definition to highlight that this framework takes a generous definition, meaning that the goal of Process Inventory is to identify every action that is performed by anyone in the organization, any customer-facing technology systems, and any outsourced third-party providers.

The result of capturing all processes is an **end-to-end process framework**. I define this through the characteristics of (1) capturing everything an organization does and (2) being able to model processes from start to finish as they traverse different parts of the organization.

Here are some characteristics of Process Inventory:

- **Comprehensive Coverage**: The goal of Process Inventory is to capture everything that a business does within an identified scope. This is achieved through an interview process that aligns with the organizational hierarchy as highlighted in Figure 2-3.

- **Accuracy Through Attestation**: Since Process Inventory is constructed through the organizational hierarchy, this provides ownership to review the accuracy of the model after its initial creation and in each subsequent maintenance review. Asking stakeholders for formal attestation encourages them to pay attention to the relevant details and ensure accuracy.

- **Alignment with Strategy**: The transparency of processes enables a clear line of sight in how each process contributes to the achievement of the organization's goals. It can be assessed in terms of its strategic importance and performance metrics.

- **Top-Down Decomposition**: High-level activities as seen by the CEO or senior leadership are made up of subprocesses, and those subprocesses can be made up of other subprocesses. This model provides the ability to drill down to the appropriate level of detail given the encountered problem.

- **Models Current State and Future State**: Capturing Process Inventory is typically done on the current inventory of processes, but it can be useful to show future state processes when executing a transformation program.

- **Process Levels**: Since this inventory is constructed by leveraging an organizational hierarchy, there is no set level for documenting process models, such as Level 3, as different organizational hierarchies can be built at different levels of depth.

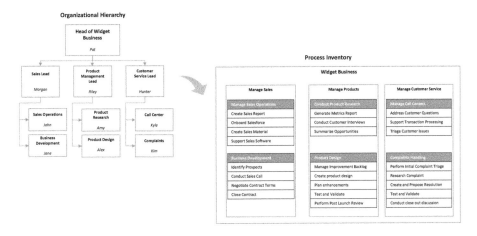

Figure 2-3. The Process Inventory Identification Process

Quality Is Paramount

Since Process Inventory serves as the common language for organizing organizational knowledge, ensuring quality is crucial. These models contribute to a repository of information interconnected with other process metadata. When stakeholders begin utilizing this information in their roles, encountering significant quality errors can undermine their confidence in the effort. Overcoming negative perceptions of poor quality can be challenging.

For each model, I will outline an approach to construction that includes multiple quality review points and stakeholder sign-offs. Adopting these quality checkpoints is of utmost importance to prevent costly or fatal mistakes. It is considered a best practice to conduct internal standards alignment reviews before seeking stakeholder attestation, thereby avoiding the need for them to re-attest if quality issues are discovered.

Process Naming

One principle that is important when constructing the inventory of processes is to provide clarity regarding the actions taking place. A good test for that is whether someone not familiar with the business unit or functional area can intuitively understand what the process accomplishes just by reading its name. One effective way to achieve this is by adopting a verb + noun naming convention. Since processes represent actions, the verb specifies the action, and the noun represents the entity on which the action is performed. Examples of good process names include "Open Account," "Submit Payment," and "Document Dispute Resolution." Additionally, when naming processes, it is advisable to minimize the use of generic verbs, such as "Manage," as they lack precision in describing the action being taken.

Furthermore, it is crucial to use the language of the business when engaging stakeholders as they are being asked to take ownership and be accountable for performance. The process names should align with their existing vernacular. For instance, if they refer to a process as "Onboard Client," it is important not to force them to call it "Open Account" just to match the terminology used by other business units.

In my experience, process owners value consistency and readability that standards bring while still allowing flexibility to align with their preferred vernacular.

Maintenance

When embarking on this work, one of the initial concerns raised is how to maintain the model's accuracy. This is a significant question, considering the constant changes that occur within many organizations, including the deployment of large-scale programs and organizational restructuring. Addressing this concern involves two key components.

Firstly, each process area must undergo periodic attestation, such as yearly, wherein the process owner identifies and highlights any changes and subsequently attests to the revised model. This ensures that updates are captured and acknowledged. Periodic attestations are not a new concept as they are used in several topics such as access controls, financial reports, and compliance reporting just to name a few.

The second aspect involves integrating this model into the organization's business management practices. Part 2 of this book will delve into this topic, encompassing the management of efficient operations, change management, risk management, and technology environment management. By instilling a sense of shared ownership among stakeholders, with everyone actively invested in maintaining an up-to-date model, integrating and attesting changes on a near real-time basis becomes more streamlined.

Process Ownership

A significant advantage of this framework lies not only in identifying the business processes within an organization but also in providing details regarding accountability for each process and process area. Process owners hold responsibility for executing processes and, in many cases, for identifying and driving changes to those processes. Since Process Inventory is built upon the organizational hierarchy, none of these accountabilities are new. However, adopting this framework enhances transparency by clarifying ownership and may lead to more defined performance metrics for both processes and their respective owners.

Figure 2-4. Process Ownership Model

As depicted in Figure 2-4, every point in the Process Inventory taxonomy will have an identified owner. This implies that the entire reporting structure will bear some level of accountability for process performance.

This structure facilitates easier maintenance of the Process Inventory when ownership transitions occur. In such cases, contacting the leader higher up in the chain allows for the identification of new owners.

Furthermore, this structure not only brings transparency to process accountability but also enables the cascading of goals throughout the organization. It ensures that lower-level teams have a clear understanding of how their efforts contribute to the organization's overarching objectives.

Omnichannel Processes

An exception to identifying processes by following the organizational hierarchy is with omnichannel processes. Many products that organizations offer allow for multiple customer contact points via various channels. These channels can include in-person interactions through physical stores or phone calls, as well as digital interactions through websites, mobile phones, or other electronic interfaces. Omnichannel aims to provide a seamless and effortless, high-quality customer experience that occurs within and between contact channels [7]. This can be achieved by providing a consistent experience to customers across all channels. However, it can become much more sophisticated by offering customers a hyper-personalized experience that leverages insights gained from the knowledge of the customer, including tracking their behavior as they interact across channels. This may also involve providing customers with the ability to start a transaction in one channel, such as the Web, and seamlessly continue it in another channel, such as physically going to a store.

A critical success factor in implementing the organization's omnichannel strategy is having a clear inventory of interactions, and by which channel, customers can interact with for a product.

A starting point for this is the product manager for each product. They can provide the list of transactions or processes associated with that product and indicate the channels in which those processes can be executed. This list should then be included in the Process Inventory for each channel. Having consistent process names across channels will enable teams to harmonize behaviors and collaborate with technology experts to develop the necessary back-end platforms that facilitate the omnichannel strategy.

Outsourced Processes

Many organizations outsource business processes to vendors for various reasons, such as not considering them part of their core value-add or lacking the necessary skills and resources. It is crucial to note that while the execution of certain processes may be delegated to a third-party vendor, the accountability for their performance remains with the organization. This means that if a vendor experiences a high-profile data breach or performance issue that impacts operations or attracts regulatory attention, the originating organization is held responsible. To address this, it is important to include the outsourced vendor processes in the Process Inventory.

Depending on the contractual arrangement, the vendor may not provide specific details on how the processes are executed. However, having clarity on the list of outsourced processes enables better monitoring of service level agreements (SLAs) and facilitates stronger management of these vendors. By monitoring performance against agreed-upon SLAs, organizations can proactively address any issues, ensure compliance, and maintain effective oversight of their outsourced processes.

Incorporating these considerations into the Process Inventory helps organizations maintain transparency, mitigate risks, and uphold their accountability even when processes are outsourced to external vendors.

Integration with Business Capability Model and Standard Process Models

In the definition I provided on business architecture and business capability models earlier, I mentioned that they are largely independent of specific organizational structures. There are also standard process taxonomy models for various industries, such as the APQC Process Classification Framework, which have adopted the same principle of being agnostic of specific organizational structures. This means that a capability or a process will be represented once and only once in those models regardless of how many business units or functional areas execute those processes.

However, this poses a challenge when trying to rationalize overlapping processes, standardize how certain processes are executed, or identify risks and implement effective controls. Leadership and practitioner teams can lose sight of these idiosyncrasies.

That doesn't mean these models lack value. They are extremely valuable in highlighting similar processes across disparate business units or functional areas. Since the Process Inventory leverages the specific vernacular of the business, it may not be immediately apparent that processes across different groups are performing the same tasks.

The ideal solution is to leverage both models and map them together, providing each stakeholder with the information they are seeking. For example, a risk team that needs to understand all the processes executed by an organizational unit will see all the processes in that area and how their execution may pose risks. On the other hand, a design team aiming to rationalize processes to create a shared services organization will gain insights into the process owners, their unique requirements, and how those must be implemented in the new organization.

Table 2-1. Highlights the Main Differences Between Process Inventory and a Business Capability or Standard Process Model

Process Inventory	Business Capability or Standard Process Model
• Constructed via the organizational hierarchy	• Agnostic of organization structure
• Represents a complete inventory of all the processes that a business unit or functional area performs	• Represents a complete inventory of all that a business can do
• Changes with organizational or process changes	• Stable and only changes with significant organizational changes
• Requires interviewing the business	• Can be obtained and leveraged immediately

Figure 2-5 shows the APQC Process Classification Framework. This diagram is their industry-agnostic model, but they also have tailored ones for different industries. The standardization is clear from the top-level view. This model is agnostic to organizational structures.

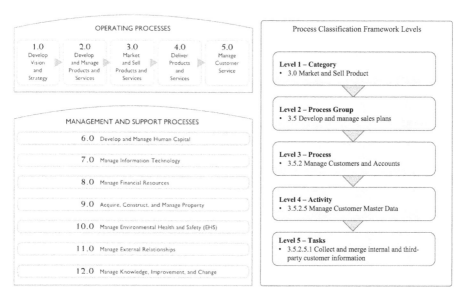

Figure 2-5. APQC Process Classification Framework

Figure 2-6 illustrates a real-world situation which is relatively simplistic, in which two different business units of the organization have sales teams. In many cases, especially with organizations with multiple business units or geographies, it can be hard to understand the overlap. Also, as you get deeper within an organization, it's possible that you'll find processes that are performed in an organization that are outside of the original mission of that group. An example is when a business unit creates a shadow IT [5] organization because they perceive or experience limitations in the central IT organization. Deciphering the details and performing alignment across the enterprise is made possible when both models are leveraged together.

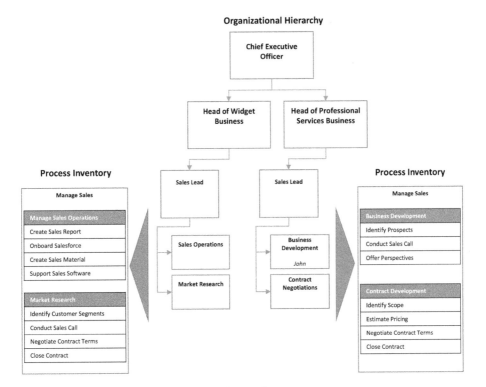

Figure 2-6. The Process Inventory Identification Process

The solution is illustrated in Figure 2-7. The Process Inventory is created then each process identified is mapped to the lowest level available and appropriate in the Standard Model.

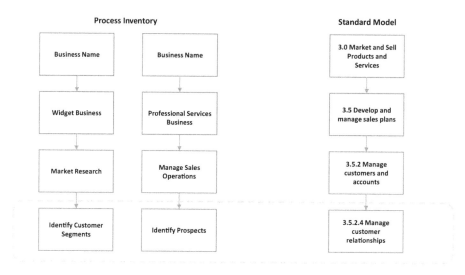

Figure 2-7. Linking Process Inventory with Standard Model

This best-of-both-worlds approach has many benefits across many use cases. It enables reporting through either lens. This is particularly useful for organizations that have become complex and are looking to optimize their operating model through optimized processes and reduced costs of doing business.

Process Mining

Process mining is an emerging concept that enables the understanding, analysis, and optimization of processes using data collected from system event logs. The first commercially available process mining tool became available in 2011, and there are now over 35 vendor tools [6] offering this capability. One of the key features of process mining tools is process discovery, where the tool automatically creates a graphical process model based on the information extracted from event logs.

While these tools offer valuable features, they should be considered as a complementary addition to manually collected Process Inventory. Process mining can be complex to implement, requiring resource-intensive effort and time, especially if an organization has a large number of systems with diverse log file formats. Implementation may necessitate changes to existing systems, data collection mechanisms, and data quality improvement efforts.

These tools do not aim to create a comprehensive and exhaustive set of all processes performed by an organization. Even if they could, organizations would still need to verify and attest to the accuracy of the output.

To fully benefit from process mining tools, the output should be harmonized with the existing Process Inventory, allowing for the alignment of metadata. This integration facilitates a more comprehensive understanding of the processes.

Conformance checking is another important feature provided by process mining tools. It involves identifying discrepancies between what humans document in the Process Inventory, process models, or procedure documents and what occurs in practice. These insights can be used to address gaps in compliance and improve the quality of documentation.

Additionally, process mining tools can analyze process performance data, including metrics such as throughput time and bottlenecks. This information serves as input for teams involved in optimizing these processes.

Process Inventory Metadata

When working with process owners to create the Process Inventory, it's important to gather as much descriptive information about the processes as possible. This information should be included in the packet when the process owner provides attestation. Table 2-2 outlines the types of operational information metadata to collect during the creation of the Process Inventory. Resource metadata, such as systems and people, can also be collected at this stage, but I will discuss that further when addressing process modeling and metadata.

Table 2-2. Highlights Metadata That Should Be Collected When Creating a Process Inventory

Metadata	Description	Source
Process Description	This should be a succinct description of the process which is understandable by everyone.	Process Owner
Process Owner	The name of the owner of that process.	Organizational Chart
Products	The product or products that the process supports.	Product Catalog
Channels	The channels or channels that the process supports.	Channel Inventory
Standard Model Alignment	The business capabilities or standard processes which each process aligns to.	Business Capability Model or Standard Process Model
Risk and Controls	The risks and control that align to the process.	GRC Risk Data Repository

Sourcing Process Metadata

To deliver on the promise of this framework, which aims to structure all knowledge and information for the organization in an ontology, data from numerous authoritative data sources need to be brought together and aligned for processing. An authoritative data source is a trusted and reliable repository of information that is widely recognized as the official or primary reference for a particular subject or domain.

In this section, I will detail how this data is conceptually linked and how the movement of data across sources facilitates this alignment.

Integrated Process Metadata Model

Figure 2-8 illustrates a conceptual model for bringing this together. The Process Inventory identifies every process that occurs in the organization in a hierarchical manner down to the process name. Operational information metadata, which provides information about the existence of each process, can be aligned with the identified processes.

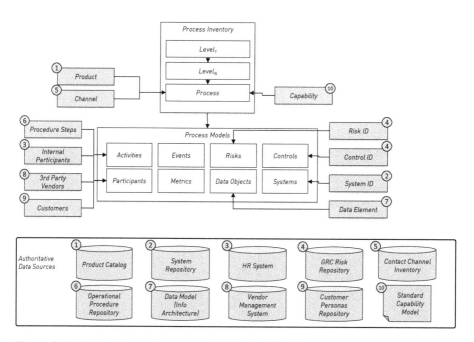

Figure 2-8. Linking Process Inventory with Standard Model

Process models are created to graphically represent how the processes are executed. Figure 2-8 shows the typical components in a process model, such as activities, participants, and systems. Many of these components represent the resources leveraged in conducting the process. This resource data is typically managed by different parts of the organization. For instance, systems are managed by IT, and risk data is managed by the risk organization. However, the ability to connect these concepts across sources has largely been absent.

These data sources typically contain a rich set of metadata about their resources. Connecting the identifiers of this data enables valuable insights. For example, connecting an activity in a process with the system that the activity leverages enables the organization to understand the programming language and the data centers that support that activity. This is very powerful for tasks like identifying the root cause of an issue, detailing the impacts of change, or determining risks that need to be mitigated. This is how the ontology is constructed for the organization, with the Process Inventory being the fundamental taxonomy.

Conceptual Architecture

Figure 2-9 represents the conceptual architecture to support the linking of data within the Process Inventory framework.

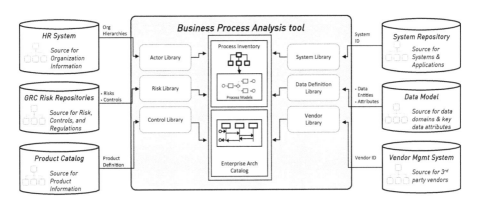

Figure 2-9. Conceptual Architecture

A **Business Process Analysis** tool is required to build and manage the Process Inventory and the library of process models associated with it. The features and a list of vendor tools containing this functionality will be detailed in Chapter 10.

Data, along with descriptive information, is migrated from authoritative data sources into the tool to construct libraries. Initially, there is a load of data, but periodic refreshes are necessary to prevent the libraries from becoming outdated. When the Process COE team creates the Process Inventory model and its associated process models, they connect the elements in these libraries to the appropriate locations within the framework. This connection of information to processes establishes the Process Inventory as the common language that links various aspects of how the organization operates. In this book, I will refer to this tool and the information it contains as the **Integrated Operational Repository** since it becomes the authoritative data source for aspects of the organization's operations.

It's important to note that the quality of the data sources is critical. If the data is untrustworthy and of poor quality, it is strongly recommended to postpone importing that data into the repository until those issues can be addressed. Poor data quality would undermine the intended purpose and could create negative perceptions of the repository.

Exporting the Common Language

Now that we have established the Process Inventory as the organization's common language and connected operational information through metadata, it is logical to export this common language to other systems that generate data. This will enable the seamless association of data across all internal systems.

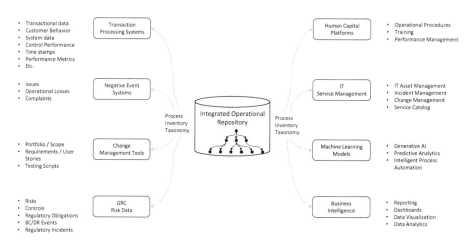

Figure 2-10. Publishing Process Inventory Taxonomy

Figure 2-10 is not an exhaustive list of systems that can align their data with the Process Inventory, but it should give you a sense of the benefits, which include

- Aligning negative events such as issues, incidents, and operational losses to process data gives triage teams access to underlying resources, reducing triage time.

- Aligning risk data results in higher-quality risk assessments, with named process owners accepting accountability for control performance. This enables more accurate reporting on the risk landscape for the board and senior leadership.

- Aligning change management deliverables brings clarity of scope, asset reuse, and stronger budget and timeline management.

- Aligning transactions in transactional processing systems provides the ability to create near-real-time monitoring dashboards, highlighting processes that are not meeting expectations.

- Aligning with human capital systems enables clarity of procedures, deployment of training, and alignment of performance metrics with process goals.

- Aligning this data with machine learning models allows for the identification of patterns that may not be accessible to humans, thereby improving numerous operational metrics.

Process Modeling and Metadata

The industry-accepted standard for documenting business processes is Business Process Model and Notation (BPMN) 2.0. BPMN 2.0 is a standard maintained by the Object Management Group (OMG). The primary goal of BPMN is to provide a notation that is easily understandable by all business users, including business analysts creating initial process drafts, technical developers implementing the technology for those processes, and businesspeople managing and monitoring the processes [8].

Most, if not all, Business Process Analysis tools on the market support native documentation of processes in this standard.

The complete BPMN 2.0 specification can be found on omg.org, and there are numerous online training resources available. My intention is not to provide education on the standard but rather to highlight how the standard enables the alignment of metadata and the implications of aligning this metadata for various use cases.

Figure 2-11 is a sample process model highlighting key components of a process model. In this section, I will highlight how the structure of the BPMN 2.0 process model is a great way to integrate this metadata in its proper context.

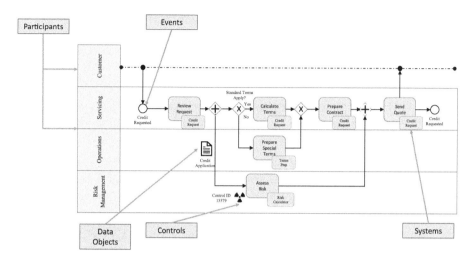

Figure 2-11. Sample BPMN 2.0 Process Model

Leveraging Metadata Libraries

When modeling processes in the modeling tool, it's important that data is standardized across models. This consistency will enable the ability to perform impact analysis across processes that leverage certain resources. To facilitate this, only data aligned in the libraries, as depicted in Figure 2-9, should be leveraged. This means hand-creating net new objects needs to be discouraged if there is an established library to choose the appropriate item.

Participants

Process models in BPMN 2.0 include lanes, which represent the participants in the process. Lanes can exist within pools, which represent the organizational units that contain the participants.

There are two types of lanes in BPMN 2.0:

- **White Box Lanes**: These lanes are used to explicitly document the activities and tasks of participants internal to the organization. They provide transparency and detail the handoffs between departments.

- **Black Box Lanes**: These lanes are used to show interaction points with external participants, typically customers or external vendors. In these cases, it may not be necessary or possible to identify their specific activities, and the focus is on the interaction points.

Both white box and black box lanes serve specific purposes based on the need for transparency and level of detail in representing the activities and interactions within a process.

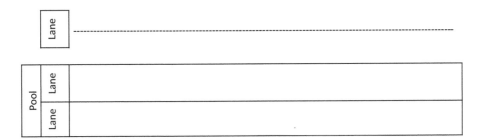

Figure 2-12. Participant Lanes

There are three types of participants that are modeled through these lanes: customers, third-party vendors, and internal teams. Here are the details of how each is sourced:

- **Internal teams** are sourced from organizational charts within the HR systems. Process modeling teams will have to determine the appropriate level of granularity to use. If lanes are defined at too low of a level, then there may be numerous lanes which will make the process models too hard to read.

- **Customers** are typically sourced from the customer experience team if one exists. Customers typically align to products or services being delivered by the organization, and they can be further segmented by the profile of the customer persona.

- **Third parties** are sourced from a vendor management system which is typically maintained by the procurement or the risk team. The focus here is on third parties that perform processing on behalf of the organization.

Figure 2-13 illustrates the load of data from their respective authoritative sources of data into the Participant Library for process modelers to use when creating lanes in process models.

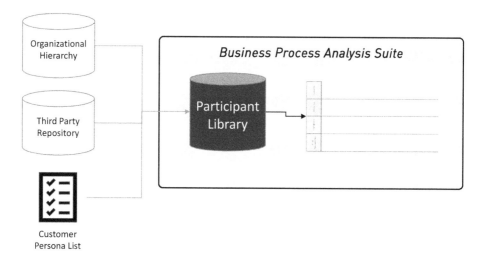

Figure 2-13. Participant Data Load

Events

Events represent occurrences that occur during business process execution. Unlike other metadata elements covered in this section, events are not sourced from an external authoritative repository; instead, they are identified through interviews with process owners and documented in process models. By building process models derived from a comprehensive list of processes provided by the Process Inventory, a powerful repository can be created for various purposes, including

- **Event-Driven Architectures**: A software design pattern in which integration and system actions are triggered through events.

- **Data State Changes**: Exclusive changes in data states occur through events. For example, a loan can transition from the application state to the approved state through an event named "Loan Approved," which alters the underlying data state in the appropriate data stores.

- **Operational Reports**: Leveraging events, operational reports can be created to provide insights into the volume and performance of underlying processes.

Events are also critical in facilitating **end-to-end process modeling** as an end event in one process can trigger the start event in another process, potentially in a different area of the business.

The events represented in business process models are only those that are visible to process owners. There are also technical events, such as data being transformed and migrated through a batch process, which will be covered in Chapter 6. When combined, these events create a powerful repository that can drive valuable insights and designs.

For this event repository to be useful, it is important to have descriptive event names. The recommended naming standard is a noun plus past tense verb, such as "Loan Approved," "Contract Signed," and "Report Delivered".

Systems

Most activities in today's digital age occur on systems. Mapping activities that occur in a business process to the system that supports those activities supports transparency of IT and facilitates better dialogue between the business and technology teams.

This level of transparency enables a rationalized Enterprise Architecture design, which will reduce complexity and redundancy. It will lead to a lower cost for maintaining the IT environment and enable greater speed to market for change items.

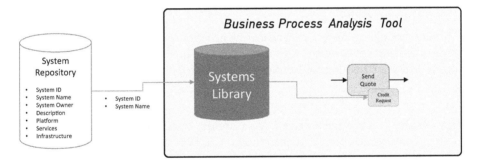

Figure 2-14. Systems Data Load

Figure 2-14 highlights how information is loaded from the source repository to the Systems Library. Each activity that leverages a system is tagged with the specific system from that library.

Data Objects

Managing the vast amounts of data that organizations generate and are required to maintain has been an ongoing challenge for most organizations. As a result, many have established dedicated data governance teams to establish and enforce policies, procedures, and guidelines for the management, quality, and security of their data assets.

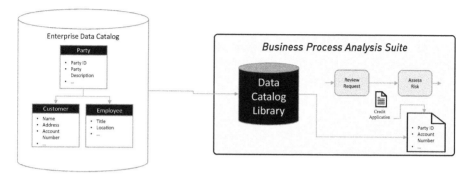

Figure 2-15. Data Catalog Data Load

Figure 2-15 illustrates the loading of data definitions from the Enterprise Data Catalog. One of the key goals of data governance is to align terms and definitions across the organization, enabling consistent application of policies and effective data stewardship. Enterprise Data Catalogs play a crucial role in achieving this consistency by identifying and cataloging the data elements used in business operations.

In process modeling, data is utilized during activities or handoffs, and this data is represented and captured through data objects. The naming convention for data objects is to align them with the business's terminology for the corresponding data.

Business Process Analysis tools enable modelers to identify the data elements associated with each data object. By aligning these data elements with the data identified in the Enterprise Data Catalog, consistency and collaboration can be promoted across different groups. For example, if one group refers to a data element as "Social Security Number" while another group calls it "SSN," mapping these terms ensures they are both referring to the same item.

This level of clarity regarding which data elements are associated with specific processes provides data governance teams with transparency when applying their policies, procedures, and guidelines.

Controls

Risk is an inherent part of conducting business. The critical aspect for any organization is to have a precise understanding of the risks involved so that leadership can make informed decisions on which risks to accept and implement appropriate mitigation strategies. Risks can arise from various sources, including operational risk, compliance risk, business continuity, and others, which may be triggered by internal or external events.

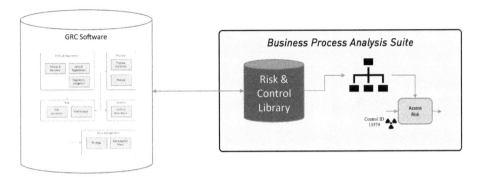

Figure 2-16. Data Catalog Data Load

Figure 2-16 illustrates the loading of risk and control information from the risk repository. Effective risk management requires a thorough comprehension of the relationship between the organization's processes, the risks associated with those processes, and the controls implemented to mitigate those risks. It is essential for organizations to maintain their risk data to perform risk assessments, design and monitor controls, and generate risk reports for the board and senior leadership. Typically, this risk data is managed using a GRC (governance, risk, and compliance) tool.

Explicitly linking risks to the processes that generate or are impacted by them brings several benefits, such as enhancing the completeness of risk assessments, aligning process owners' accountability for control performance, and improving monitoring and reporting capabilities.

This process-risk linkage also creates a two-way flow of data. The GRC tool benefits from having a comprehensive inventory of processes as part of its data model to ensure completeness, while the modeling team, in collaboration with process owners, gains insight into the specific controls they need to design and integrate into their processes.

Customer Personas and Customer Journeys

Providing customers with a great experience is key to driving customer loyalty, differentiating from competitors, improving brand reputation, and gaining valuable customer insights that lead to increasing revenues. This drives many organizations to anchor their digital transformation program on the goal of improving customer experience.

This is why many are creating dedicated customer experience (CX) teams. These teams have adopted an ethnographic research methodology that provides them with a deeper understanding of customers' needs, expectations, and behaviors. This outside-in analysis gives organizations valuable insights into how they need to change to meet their customer experience aspirations.

These CX efforts typically focus on understanding customers through customer personas and documenting their experiences interacting with products and services in a customer journey.

Customer personas are fictional representations of customers who use your products or services. They often include information about demographics, lifestyle, behaviors, goals, motivations, pain points, and communication preferences.

Customer journeys are the end-to-end set of interactions that a customer has with a product or service. They usually include information about the experience that ties to the customer persona, such as touchpoints, customers' needs, emotional reactions, and pain points.

Understanding customers through these artifacts is imperative in defining the CX strategy. Organizations can choose to reinvent the customer experience entirely or focus on tactically addressing current pain points. Regardless, they provide a basis for understanding customers and the organization, which should lead to success.

Astonishingly, only 25% of CX professionals say their companies' CX programs improve customer experience according to a study by Forrester [9]. There are many reasons for this, but one of the most prominent is the failure to identify the root causes of poor CX.

Even if the root causes can be understood, coordinating change across the organizational silos that need to collaborate to implement the change is a significant undertaking.

Linkage to Process Inventory Framework

A great characteristic of customer journeys is that they capture every touchpoint a customer has with an organization throughout their relationship life cycle. This is insightful as it covers the end-to-end process for the product or service, crossing organizational boundaries such as marketing, sales, back-end operations, channels, and technology platforms.

Since the Process Inventory aims to create a complete and accurate inventory of the organization's processes, it is important that each touchpoint identified in a customer journey is represented in the Process Inventory. This relationship is illustrated in Figure 2-17. By mapping the customer journey interactions with the processes in the Process Inventory and aligning metadata, it enables traceability from the customer's perspective through each resource that supports those interactions.

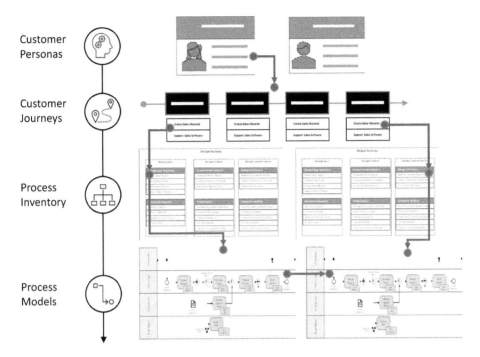

Figure 2-17. Customer Journey—Process Inventory Alignment

This approach allows for precise identification of root causes, enabling the development of appropriate solutions. However, implementing such changes may not be trivial as it may require coordinating change efforts across multiple lines of business, geographies, and practitioner teams.

The changes, along with their comprehensive set of impacts, can be estimated and incorporated into the change portfolio investment process. This provides the change investment committee with a solid business case for prioritizing and allocating discretionary change expenditure related to customer experience. If funded, this ensures that all practitioner teams are aware of the full range of impacts and have clear accountability for implementing the required changes.

Many organizations strive to build a culture of customer centricity, but sometimes this goal may be lost on teams that are several levels removed from direct customer interactions. In such cases, it becomes challenging for them to establish a direct connection between their day-to-day tasks and their impact on the customer. The structure described earlier provides the necessary clarity, enabling everyone to be accountable for their part in delivering an enhanced customer experience.

Value Streams

Value streams are the end-to-end process from initial conception through to delivering value to an end customer or stakeholder.

Value streams and customer journeys are very similar in that they are both end-to-end views that cross organizational boundaries and leverage specific processes identified in the Process Inventory. The main difference is that customer journeys are from a customer's perspective, an outside-in view, while value streams are from an internal perceptive, an inside-out view. The modeling standards and techniques for connecting to specific processes, as depicted in Figure 2-17, should be consistent.

Key Takeaways

- **Ontology** is a construct for representing an organization's knowledge. The Process Inventory serves as the anchor framework, ensuring consistent representation and alignment to drive business value from this knowledge.

- **Process Inventory** is a framework designed for capturing and managing a comprehensive and accurate inventory of the processes performed within an organization.

- **Metadata** is sourced and aligned from various authoritative data sources to provide context for operational information and the utilization of resources within the processes they support.

- **Additional models** and modeling techniques are required to understand the organization from diverse perspectives. These include BPMN process models, customer personas, customer journeys, and value streams.

In the next chapter, we will explore key trends in digital transformations as well as understand the components of a successful digital transformation program.

Defining the Digital Transformation Program

We'll explore the critical role of building a digital strategy as the foundation for successful digital programs. When articulating a digital strategy, it's essential to consider key trends that are reshaping business models and transforming how organizations operate. These trends encompass new innovation models, a heightened focus on the customer, and the recognition of data as a strategic asset.

We will delve deeply into a methodical approach for establishing the digital transformation program and crafting a transformation roadmap aligned with an organization's unique context and strategic requirements. Finally, we'll

© Michael Schank 2023
M. Schank, *Digital Transformation Success*,
https://doi.org/10.1007/978-1-4842-9816-9_3

cover how the output of the digital strategy plays a pivotal role in defining the Process Inventory strategy, which is essential for determining the priority models, use cases, and resources to apply within this framework to contribute the highest value.

John Deere's Digital Transformation

John Deere's digital transformation journey showcases that not only digitally native companies can excel in adopting digital technologies, but also well-established companies can maximize business gains by successfully transitioning to the digital world.

Founded in 1837 by John Deere [1], the company started as a blacksmith shop in Grand Detour, Illinois, serving as a general repairman and manufacturer of agricultural tools. They gained recognition for pioneering the self-scouring steel plow in 1837, a revolutionary invention that revolutionized farming practices. Fast-forward to the twenty-first century, John Deere has become a global leader in the agricultural industry, with a revenue of $52.77 billion and a workforce of 82,200 employees. By demonstrating a commitment to leveraging technology to drive innovation, enhance customer experiences, and optimize internal operations, John Deere has transformed its products and internal processes to stay ahead in the rapidly evolving landscape.

Innovations in customer products have been a hallmark of John Deere's digital transformation. They unveiled a fully autonomous tractor equipped with six pairs of stereo cameras that enable 360° obstacle detection and distance calculation. The machine continuously checks its position with GPS technology to automate movement within an inch of accuracy [2].

In 2017, John Deere acquired Silicon Valley technology company Blue River to apply artificial intelligence to agriculture. Leveraging machine learning and computer vision technology from this acquisition, they developed an autonomous "See and Spray" system, which uses cameras to identify and spray weeds with precision, reducing herbicide usage by 80–90% [3] compared to the traditional blanket spraying of chemicals.

John Deere built a digital ecosystem that empowers farmers to access and analyze farm-related data, optimize equipment utilization, and collaborate with ecosystem partners for valuable insights. They created a cloud-enabled JDLink system that connects and manages all the machines on a farm. Additionally, the AI-based data platform, John Deere Operations Center, allows customers to access farm-related data and insights. This transformation has enabled John Deere to create an ecosystem beyond just selling farm equipment, offering a suite of smart products such as farm equipment, irrigation systems, speed optimization systems, and weather data systems, all connected through Internet of Things (IoT) technologies [5]. They have evolved their business model from being solely a products company to a services company with an additional revenue stream via subscription fees.

Furthermore, John Deere didn't limit its digital transformation to customer products but focused inward on enhancing internal operations. The company is deploying 5G in all its manufacturing facilities [6] to expand factory capabilities. This includes the implementation of edge computing, analytics, autonomous devices, and a suite of smart applications such as real-time location systems, asset tracking, inventory management, wearables, building automation, and robotics. These initiatives drive operational cost savings and contribute to the goal of creating smart, connected factories and supply chains.

Tami Hedgren, manufacturing lead for tractors and combines, highlights the significance of these efforts, stating, "With Smart Connected Factories, we will identify issues before they become problems and have solutions ready before they become disruptions. This will help make us more efficient and our customers more productive." [7]

Through these strategic initiatives, John Deere positioned itself as a leader in the digital revolution. The company's forward-looking approach aims to drive revenue growth, increase market share, and deliver superior customer experiences in the agricultural industry. By embracing digital transformation, John Deere demonstrates its commitment to remaining at the forefront of innovation and serving the evolving needs of farmers worldwide.

Digital Strategy Trends

The first step in seizing on a digital opportunity is to establish a digital strategy. A digital strategy is a comprehensive and forward-thinking plan that guides organizations on how to harness the power of digital technologies to deliver business results in the digital age. The digital strategy, at a minimum, should be aligned with the corporate strategy, and in many cases, they are one and the same.

Each organization and the industry they serve are unique, necessitating an examination of all aspects of their business model to identify vulnerabilities and opportunities that can provide a competitive advantage. The outcome of this process should be a vision for the future, detailing their digital aspirations, and a prioritized roadmap to achieve these aspirations.

For many organizations, this transformation may be disruptive as it requires challenging existing processes and cultures that reinforce a particular way of working. Embracing new practices will entail building new muscle memory in reimagined business processes, necessitating significant investments in time, effort, and financial resources. The digital strategy must inspire and motivate employees, stakeholders, and customers, providing clear direction and purpose.

The external environment is prone to change during the digital program, requiring a digital strategy that envisions a culture of innovation that is agile and adaptable, capable of capitalizing on emerging trends and technologies.

In this section, we explore the top digital trends driving transformational change and revolutionizing the way companies operate, engage with customers, and create value. Understanding these trends allows businesses to determine relevance to their context and chart their course toward a digital future.

Business Model Disruption

The digital age has brought an unprecedented level of disruption to traditional business models. This represents a threat to established businesses as smaller upstarts, and some larger innovative companies such as Apple, have leveraged technological advancements to introduce new ideas and value propositions, addressing unmet customer needs with greater convenience, efficiency, and affordability, to capture market share. In many cases, these challengers are unburdened by the complexities of outdated technology systems, complicated organizational structures, and even high regulatory requirements. Classic examples include Netflix displacing Blockbuster Video, Amazon displacing Borders Group in selling books, Uber displacing many taxi services, and Airbnb challenging existing hospitality businesses. This era also brings opportunities, not only to new digitally native startups but also to established businesses that can disrupt their own organizations with a re-envisioned business model, a culture of innovation, and the agility to transform how they operate. In this section, we'll explore some of the new business models that are emerging.

The dot-com boom that started in the mid-1990s marked the beginning of the **ecommerce business model**, which is defined as enabling customers to buy and sell goods and services over the Internet. This business model, which has challenged traditional brick-and-mortar businesses, has evolved with the maturation of smartphones, tablets, and other Internet-connected devices and apps. This area has become increasingly competitive as ecommerce is projected to account for 20.4% of global retail sales by the end of 2022, up from only 10% five years earlier [8]. A couple of recent trends have emerged which should be considered. One trend is direct-to-consumer (D2C) ecommerce, where consumer brands establish a direct sales channel to customers to form a deeper connection and maintain control of their brand experience. Successful examples of D2C ecommerce include Warby Parker for eyewear and Dollar Shave Club for shaving products, both of which have effectively bypassed traditional retailers to engage directly with their customers. Another trend is the integration of ecommerce presence with brick-and-mortar operations through an omnichannel strategy, providing customers with a seamless experience across both channels. Walmart, which began with physical stores, has heavily invested in building its ecommerce channel and integrated the experience with features such as "Pickup Today" and "Ship to Store."

The global subscription market size is expected to increase from $72.91 billion in 2021 to an expected $904.2 billion by 2026 [9]. This underscores another business model shift to that of the **subscription business model**. In the digital era, companies are finding that subscription models help organizations drive greater customer engagement from which they can gain better insights into behaviors and they are provided a predictable stream of revenue. The migration of software to the cloud has driven more software providers to move away from traditional licensing models to subscription-based models through software as a service (SaaS). In this model, customers purchase subscriptions to software hosted in the vendor's cloud environment, which provides them a cost-effective solution that can scale on demand, and they are provided with regular software updates.

The model that may have had the most success in this era is the **platform business model**, in which a company creates a platform that connects multiple groups of users. These models allow enterprises to set up powerful ecosystems for value exchange and innovation among participants [10]. Some of the largest and most successful companies by market capitalization in this era, such as Apple, Microsoft, Amazon, Alphabet (Google), Facebook, Uber, Airbnb, and Alibaba, are either based on or prominently integrate this model. Established companies are also having success setting up platforms. General Electric, founded in 1892, has set up, through GE Digital, the Predix platform as a service (PaaS), which is an Industrial Internet of Things (IIoT) platform that provides edge to cloud connectivity, processing, analytics, and services to support their customers' industrial applications. This provides their customers with data-driven insights, predictive maintenance solutions, and improved operational efficiency while providing GE with a recurring revenue model, access to data to drive additional innovations, and strategic positioning as a leader in IIoT.

Democratizing Innovation

The digital technology landscape is rapidly evolving, and this evolution doesn't appear to be slowing down anytime soon. That means the success of a digital strategy is dependent on building a culture of innovation.

The traditional model of innovation relied on the top-down hierarchy or a dedicated R&D department to identify ideas and drive solutions in products, services, and business processes. Others may be constrained by their leadership, hindered by organizational silos, or lack the tools and access to information to pursue their ideas. Digitally maturing companies are finding success by sourcing innovative ideas and solutions externally through partner ecosystems and internally by promoting and rewarding cross-functional collaboration. A recent study found that digitally innovative organizations grew their revenue more than twice as fast as those that haven't built this capability [11].

Open innovation is the practice where organizations don't solely rely on their own internal knowledge, sources, and resources for innovation but also utilize multiple external sources, such as customers, partners, and the public at large, to drive innovation [12]. A compelling example of successful open innovation is LEGO. In 2004, the company faced a crisis and was on the verge of bankruptcy due to a series of unsuccessful products that failed to excite customers, which was compounded by increasing competition from video games and online activities. To find new product ideas, LEGO turned to a different source—their customers [13]. They introduced the LEGO Ideas platform, allowing fans to upload product ideas, and if an idea received 10,000 votes, LEGO would review it for possible production [14]. This approach not only led to the creation of products that resonated with their customers but also helped build a community of loyal enthusiasts.

Democratizing innovation is expanding ideas and innovation internally. This requires building a culture of innovation and capabilities in people to explore ideas. This happens to coincide with the disruptive impact that generative AI and other advanced automation technologies will have on the workforce as routine and redundant tasks are eliminated. Organizations will have to shift the workforce toward higher cognitive activities that require critical thinking and problem-solving skills. Many employees have developed deep expertise in their areas and just need leadership to build an environment around them where they are encouraged to pursue their creativity, connect dots, and create novel solutions that generate business value. This starts with a philosophy and tone that removes hierarchical barriers, values openness and experimentation, and rewards initiative. This also means providing training, breaking down organizational silos through cross-functional teams, and giving people access to resources, tools, and data for them to understand the big picture.

A great example of getting this right is the innovation powerhouse, 3M [15]. 3M has created a wide variety of innovation centers and technical forums to facilitate building a network among scientists, employees, and customers, where they freely exchange their ideas and discuss future projects. They have implemented a 15% rule, which encourages employees to dedicate that portion of their time to innovation. This concept traces its roots back to 1914 when William McKnight, the company's general manager at the time, instituted the philosophy of "Listen to anybody with an idea" [16]. This approach has led to the development of several successful products, such as the Post-it Notes and Scotchgard. 3M has set a goal of 30/4, meaning they expect 30% of their revenue to come from products created within the last four years.

Focus on the Customer

The rapid advancement of technology has compelled organizations to embark on digital transformation journeys. However, many successful companies are shifting their perspective to focus on customer engagement as the core of their transformation strategy, with technology as a critical enabler.

This approach focuses on viewing the business from the outside-in—that is, from the customer's point of view—to redefine customer experiences, relationships, and processes. Statistics demonstrate the validity of this approach as 84% of organizations that focused on improving customer experiences increased their revenue and 79% reported significant cost savings. Deepening relationships with existing customers partly explain these stats as acquiring new customers can cost as much as five times more than retaining existing ones [17]. Nowadays, customers are heavily influenced by ratings and endorsements, with 85% reading online reviews before making a purchase, making a strong brand imperative in acquiring new customers [18].

A critical aspect of success in this endeavor is to build a companywide culture of commitment to customer centricity. This means aligning mission, values, and incentive systems to this goal. This culture fosters a continuous feedback loop, encouraging companies to listen and adapt to customer needs. Tesla, the electric vehicle pioneer, stands out for its customer-first approach, and they have been rewarded with unparalleled customer loyalty as a staggering 80% of customers buy or lease another Tesla for their next car [19]. Handling everything from production to sales in-house, Tesla maintains complete control over the customer experience, where most car companies put sales and service in the hands of third-party dealerships. Notably, Tesla's transparent communication during a previous manufacturing issue further solidified its customer relationships as Elon Musk sent personal responses to customers who tweeted at the company with honest updates on the situation.

Gaining a deep understanding of the customer's needs from their perspective is essential. A standard method for doing this is creating customer personas, which detail a customer's perspective. Clothing retailer Lululemon underscores the success of this approach. Founder Chip Wilson anchored the company's strategy on a persona he named Ocean [20]. Ocean was a 32-year-old professional woman who makes $100,000 a year, is engaged, owns a condo, travels, is fashionable, and works out an hour and a half a day. The organization studied Ocean, who served as the inspiration for their merchandise design. This design innovation has had a transformative effect on the fashion industry, establishing them as pioneers in the emerging fashion category known as athleisure. This approach can lead to an end-to-end process view via a customer journey, in which organizations assess and improve the experience the customer has while using their products and services.

Additionally, building and maintaining data about customers to create a 360-degree view of their preferences and past interactions is essential in identifying their needs at any point in time and predicting their behavior. This is valuable in personalizing interactions, recommending products a customer might need, and identifying solutions to customer issues.

With the additional insight gained about the customer and by delighting customers and exceeding their expectations, organizations can drive a higher net promoter score (NPS), which is a standard measurement of customer loyalty and satisfaction measurement taken from asking customers how likely they are to recommend your product or service to others.

Another way to drive NPS and financial performance is to drive engagement and build a community of loyal customers by building social media channels. Nike has done this by creating a membership program that gives customers access to discounts, events, access to exclusive merchandise, and fitness communities via the Nike Training Club and Nike Run Club apps. These apps provide members access to training programs, at-home workouts, world-class trainers, wellness and nutrition guidance, and more. Through this program, they have built strategic partnerships with retailers such as Dick's Sporting Goods, which will allow customers to link rewards programs and give customers personalized shopping experiences and discounts across multiple channels [21]. The company has about 160 million active members who engage with the brand on a regular basis. This engagement, and their increased direct-to-consumer approach, has paid off for the bottom line as they announced their fourth-quarter (Q4) and annual performance for the fiscal year ending May 31, 2021, with annual profits soaring 196% [22].

Data as an Asset

The digital era has ushered in an unprecedented explosion of data. From the decade ending in 2020, the amount of data created, captured, copied, and consumed in the world increased from 1.2 trillion gigabytes to 59 trillion gigabytes, representing almost 5,000% growth [23]. With the rise of social media, online transactions, Internet of Things (IoT) devices, and other technology enhancements, the pace of data growth is only accelerating. The regulatory environment regarding data adds another layer of complexity as regulations such as GDPR (General Data Protection Regulation) in Europe, CCPA (California Consumer Privacy Act), HIPAA (Health Insurance Portability and Accountability Act), and numerous others are imposing stringent requirements on how data must be handled and protected. This is leading the management and governance of data to become a high priority for many organizations.

Data can be a source of competitive advantage for organizations that recognize its value as an asset. Those who can effectively manage and harvest it to gain valuable insights and make stronger decisions will gain an edge. Data not only helps companies understand their customers better, as was just covered, but it's critical in the adoption of new technologies such as machine learning, and it can fuel innovation in products, processes, and business models. That is why developing a strategy for the use and management of data must be a consideration for a digital strategy.

This explosion of data combines with the emergence of AI capabilities, leading organizations to build stronger data analytic capabilities where decisions are made with empirical information rather than gut feeling. This starts with the ability to gather data from multiple input sources with quality that decision-makers can trust. To unlock this potential, advanced analytical models need to be created to identify patterns, predict trends, and optimize decision-making. To be effective, these models need to work backward by first identifying the business outcome to be optimized. This may require a culture shift where leaders embrace this new approach and decision-makers in the business partner with data scientists. An excellent example of this strategy is Walmart, the world's largest retailer, which has fully embraced a data-driven approach with AI and machine learning to optimize its supply chain and deliver enhanced customer experiences. With hundreds of in-house data scientists dedicated to various aspects of the business, Walmart's cutting-edge AI technology has evolved from predicting sales demand to understanding and fulfilling customer preferences. Through advanced robotics, machine learning, and predictive analytics, Walmart's supply chain is becoming more efficient, enabling next- or two-day shipping to 95% of the US population and increasing inventory accuracy [24].

As organizations conduct their regular business operations and accumulate vast amounts of data, some are recognizing the unique value their data holds for other entities. This realization has led to the creation of new revenue streams as they monetize their data. Mastercard is a great example of this, with about 3 billion cardholders making approximately 90 billion transactions yearly at around 70 million merchants through about 40,000 banks and financial institutions in about 210 countries and territories [25]. This represents valuable insights into the purchasing trends of consumers that consumer-facing businesses can leverage to develop a holistic view of different customer segments. Mastercard established the Data & Services unit, which leverages anonymized and aggregated transaction data to offer clients a portfolio of services, including reports, data products, analytics solutions, and consulting services. Monetizing data has become a significant source of revenue for Mastercard and added value for their clients.

Defining a digital strategy that extracts maximum value from data must start with a commitment from the top. Many organizations are hiring a Chief Data Officer, who reports directly to the CEO. The chief data officer, or an equivalent senior-level data leader, will be charged with creating a data strategy. This strategy must lead with business objectives and include the definition of a data management program that consists of data governance and quality processes, data privacy and compliance policies, training and cultural alignment, a data architecture vision, and the required data and analytics capabilities to enable data-driven decision-making.

Defining the Digital Program

As each organization and the industry they serve are distinct, defining a digital strategy and executing change through a digital program will require organizations to critically assess their own threats and opportunities to identify the competitive advantage they need to pursue. The digital trends that I just covered, while not exhaustive, highlight what must be considered when doing this assessment.

Sunil Gupta, a professor at Harvard Business School and author of the book *Driving Digital Strategy*, highlights the keys to success in this journey as "four things: One is your business strategy; the second is about your operations and value chain; third is about how you engage with customers; and fourth is how you structure the entire organization" [26].

The approach in Figure 3-1 represents how each of these keys can be considered in a structured manner. While this appears sequential, most times it's executed iteratively as organizations test new business models and improve strategies and designs based on those insights.

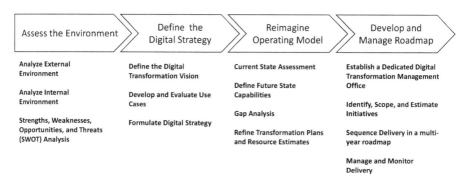

Figure 3-1. Defining the Digital Program

Assess the Environment

In this step, insights are gathered and analyzed from both external and internal sources to identify opportunities and threats, as well as assess the strengths and weaknesses that need to be addressed during the transformation.

Analyzing the external environment can be facilitated through the PESTEL framework and the Five Forces analysis. The PESTEL framework offers valuable insights into the macroenvironmental influences that impact businesses, encompassing six key factors: political, economic, social, technological, environmental, and legal [27]. The Porter's Five Forces covers the competitive forces of competitive rivalry, supplier power, buyer power, threat of substitution, and threat of new entry [28].

I will highlight how some of these forces may impact digital strategy:

- **Political influences** pertain to potential laws and regulations surrounding new technologies. We are seeing that play out right now with debates in Washington, DC, on how to regulate artificial intelligence.

- **Social influences** are currently shaping customer behavior, especially among tech-savvy younger generations, underscoring the need to align digital strategies with evolving preferences.

- **Legal considerations** entail compliance with existing laws and regulations, which hold critical implications for digital strategies. In some industries, the regulatory environment is so onerous that it creates a barrier to entry for digitally native startups. This is the case for Fintech companies that build technology to enable digital access to financial services but can't directly compete with traditional banks due to the prohibitive cost of compliance.

- **Competitive rivalry** is where you assess the strengths and weaknesses of your competition in your industry. For established players, this could include threats from digitally native startups.

- **Buyer power** is evaluating the power of your customers to switch to competitors, which would give them greater bargaining power in establishing pricing.

Performing an internal analysis requires leaders to honestly assess the strengths and weaknesses of internal capabilities to adopt a digital agenda. For established companies, there are many strengths, such as the quality of their assets, the loyalty of existing customers, and the expertise of their people. However, several weaknesses can exist if the culture isn't aligned with agile ways of working, the organizational structure is siloed and complex, data isn't managed effectively, and technical complexity becomes burdensome.

Internal and external analyses are summarized in a SWOT analysis, which categorizes the organization's strategic position internally as strengths and weaknesses and externally as opportunities and threats. This comprehensive analysis provides leaders with the needed information from which to develop the digital vision by defining for them where to focus their digital energies.

Define the Digital Strategy

When defining the digital strategy, it's essential to be bold and set an ambitious tone throughout the process. Advancements in technology and changing customer expectations are leading innovative companies to disrupt traditional business models and displace previous market leaders. Some new business models are subject to a network effect that creates a winner-take-all situation for first movers and fast followers [29].

This leads many organizations to adopt an "art of the possible" approach, which means that idea generation is not bound by the status quo, existing constraints, and preconceived notions. This fosters creative thinking and innovation, which is the key to discovering groundbreaking ideas that have the potential to revolutionize the organization and their industry. The result is a broader set of ideas that can later be evaluated and refined based on feasibility and potential impact.

According to BCG, "Only 33% of organizations successfully meet the challenge of digital disruption. Those that do tend to make big strategic bets—on the order of 10% of their market capitalization [30]." Winning digital strategies aim to move the needle in terms of value creation.

The key to maintaining alignment is to have your digital strategy anchored in a strong definition of "Why" as expressed in the **digital vision statement**. The vision statement should clearly state the objectives of the transformation and communicate the expected outcome when it's complete. The vision statement should inspire stakeholders to act and facilitate decision-making along the transformation journey.

As part of this process, it's important to identify the value that is expected for the organization via high-level digital transformation goals. Figure 3-2 illustrates some sample goals that can be adopted. Identifying goals will be important for evaluating and prioritizing transformation options and use cases as well as defining success criteria for the program.

Figure 3-2. Digital Transformation Goals

The next step in this process is to develop transformation use cases, which are specific scenarios that the organization aims to implement or improve using digital technologies and solutions. Use cases are essential in evaluating, planning, and executing specific digital priorities. Broadly, there are two categories of use cases: strategic use cases and operational use cases.

Strategic use cases are focused on innovating offerings, services, and products that a business provides to customers to generate revenue. On the other hand, operational use cases are focused internally on the operating model, which includes culture, employee talent, supporting processes, partnerships, use of technology, and data to support the generation of revenue.

Each of the proposed use cases is detailed with a description, objectives, value proposition, and benefits. Leadership will assess each of the use cases based on the benefits for the business to determine priority for implementation.

The culmination of this step is to summarize the digital strategy in a document that covers the vision, goals, initiatives, key priorities, and other important information. This strategy, which is essential in defining how to win in this agenda, can be shared broadly with stakeholders to build support and collaboration when starting the program.

Reimagine Operating Model

Executing an ambitious digital transformation strategy can have profound implications for how legacy organizations operate. It requires not only leveraging digital technologies to maximize business value but also cultivating organizational agility and adaptiveness to respond promptly to changes in the external environment. As shown in Figure 3-3, the operating model serves as the backbone of the organization, where various components, such as resources, capabilities, processes, and technologies, come together to deliver on its mission and objectives.

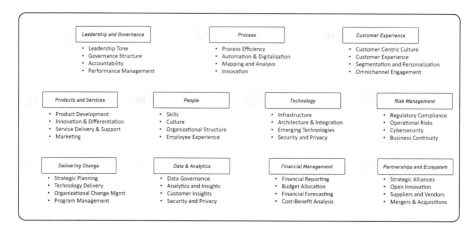

Figure 3-3. Operating Model Components

There is an intricate interplay between the components in Figure 3-3 which has a crucial role in enabling the organization to achieve its goals. For instance, the right combination of people and talent, supported by effective processes and technologies, is essential to drive innovation and adapt to rapidly changing market conditions. Similarly, a well-structured governance and decision-making framework ensures that the digital transformation initiatives align with strategic objectives and are monitored for progress.

In many organizations, the operating model evolves naturally as the business evolves. While this may work fine in regular circumstances, it presents challenges when executing on a transformational agenda. Hence, proactively defining and articulating the future state operating model becomes paramount to aligning the digital strategy with day-to-day execution.

By explicitly identifying the connections between the various components of the operating model and their roles in supporting digital transformation, organizations can better understand the intricacies involved. This understanding empowers them to identify potential bottlenecks, anticipate challenges, and align their transformation initiatives more effectively to drive successful outcomes.

Performing a current state assessment, by leveraging this framework, ensures that all existing components are considered, reveals the strengths and weaknesses of the organization, identifies areas for improvement, and serves as a starting point for the transformational journey.

Defining a future state operating model that aligns with the digital vision and identifying gaps that need to be addressed are pivotal steps in bridging the connection between the current operating model's complexity and the digital transformation journey's success. Together, these activities provide a clear pathway for organizations to navigate the complexities and challenges associated with transforming into a digitally powered enterprise. It also enables teams and functions across the organization to understand more clearly how their efforts support success in the transformation.

Develop and Manage Transformation Roadmap

Executing on a digital transformation journey is a significant undertaking that demands leadership commitment, thoughtful planning, and rigorous execution. These programs require large investments and multiyear coordination across disparate business and functional units, which must balance the needs of ongoing business operations. Dependencies must be managed, and the inevitable challenges will have to be overcome. Without a solid execution plan, even the strongest digital strategies will result in missed expectations, frustrated stakeholders, and cost overruns. In this phase, I'll cover some of the best practices that organizations are implementing to deliver on their digital agenda.

Transformation efforts require versatile leadership to navigate disparate stakeholders, change the capability and culture of the organization, and keep everyone focused on the transformational goals. This is leading to the emergence of the chief transformation officer (CTO) or a similar role that ideally reports to the CEO or, at a minimum, has a seat at the leadership table, signaling to the organization that top management is serious about the transformation and committed to its success [31]. An effective CTO typically has broad experience, especially across business and technology domains, and they have earned trust and credibility across the organization, which is critical in mediating the inevitable organizational friction. They must be capable of driving the big picture toward the strategic vision while also rolling up their sleeves to direct the details of the program.

CTOs will establish and lead Transformation Management Offices (TMO). TMOs provide a central point of planning and coordination across all digital initiatives. They are responsible for establishing consistent processes, accountability, frameworks, and tools that govern the effort with transparent reporting of risks, milestones, and benefits being gained.

A critical action for the TMO is to create and maintain the execution road-map. This involves leveraging transformation use cases and future state operating model designs to identify specific initiatives with logical scope that can be executed as a unit. Detailed planning for each initiative is undertaken to refine scope, identify dependencies, and determine resource requirements across functional areas. This team will coordinate project planning, identifying resource requirements across each type, and determining projected timelines and costs for each initiative.

Identifying the right talent for success is a crucial part of this process as many organizations may not have sufficient capacity or capability to drive such a large effort. Organizations will need to build internal capabilities through targeted training and hiring talent externally. In many cases, partnerships with external service providers can bridge the talent gap, provide additional capacity, and bring in fresh perspectives and expertise.

Sequencing initiatives in a multiyear roadmap requires a deep understanding of dependencies and balancing between quick wins that demonstrate results with foundational priorities, such as a new enterprise data platform, which requires a greater duration but is necessary to deliver on some big bets.

The chief transformation officer and the Transformation Management Offices must instill a culture of delivery and build monitoring processes that provide transparency on the status of efforts and their progress toward their goals so that, if needed, leadership can take corrective actions.

Establishing a Process Inventory Strategy

As established in Chapter 1, a key to success in transforming the organization is gaining alignment with processes through the Process Inventory framework. This is core to rebuilding the capabilities of the organization as the vertical and horizontal alignment that Process Inventory will enable is essential for enterprise agility.

To capitalize on this promise, it's crucial to thoughtfully create a strategy for implementing the Process Inventory framework. Creating required models, aligning metadata, and implementing use cases, such as those covered in Part 2 of this book, will be a multiyear effort. A winning approach is to start small, perhaps with a pilot in a single business unit, to demonstrate the value of this approach, and then scale it more broadly after the model is proven.

The best place to start is with the output of the digital strategy as it will detail the goals, use cases, and operating model impacts in the transformation. For instance, if a priority goal is to improve customer engagement, then that would mean creating a customer experience capability that builds and analyzes customer personas and customer journeys and aligning it with Process Inventory. If the goal is to increase operating efficiency, then detailing process flows with the resources leveraged may be a priority.

A business case for this framework and the resources to enable it will be required to gain alignment across leadership, which means showing how this directly supports the digital strategy will increase the chances of obtaining needed financial and stakeholder support.

The business case, like other initiatives seeking funding, needs to detail the plan, process use cases, points of collaboration, the resource plan, and the financials to get started. This should be integrated into the digital roadmap that the TMO is managing so that process dependencies across other digital initiatives can be identified and tracked.

Key Takeaways

- **Defining a digital strategy** is an important step to clarify the goals of the transformation, which is critical for aligning all efforts with those goals.

- **Key trends** are emerging in this digital era that are reshaping business models and transforming how organizations operate.

- **Creating a digital program** requires a meticulous approach that considers all opportunities and implications in defining and managing an optimal transformation roadmap.

- **Articulating a Process Inventory strategy** is important for defining the priority models, use cases, and resources necessary to apply this framework and contribute the highest value.

In Part 2 of this book, we'll explore how to apply the Process Inventory framework to transform organizational operations. This exploration begins with the next chapter, which focuses on leveraging this framework to drive operational excellence.

Applying Process Inventory to Transform Ways of Working

Driving Operational Excellence

This chapter explores several key aspects that contribute to achieving operational excellence. We'll start by defining operational excellence as the driving force behind comprehensive operational improvement efforts. Then, we'll delve into the Lean Six Sigma methodology, highlighting its role in process optimization. Additionally, we'll detail how the Process Inventory directly enhances the effectiveness of Lean Six Sigma initiatives.

Operational excellence extends beyond process improvement, so we'll also explore several other critical programs that are essential for achieving organization-wide operational excellence. Throughout, we'll emphasize the pivotal role that the Process Inventory plays in these efforts.

The Impact of the Toyota Way

The story of Toyota's operational excellence and advancement of the Lean methodology is one deeply rooted in history, philosophy, challenges, and remarkable achievements. The journey of Toyota's success, as driven by the

© Michael Schank 2023
M. Schank, *Digital Transformation Success*,
https://doi.org/10.1007/978-1-4842-9816-9_4

Toyota Way and the Toyota Production System (TPS), serves as a remarkable case study of how a company's core principles can transform the automotive industry and business practices globally [1].

Toyota was established in 1937 by Sakichi Toyoda and his son Kiichiro Toyoda. The company's journey toward operational excellence finds its origins in the ideals of Sakichi Toyoda. He was not only an engineer but also a visionary whose philosophy emphasized continuous improvement and dedication to contributing to the greater good. This philosophy is distilled into the "five main principles" of adhering faithfully to responsibilities, pursuing knowledge and innovation, practicing practicality, fostering a welcoming work environment, and upholding respect for spiritual values while maintaining gratitude. These principles guide Toyota's actions even today.

Post-World War II, Toyota faced unique challenges, starkly different from those of American automakers. While competitors, such as Ford, embraced mass production, economies of scale, and big equipment to produce large volumes of parts as cheaply as possible, Toyota couldn't follow this model as the Japanese market was much smaller and they didn't have sufficient cash on hand. This challenge led to a crucial realization: shorter lead times and flexible production lines were needed to manufacture diverse vehicle models on a single assembly line, fostering a culture of waste elimination and quick cash turnover to pay suppliers.

Kiichiro Toyoda's vision for the Koromo plant laid the groundwork for the revolutionary Kanban system. Initially documented using slips of paper, this system aimed to produce required parts each day, necessitating flow production across every operation. Quality became paramount as Toyota recognized that JIT (Just-in-Time) required impeccable quality at each step. Standardized work, JIT, and the development of the Kanban system formed the backbone of the Toyota Way. The Toyota Production System (TPS) emphasized "getting the facts" and identifying root causes—a scientific mindset that continues to drive Toyota's success.

Toyota's adherence to the Toyota Way yielded remarkable results. The company consistently delivered top-quality vehicles, witnessed steady growth in sales, and achieved consistent profitability. Toyota built massive cash reserves, which further funded innovation, contributing to society and local communities. Financially, Toyota's net profits outshone competitors by a staggering margin; they were the world's first automobile manufacturer to produce more than ten million vehicles per year, a record set in 2012 [2], underscoring the potency of their philosophy.

The story of Toyota's journey to operational excellence is one of continuous evolution rooted in a distinct philosophy. The Toyoda family's ethos—embracing challenges, innovation, and contributing to society—served as a guiding light. Toyota's paradigm-shifting approach, with lean principles at its core, heralded the decline of traditional mass production and ushered in a new era of lean production practices. The Toyota Way stands as a testament to the power of principled thinking and a relentless pursuit of excellence. From its origins to its operational achievements, Toyota's journey resonates as an inspiring case study of how a commitment to innovation, pragmatism, and continuous improvement can pave the way for enduring success in a rapidly evolving world.

Organizational Inefficiencies and Complexity

British naval historian and author Cyril Northcote Parkinson published an essay in the Economist in 1955, where he detailed his observations of the British navy's evolution from 1914 to 1928. This essay came to be known as "Parkinson's Law" found that despite a reduction of navy ships by two-thirds and personnel by a third during those years, he noted that the number of bureaucrats had increased by almost 6% annually [3]. The observation was clear: fewer personnel and reduced workload, yet the administrative ranks continued to expand. Parkinson's opening line poignantly stated: "It is a commonplace observation that work expands so as to fill the time available for its completion." In bureaucratic organizations, headcount tends to expand to consume the available budget. Parkinson identified two forces at play: the "multiplication of subordinates," wherein officials prefer subordinates to rivals, and the phenomenon of officials creating work for one another. Subsequent studies further explored the repercussions of this surplus headcount, revealing that in larger group settings, unanimous decisions can become elusive as subgroups form to block one another.

Along with these complexities, many organizations face additional challenges with system proliferation, often resulting in overlapping functionality and stifling IT spending. Complex vendor relationships, an explosion in the growth of data, increasing risks, and evolving regulatory requirements further compound challenges to operational efficiency.

In this context, costs and headcount become bloated. More importantly, getting things done becomes challenging, which doesn't bode well when attempting a change as significant as digital transformation. Changes can become time-consuming and expensive, or worse, encounter resistance as teams undermine efforts to protect their turf. It becomes almost impossible for leadership to identify which resources are essential for the organization.

Significant investments have been made in efficiency efforts, utilizing both internal resources and external consultants, with the goal of identifying and reducing waste and inefficiencies. Despite these investments, the collective benefits often fail to materialize, often due to a narrow focus on specific processes or business areas. The absence of a broad, enterprise-wide perspective can lead to a situation where efficiencies gained in one area are offset by waste accumulating in another.

Operational Excellence

As a response to this challenge, a comprehensive concept known as operational excellence has emerged, which strives to achieve optimal performance across the organization.

Operational excellence is a state in which the organization is achieving and maintaining the highest level of performance aligned with its vision and goals. While this state may not be achievable as there is always room for improvement, this defines a philosophy that directs efforts toward creating a purpose-driven culture of continuous improvement throughout the organization. This enables efficient resource utilization and the elimination of waste to deliver a sustainable competitive advantage. This program empowers organizational agility in the face of change while maximizing overall company performance and creating exceptional value for customers and stakeholders.

Keys to Operational Excellence

The starting point for driving operational excellence is to be clear about what that means in the context of your organization. This requires leadership to articulate a **vision for the future that identifies and prioritizes the goals** that are important in operating the organization. Figure 4-1 illustrates sample goals for consideration in this exercise. Furthermore, a definition of the aspirational or ideal state design can be created, which outlines key design concepts to focus on, but there should be some recognition that this is a long-term journey, and this design will likely evolve and adapt as lessons are learned and as the external environment changes. The importance of this future state vision and goals is to define and serve as an important "why" or purpose that will motivate internal and external stakeholders and ensure that every effort and action is aligned toward this shared purpose.

Figure 4-1. Sample Operational Excellence Goals

The **scope of this effort should be enterprise-wide,** or for large and complex organizations, a significant business unit. Traditionally, many improvement efforts have been focused on a small set of processes to identify inefficiencies and implementing local solutions. This fails to recognize that organizations are composed of multiple functional domains and customer touchpoints cut across multiple business areas, which means that local solutions may address that problem but will have minimal impact on the overall operating environment. Figure 4-2 illustrates the various components of the operating model, which when considered holistically can drive needed synergies across these functional domains, remove silos, foster collaboration, and propel a higher level of operational performance.

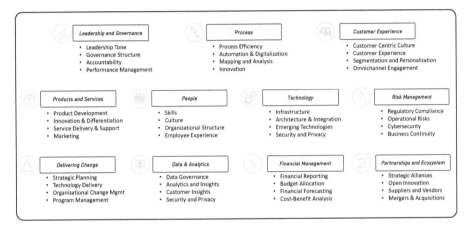

Figure 4-2. Operating Model Components

Operational excellence **programs can vary in scope and size**. They can be sizable programs with a significant multiyear investment, involving numerous workstreams, or they can be less formal and driven by a cultural shift toward incremental improvements through methods such as Kaizen events—short cross-functional workshops focused on a targeted area or process. Regardless, a program structure, perhaps through a Program Management Office, should be set up to ensure that all efforts are aligned to the future state vision. They should define success and establish key performance indicator (KPIs) targets to measure progress. KPIs should be collected and published regularly to provide insights into the effectiveness of improvement efforts.

A program of this nature needs to have **strong leadership** that communicates the vision, progress, and benefits to the entire organization. Consistency and commitment are key; leaders must walk the talk and demonstrate through their actions that they are modeling their behavior and being accountable for the success of this endeavor.

Leadership must **cultivate a culture of continuous improvement**. People, at all levels of the organization, are the engine that will drive operational excellence as they have developed deep expertise in their domain. The emphasis on critical thinking and questioning every assumption will lead to valuable insights and perspectives as to how to optimize processes. In the Toyota Way, people were at the center of the philosophy, and they were expected to spend a lifetime working to perfect their craft [1].

In traditional models, innovation was driven exclusively by the hierarchical structure or specialized efficiency teams. However, in the **democratic innovation** model, employee engagement and contributions must be encouraged. Leadership needs to remove barriers, arm employees with tools and data, enable cross-functional collaboration, and set the tone where everyone can pursue their innovative ideas. Failed ideas will inevitably occur, but this should be viewed as a learning opportunity, and the reward system should value openness and recognize employee initiative.

This will lead to the side effect of an engaged and high-performing workforce. According to Herzberg's two-factor theory [4], employee satisfaction can only be negatively impacted by not providing sufficient salary, job security, status, etc. Positive motivating factors such as challenging work, achievement, recognition, and opportunities drive greater engagement. In other words, **employees seek empowerment to find purpose in their work**. Empowering employees to make decisions and contribute to process improvements enhances their sense of ownership and accountability.

Operational Excellence Outcome

Organizations that have been successful in their pursuit of operational excellence are driven by a strong purpose, which empowers motivated employees to deliver superior customer service and value for shareholders. The organization operates with minimal waste, produces high-quality outputs, optimizes processes, and mitigates risk. This increased efficiency provides the agility needed to respond rapidly to changing competitive and environmental pressures.

Lean Six Sigma

While operational excellence provides the holistic vision, purpose-driven culture, and program for achieving a high-performing operating environment, Lean Six Sigma offers a rigorous and structured methodology, a set of tools, and techniques to aid in managing and improving quality and performance, as well as solving potentially complex problems to enhance processes. The term "Lean Six Sigma," an integration of two distinct methods, was introduced in the 2001 book *Leaning into Six Sigma: The Path to Integration of Lean Enterprise and Six Sigma* [5].

Lean, as a term, was conceived by John Krafcik, a researcher at MIT, while studying the performance attributes of the Toyota Production System [6]. He commented at the time, "It needs less of everything to create a given amount of value, so let's call it Lean." The world of Lean thinking grew rapidly, focusing on reducing non-value adding activities or waste, known as "muda" in Japanese. The Lean approach is truly about understanding how the work gets done, finding ways to do it better, smoother, and faster, and closing the time gap between the start and end points of processes.

Six Sigma is a highly disciplined approach focused on delivering near-perfect products and services by minimizing the variants within a process and identifying the causes of defects. Its roots trace back to the US in the 1980s at Motorola, during a time when they were struggling to compete with foreign manufacturers. They set a goal of achieving tenfold improvement in five years, centered on a plan for global competitiveness, participative management, quality improvement, and training. The term "Six Sigma" was coined by Motorola quality engineer Bill Smith, signifying an improvement measurement derived from a statistical term denoting three or four defects per million.

Six Sigma was further popularized by General Electric in the 1980s after Jack Welch, the dynamic CEO at that time, became a champion of the cause. After an initial successful pilot, it became evident that Six Sigma projects could yield attractive financial benefits. Welch mandated the use of Six Sigma across the entire group of GE businesses [7], stating, "We are going to shift the paradigm from fixing products to fixing and developing processes, so they produce nothing but perfection or something very close to it."

Lean and Six Sigma complement each other perfectly as central to both methods is the recognition that "process" is what needs to be improved. Six Sigma enhances the efficiency-driven Lean considerably through its strong roots and toolkits for measurement and data analysis. Lean Six Sigma (LSS) is a powerful approach for delivering necessary process improvements to drive operational excellence.

Lean Six Sigma Principles

Lean Six Sigma has a foundation of seven core principles, which represent the essence of the methodology. We'll delve into these principles as it's critical to understanding how Lean Six Sigma drives continuous improvement.

Principle #1: Focus on the Customer

To deliver the best customer experience, it's essential to understand your customers' wants and needs. The aspects of your service or offering that customers consider most crucial are referred to as CTQs (critical-to-quality) requirements in Lean Six Sigma. CTQs serve as the foundation for defining metrics that assess meaningful improvements and measure the effectiveness of those improvements.

Since Lean Six Sigma is focused on the value stream—the end-to-end process from initial conception through to delivering value to an end customer or stakeholder—it's important to recognize that value streams can encompass multiple internal stages involving various suppliers. In the context of Lean Six Sigma analysis, customers are defined as anyone who receives the output of a process. This definition includes both internal stakeholders and external customers.

To establish the boundaries of a process, a SIPOC diagram is created, documenting the following components: suppliers (providers of inputs), inputs (required resources), process (the actual steps), outputs (results or products), and customers (recipients of the outputs). This high-level tool helps identify stakeholders, segment customers, and centralize conversations around a unified process definition.

Understanding customer needs is achieved through a method known as Voice of the Customer (VOC). This involves interacting with them using techniques like interviews, focus groups, performing observations, and surveys. By actively listening to your customers, you can gain insights into their needs, preferences, and pain points. The insights derived from VOC sessions facilitate the development of critical-to-quality (CTQ) requirements. These requirements transform customer need statements into specific product or service requirements.

Requirements are refined further through Kano analysis, which assesses the value that customers place on features of a product or service. This process ensures that the most impactful requirements are given priority. Subsequent analysis is carried out to determine how each requirement could be quantified using metrics or measures. These quantifications form the foundation for establishing targets and identifying methods for metric collection.

Principle #2: Identify and Understand How Work Gets Done

The Japanese word "gemba," translating to the "actual place," refers to where the action takes place. The central concept of this principle emphasizes that Lean Six Sigma practitioners should engage stakeholders directly in the work environment. This immersion allows them to gain an appreciation of how processes are executed. Through documentation and in-depth analysis, practitioners aim to comprehend the challenges and identify opportunities for improvement.

A fundamental aspect of comprehending work involves process mapping, which serves to confirm understanding, facilitate stakeholder discussions, and provide a foundation for analysis. Various models can be constructed, tailored to the desired level of granularity and the focus of the study.

A value stream map documents the end-to-end process, including stages, activities, and handoffs as it crosses organizational boundaries to deliver customer value. This higher-level representation is designed to cover both value-adding activities and non-value-adding activities that introduce waste and inefficiency.

Process models are constructed to document how high-level activities in a value stream map are executed, including specific actors, activities, cross-functional handoffs, and leveraged resources.

A spaghetti diagram represents the flow of people, materials, and equipment in a physical space, with the intent of identifying unnecessary movement in the process.

This principle extends beyond documenting processes to include several analysis techniques. During observations, the analysis team should identify and collect relevant performance data such as the overall timeline, number of people involved, and wait times and document those on the process maps themselves. Moments of truth should be noted, which are points of interaction with external customers as they hold a higher significance in customer satisfaction or dissatisfaction. Finally, an exercise called process stapling is conducted to following the process, not from the perspective of the person operating the process but from the perspective of the thing going through the process to understand the flow to identify bottlenecks, idle time, or any other inefficiency.

Principle #3: Manage, Improve, and Smooth the Process Flow

The focal point of this principle is the identification and resolution of bottlenecks, which are process steps lacking the capacity to meet demand, and constraints, which impede the overall performance of the end-to-end process. Employing the theory of constraints, a standardized methodology is used to detect and address these limitations. This can involve subordinating other process steps to align with the constrained step, thereby preventing overproduction, or elevating the constraint itself by enhancing its capacity. The approach is an iterative one, involving the continuous identification and resolution of constraints until the end-to-end process achieves satisfactory performance.

Principle #4: Remove Non-value-added Steps and Waste

This principle focuses on streamlining processes by identifying and eliminating activities that do not directly contribute to customer satisfaction while also addressing various types of waste that can hinder agility, efficiency, cost savings, and quality.

Value, within the context of Lean Six Sigma, pertains to any activity or process step that directly contributes to fulfilling customer needs and requirements. To evaluate the value of each step, three general criteria can be leveraged:

- Does the outcome matter to the customer?

- Does the activity either physically alter the product or service, or is it indispensable for a subsequent step?

- Is the activity executed correctly the first time?

While these criteria serve as a starting point, they are somewhat vague and require interpretation. Therefore, it is imperative for each organization to establish its own definition that aligns with its specific context.

To further guide the identification of non-value-added steps and waste, Taiichi Ohno, a former Toyota executive and often referred to as the "father of the Toyota Production System," developed a list of seven wastes applicable to manufacturing processes. Over time, this list expanded to encompass eight wastes applicable to various types of processes across different organizations:

- **Transportation**: Unnecessary movement of materials or products that can lead to waiting times, increased resource consumption, and potential loss or damage.

- **Inventory**: Excessive levels of raw materials, work in progress, or finished goods that contribute to longer lead times, obsolescence, higher costs, and delays.

- **Motion**: Wasted efforts due to unnecessary physical movement, such as bending, twisting, or walking, often caused by suboptimal equipment placement or information access.

- **Waiting**: Delays caused by people being unable to proceed with their work, leading to idle time and inefficiencies.

- **Overproduction**: Generating more products or services than needed, resulting in overstaffing, unnecessary storage and transportation costs, and excess inventory.

- **Overprocessing**: Executing more steps than necessary, consuming resources without adding value.

- **Defects**: Rework or errors caused by failing to meet critical-to-quality (CTQ) requirements.

- **Skills**: Underutilizing the skills and potential of people within the process.

The analysis of removing non-value-added steps begins with process models, where non-value-add and waste are documented based on established criteria. Capturing the processing time or, if possible, estimating the cost of each step is crucial for constructing a business case, particularly when the elimination of these steps requires an investment.

Principle #5: Manage by Fact and Reduce Variation

At the core of this principle lies the emphasis on making decisions based on factual data, rather than assumptions or intuition, to achieve process consistency. Uncontrolled variations in processes can lead to quality issues, so it's in an organization's best interest to achieve a consistent, reliable, and predictable level of performance. This means collecting data, calculating for variation, and interpreting calculations correctly to determine if actions are required.

Standard deviation is a calculation method for assessing process variation. It quantifies the extent to which individual data points deviate from the average or mean. A smaller standard deviation indicates that data points cluster tightly around the mean, highlighting consistent and predictable outcomes. Conversely, a larger standard deviation suggests greater data spread, indicating higher process variability and less predictable results. Investigating the nature of variation, whether common (expected) or special (unexpected), will determine if further root cause analysis is needed.

Control charts play a pivotal role in identifying and differentiating between common and special cause variations. These charts depict the process average and upper and lower control limits (UCL and LCL). Placed at plus and minus three standard deviations from the process average, these limits serve as reference points for assessing process stability.

While this topic can be explored further, including additional chart types like histograms and Pareto charts, the key takeaway is that calculating and understanding variation is essential for effectively managing variations and delivering high-quality processes.

Principle #6: Involve and Equip the People in the Process

This principle recognizes that the success of any improvement initiative hinges on involving the people in the process, equipping, and empowering them to challenge and enhance the way work is executed.

Achieving results thrives on collaboration rather than isolated efforts. A collaborative approach engages every organizational level. Employees, with their valuable insights into processes, hold the keys to understanding nuances and overcoming challenges. Their active participation in process improvement discussions fosters a sense of ownership and accountability. Empowered individuals become the driving force behind innovation, propelling solutions aligned with organizational objectives.

Empowering employees to identify and resolve problems not only boosts morale but also nurtures a culture of continuous improvement. Empowered individuals become change agents who inspire others. This culture embraces challenges and perceives them as opportunities for learning and growth, aligning perfectly with a growth mindset.

Equipping employees with the necessary tools and skills is critical. Offering training and development initiatives positions individuals for success in process improvement endeavors. By honing problem-solving and analytical skills, organizations cultivate a workforce adept at identifying inefficiencies, addressing challenges, and implementing sustainable solutions.

This culture thrives on transparent communication, robust feedback loops, and recognition of achievements and initiatives. A shared commitment to ongoing enhancement propels the organization forward, fostering adaptability in the face of evolving challenges.

Principle #7: Undertake Improvement Activity in a Systematic Way

This Lean Six Sigma principle emphasizes the importance of a structured, systematic problem-solving methodology for conducting improvement efforts to enhance existing processes. This methodology is best used when confronted with complex problems where causes and solutions are not readily apparent and when collaboration from individuals with diverse expertise is required.

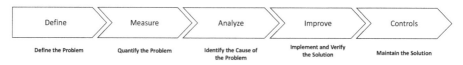

Figure 4-3. DMAIC Framework

A critical factor in the success of a DMAIC (Define, Measure, Analyze, Improve, and Control) project is to clearly identify and describe the problem, purpose, and objectives through an improvement charter, which marks the start of the effort. The improvement charter includes the following components: a compelling business case, a concise problem statement, measurable goals, a well-defined scope, critical-to-quality (CTQ) factors, roles, milestones, and more. This charter, important for gaining alignment from sponsors and team members, should be considered a living document that evolves as the team gains a deeper understanding of the problem.

A great way to validate the quality of the improvement charter is through the 5Ws (and 1H) tool. This means ensuring that it clearly addresses the what, why, when, how, where, and who aspects in a manner that all stakeholders can easily understand.

Maintaining a pulse on progress through informal reviews with sponsors and formal tollgate reviews at the conclusion of each DMAIC phase ensures that the initiative remains aligned with its original objectives. Tollgates play a crucial role in validating the proper completion of the latest phase and the production of high-quality outputs. They also offer an excellent opportunity to revisit the improvement charter based on new insights, evaluate lessons learned, assess team dynamics, review milestones, validate assumptions, and reexamine goals.

Process Inventory Enhances Lean Six Sigma Effectiveness

The main criticism of Lean Six Sigma programs is that management adopts the methods and tools, trains their people, and expects amazing results which never materialize. They fail to realize that this success requires an enterprise-wide culture change toward a philosophy of critical thinking and continuous improvement. While there is no substitute for leadership, Process Inventory can significantly increase the effectiveness of process improvement efforts.

Sustained Knowledge Management

Optimizing processes is an iterative pursuit that entails experimenting, analyzing results, designing further solutions, and repeating these steps. This process can take place over the span of several years or more, with potentially different teams performing the analysis. Without maintaining process documentation, each team may define the problem uniquely and map the process with different boundaries. I've personally seen this many times where each new team comes in and starts their analysis with a blank sheet of paper. This not only inefficiently uses time but can also lead to poor results as past lessons and failures don't serve as a guide for future solutions.

Process Inventory, and the information governed in the Integrated Operational Repository, solves this by providing an authoritative source of process information within the environment. This provides analysis teams with an inventory of processes, their boundaries, identification of process ownership, and if process models have been created, process activities and connections upstream and downstream, as well as all the resource and operational information captured in the metadata.

If the Integrated Operational Repository is populated, then the Process Inventory should be leveraged to define scope with precision. Analysis should begin with this information, and stakeholder discussions should focus on identifying information gaps and brainstorming solutions.

If this process area has not been documented yet, then new analysis efforts represent an opportunity to create proper documentation. This means working with the Process COE to create the Process Inventory, as well as developing value stream maps and process models following the defined modeling standards. This will ensure that future improvement efforts will have maintained documentation to drive further improvement.

Transparency

One barrier to enabling the culture of continuous improvement is arming individuals with information about how processes work so they can create novel and innovative solutions. In many cases, detailed understanding is locked in a select few subject matter resources, which means any analysis efforts will be dependent on getting their valuable time. Having a transparent source of information that is accessible to everyone solves the issue of the limited subject matter experts and allows innovation to be democratized to everyone.

Ownership Model

Diffusion of responsibility [8] is a sociopsychological phenomenon wherein a person is unlikely to take responsibility when they assume that others in the environment are accountable. Essentially, if everyone is accountable, then no one is accountable. This hinders attempts to transform the culture toward a state where everyone actively drives improvements. A key strategy to avoid this situation is to clearly define accountability, set expectations and goals, and reward initiative and results on an individual level. Process Inventory plays a crucial role in this by defining ownership for each process.

Process Inventory

Figure 4-4. Process Ownership Model

Furthermore, the hierarchy of ownership, as illustrated in Figure 4-4, encourages everyone to contribute solutions that align with their scope of responsibilities and facilitates effective collaboration down the hierarchy. In this concept, lower-level process owners should be focused on ways to improve the process, while managers and leaders should be focused on higher-level strategies for success, such as whether is this process redundant and should be moved to a shared service team, should the process be outsourced to an external vendor, and do we have the right talent sourcing strategy.

Collaboration and communication along the hierarchy integrate perspectives at different levels and optimize processes for the organization.

Cross-Functional Coordination

Processes rely on various resources, including people, systems, data, controls, and vendors, all of which are managed and governed by distinct functional groups. By connecting all this information through the metadata library, tracing ownership back to these groups becomes possible, enabling cross-functional validation before deploying solutions.

This integration is particularly useful as many processes are heavily dependent on technology for their performance. I've witnessed several Lean Six Sigma efforts conclude without actual improvements but with a list of system changes requiring prioritization for funding. Such clarity empowers business and IT leaders to collaborate to define an optimal IT environment aligned with the business's needs.

Leveraging Technology to Design Improvement

The advancement of technical capabilities can be harnessed to identify problems and devise solutions for process optimization. A prime example of such progress is the emergence of digital twins. A digital twin serves as a virtual representation of a physical object, system, or process, effectively capturing real-time data from its physical counterpart [9] to leverage artificial intelligence to conduct simulations, analyses, and predictions. This presents an exciting opportunity where technology aids in process analysis to pinpoint areas for improvement and define solutions.

Digital twins find their primary application in the manufacturing sector, where Internet of Things (IoT) sensors supply real-time data for their virtual counterparts to analyze. Across all industries, Process Inventory assumes the role of providing the virtual representation of all process areas, enabling technology to take on the role of an analyst. Further details on this concept are explored in Chapter 6.

Additional Operational Excellence Methods

While Lean Six Sigma is an important methodology for improving the performance and quality of processes, there are many other programs that contribute to achieving operational excellence. This highlights the crucial aspect that achieving operational excellence demands a comprehensive organizational effort where all functions are aligned toward the organization's objectives. Here are a few additional programs that hold significance, along with their with the ways that Process Inventory supports their success.

Enterprise Architecture

In today's digital age, the performance of processes is highly dependent on the systems and architecture they run on. Plus, a significant amount of operating costs is dedicated to maintaining the IT environment. Enterprise Architecture is responsible for defining the IT vision and governing the alignment of technologies with processes and business strategies. By optimizing the IT infrastructure and integrating diverse systems, a well-run Enterprise Architecture function can promote agility and adaptability, driving continuous improvement and innovation across the organization.

Data Governance

The digital era has ushered in an unprecedented explosion of data. Data, if managed well, can be an asset that brings a competitive advantage. When managed poorly, it can lead to many operational issues such as inaccurate decision-making, poor process performance, low-quality customer service, high cost, and compliance issues. The data governance program is accountable for ensuring the availability, accuracy, and integrity of data. They establish data governance policies, define quality processes, design data architectures, unlock the power of data-driven insights, and more. A commitment to optimizing the data environment is a critical part of an operational excellence program.

Process Inventory and the details collected in process models, through data objects, provide data governance teams insights into which data each process uses and how it's leveraged. This information, especially when mapped to an enterprise data glossary or data model, can enable higher data quality by eliminating redundancies, inconsistencies, and inefficiencies in data storage, management, and usage. If process modeling is combined with system sequence diagrams, this can capture the end-to-end journey of data as it moves from source to destination, providing insights into transformations, bottlenecks, and compliance with data policies. Process Inventory provides a clear ownership model from which to coordinate data quality efforts.

Risk Management

Managing risk effectively holds significant importance for many organizations, particularly those operating in highly regulated industries. Establishing a program capable of proficiently identifying and controlling risks is paramount for informed executive decision-making, ensuring compliance with laws and regulations, mitigating financial risks, safeguarding business continuity, fostering customer trust, and upholding the organization's reputation.

The ways in which Process Inventory can support the effective management of risk are covered in Chapter 7.

Operating Model Design

Leadership faces numerous considerations when structuring their organization, encompassing factors like insourcing vs. outsourcing, centralization vs. decentralization, geographical location, roles and responsibilities, and others. These decisions directly impact the organization's performance, which makes it a key consideration for an operational excellence program. An effectively designed operating model not only aligns business strategies with execution but also provides role clarity, eliminates redundancies, enhances customer service, and exhibits adaptability to changing circumstances.

Process Inventory offers leadership a transparent view of the processes performed and owned by each group and their alignment with the organization's performance objectives. When every process in the Process Inventory is correlated with a business capability model or a standard process model, it enhances visibility into potential process overlaps or redundancies. This heightened visibility serves as a catalyst for evaluating these processes, potentially leading to their rationalization through the creation of shared service functions and the standardization of similar processes. Such actions enable organizations to optimize their operating models to effectively align with the goals of operational excellence.

Supply Chain Management

Supply chain management plays a pivotal role in achieving operational excellence by optimizing the flow of goods, services, and information across the value chain. Effective supply chain management minimizes lead times, reduces costs, and enhances collaboration with suppliers and partners. It enables organizations to respond swiftly to market demands, reduce waste, and ensure consistent product quality.

Process Inventory supports supply chain management by linking the value chain in a value stream map and providing lower details to specific processes as previously discussed in this chapter.

Customer Experience

Providing superior customer experiences and engagement is a prominent goal in many business strategies. To deliver on that commitment, it requires a deep understanding of their customers, what motivates them, what pain points they experience, and how their needs evolve over time. This comprehensive understanding enables organizations to design products, services, processes, and experiences to address specific customer preferences and anticipate emerging trends. This has led many organizations to create dedicated customer experience functions that are focused on creating deep insights by studying their customers.

Chapter 2 covers the linkage between customer personas, customer journeys with processes in the Process Inventory, and the alignment of metadata; it enables traceability from the customer's perspective through each resource that supports those interactions. This enables precision in root cause analysis enabling the development of appropriate solutions to address issues or capture opportunities.

Process Inventory Powers Operational Excellence

This is just a small sampling as Process Inventory can power effectiveness in other programs such as vendor management, IT operations, issue management, and more. The key to optimizing how the organization operates and delivers on operational excellence goals is having a shared deep understanding of the organization's processes through Process Inventory. Process Inventory facilitates alignment to operational excellence goals, keeping each program focused on the organization's priorities. Process Inventory empowers the organization to streamline its operations, enhance quality, and achieve remarkable efficiency and adaptability in the challenging competitive landscape.

Key Takeaways

- **Operational excellence** is a state in which the organization is achieving and maintaining the highest level of performance aligned with its vision and goals. It requires an organization-wide purpose-driven culture of continuous improvement.

- **Lean Six Sigma** offers a cultural philosophy, rigorous and structured methodology, and a set of tools and techniques to aid in managing and improving quality and performance, as well as solving potentially complex problems to enhance processes.

- **Many more programs,** in addition to Lean Six Sigma, play a critical role in driving operational excellence success.

- **Process Inventory** powers effectiveness and facilitates alignment across all these programs toward operational excellence goals.

In the next chapter, we will delve into how the Process Inventory framework can transform the change process.

Transforming the Change Process

What You Will Learn

In this chapter, we will delve deep into the change process, a broad term encompassing any change in organizational capability, regardless of size and scope. You will gain an understanding of prominent change methodologies, including the strategy process, project portfolio management, Agile, Waterfall, and organizational change management.

We will explore how the Process Inventory framework can transform these methodologies by enabling alignment among all stakeholders and deliverables, ensuring that efforts remain focused on the strategic objectives of change. You will discover how it enhances the strategy development process, streamlines project portfolio management, provides clarity in scope and impact analysis, improves the handling of requirements and user stories, facilitates rigorous testing, and empowers effective change management for

© Michael Schank 2023
M. Schank, *Digital Transformation Success*,
https://doi.org/10.1007/978-1-4842-9816-9_5

people. Furthermore, you will find that project management becomes significantly more effective due to the transparency and traceability that the Process Inventory framework provides.

BBC Digital Media Initiative Transformation Failure

In 2008, the British Broadcasting Corporation (BBC) launched an ambitious project aimed at modernizing production operations and transforming how the organization manages data and provides content to audiences, all while reducing costs [1]. The business transformation program was named the Digital Media Initiative (DMI), which involved strategic investments in infrastructure, people, and production processes. A key aspect of the digital transformation was overhauling the BBC's data management system, with significant efforts dedicated to enabling staff collaboration on audio and video content and providing access to archived material.

From the outset, the program suffered numerous delays and rising costs. The BBC had awarded a contract, without running an open procurement process, to technology conglomerate Siemens to be their technology delivery partner. That contract was canceled a year later due to poor performance. The BBC brought the work in-house, but the struggles remained as they didn't have the technical capability to deliver the program.

In 2013, the BBC announced that DMI was shut down, and they would be writing off £98 million in unusable technology. These financial losses were a significant blow to the organization, drawing criticism and public scrutiny over the misuse of public funds. PWC performed a postmortem review [2] of how the program was managed and found numerous issues.

The program lacked adequate oversight and governance. It lacked an Executive Steering Committee, which could have challenged program management on progress toward their goals. The Finance Committee assumed some of that role, but their expertise primarily restricted them from challenging the financial costs and benefits. The program did not provide clear and transparent reporting on progress against the plan, cost to complete, and delivery of benefits. The risks and issues logs were not kept up-to-date and were missing several critical items, and the risks and issues captured focused on technology risks and issues rather than the ability of DMI to drive operational change to business practices. The program also lacked an effective assurance plan needed to audit program management practices and risks.

They lacked a solid approach to delivering the program. The BBC team didn't understand the methodology employed by Siemens. When they brought the work in-house, they lacked a structured approach with proper phases and tollgate control to monitor delivery. The PWC report stated that they would have benefited from a proper Design Authority, which could have advised the program on the technical designs and the linkage to business outcomes.

Finally, it appears that the program was run predominantly from a technology point of view and lacked proper engagement from the business. The report found no evidence that the program had a business sponsor with an active role in the program. Their delivery roadmap didn't provide clarity as to when benefits to the business would be delivered, and they failed to engage business stakeholders to sign up for delivering those benefits.

Defining Change

Change is constant in organizations, but it becomes more prominent when an organization is adopting a digital agenda. There are several triggers for change, such as a shift in strategy or business model, response to competitive pressures, meeting customer expectations, adopting new technologies, regulatory changes, or any many other reasons. Implementing change can have impacts across one or more of the following: customers, products, services, risk and compliance, people, third-party vendors, employees, technology, data, or infrastructure.

Change can take on different forms based on its size and scope. There are large transformation efforts that redesign the organization's core capabilities to adapt to changing market conditions, capture new opportunities, and address significant challenges. Additionally, there are large mergers, acquisitions, or divestitures that require merging or splitting the resources of the organization within a compressed timeline. These endeavors also encompass significant changes and have wide-ranging impacts on the organization. These efforts typically span the enterprise, require multiple years of effort, and involve substantial funding, often in the range of tens or hundreds of millions.

On the other end of the spectrum, there are small projects focused on deploying small enhancements or fixing defects. Some changes may not involve technology at all and may instead entail organizational restructuring or cultural transformation.

Implementing change, especially for large transformation efforts, is one of the most complex endeavors an organization must undertake due to the following factors:

- **Coordination** across multiple stakeholder groups and practitioner teams, each with their own interests and perspectives, to deliver on the expected change.

- **Complexity** of the organization, its processes, and the systems means identifying the impacts and the precise changes that need to occur may take substantial effort.

- **Organizational culture** may be an impediment, especially for large change, as disruption to the status quo may be faced with resistance.

- **Interdependencies** can be difficult to understand and manage, missing key ones can result in delays or disruptions.

- **Risk**, when deploying change, can be heightened, or new risks can be introduced, requiring a deep understanding to implement and test appropriate mitigating controls.

- **Resource effort** can be significant, especially if the organization doesn't have the required skills in-house. Managing an external vendor adds another layer of complexity.

- **Duration** for large efforts may take years, which may result in fatigue especially if the change initiative requires long hours for key resources.

Change management is a systematic approach and set of methodologies, processes, and techniques employed to effectively navigate these challenges and deliver on the intended business objectives. It aims to address the complexities and uncertainties associated with change.

For the delivery of technology changes, there are several software development life cycle (SDLC) methodologies, which are processes for planning, creating, and deploying information systems. The two most prominent SDLC methodologies are Waterfall and Agile. While organizations may support both methodologies, the choice depends on the characteristics of the change effort and the specific project requirements. Additionally, two other disciplines play important roles in the change management process: organizational change management and project management.

Waterfall is characterized by a series of sequential phases, where each phase depends on the deliverables of the previous phase [4]. It follows a linear and structured flow and typically includes control tollgates for quality confirmation and approvals before progressing to the next phase. Waterfall is appropriate for complex system integration efforts, where the scope and requirements are stable, the project has a fixed timeline, and iteration is not required.

Agile is an iterative development process that emphasizes collaboration within cross-functional teams, including product owners, developers, testers, and DevOps members [5]. Agile is suitable when the solution has limited interdependencies, requirements are subject to change, and continuous product management input is needed. It is particularly effective when there is a focus on innovation and continuous improvement.

Organizational change management involves the planning, executing, and monitoring of activities that facilitate the adaptation of individuals and organizations to new ways of working and technologies. It entails recognizing and addressing the impacts on people, as well as understanding, preparing for, implementing, and sustaining changes within an organization. The ultimate objective is to maximize the benefits and minimize the negative impacts associated with those changes.

Project management is the practice of guiding a team to achieve all project goals within the given constraints. The discipline of project management is focused on planning, organizing, monitoring, and controlling programs or projects that are created to execute change.

Challenges in Executing Change

I mentioned in Chapter 1 that 70% of digital transformation failed to reach their goals. Those challenges extend to smaller efforts, and 9.9% of every dollar dedicated to change initiatives is wasted due to poor performance [8].

The top challenges in change initiatives, as defined by Forbes [9], are

- **Lack of Clarity and Execution Strategy**: The primary goal of projects is to solve a business problem. This requires a clear consensus among the entire group of stakeholders on the definition of the business problem and a robust execution strategy to deliver software that addresses the business objectives.

- **Inability to Reach Consensus on Priorities**: Project sponsors and project teams are not clearly aligned on the top priorities for the project.

- **Not Starting with the End Customer**: Change initiatives can begin with a great idea that is implemented, only to discover that the problem they solved wasn't the problem their customers faced. Doing the hard work of deeply understanding your customers, their desires, and what they're willing to pay for sets the ceiling on project performance and can help refocus a team when things derail.

- **Unclear Scope and Requirements**: A common reason for project failure is unclear requirements and a lack of detailed explanation of the vision for the initiative.

- **Working in Silos**: A major reason for failure is when teams embark on a journey to build something that is either not a business need or does not address the right problem, which is a symptom of misalignment between the business and technology.

- **Lack of Coordination and Detailed Planning**: Many projects fail due to a lack of good coordination and detailed planning. Teams need to implement a bottom-up planning process that identifies dependencies between deliverables and includes effort and duration estimates from critical resources.

- **Friction Caused by Undefined Roles**: Undefined or unclear role expectations create friction in project teams. Lack of clear accountability leads to quality issues in work products and the delivered change.

A Vision for Change Fueled by Process Inventory

In Chapter 1, I covered how the root cause of digital transformation failures is often a lack of strategic alignment. This same root cause underlies many challenges in the change process. Process Inventory addresses this by providing an anchor for all change efforts, regardless of size or type, to a comprehensive and accurate inventory of processes. It offers a consistent business-oriented lens through which to align vertically, from business strategy to the lowest level of implementation. Additionally, it enhances accountability and collaboration by aligning resources horizontally with the processes impacted by change. Process Inventory increases the effectiveness of organizational change management and project management by equipping these teams with more granular details on the impacts of change. Lastly, it establishes a sustained knowledge management structure that promotes continuous improvement and optimization.

Vertical alignment begins by aligning the outcomes of the strategic planning process with the process areas and customer touchpoints affected by the updated strategy. This enables the project portfolio team to assess priorities and estimate the size of change objectively, guiding the allocation of the change budget toward the highest priority business goals. Process Inventory provides a common language that serves as a business-oriented anchor for all deliverables in the change methodology, including scope, requirements, agile deliverables, design documents, testing, risk management impacts, and deployment and monitoring. This top-down traceability creates a linkage from leadership to lower-level resources executing the change, significantly minimizing any gaps in understanding.

Horizontal alignment is facilitated by identifying all impacted processes and the resources that support them. Each process in the Process Inventory framework is assigned an owner, making the accountability model clear. Furthermore, as each process is connected with the resources it leverages during execution, accountable resources within the various practitioner teams can be identified with precision. This not only facilitates effective planning by determining the scope for each resource but also allows for accurate effort estimation. Additionally, by detailing the interdependencies between processes, the Process Inventory framework enables identification of dependencies when delivering change.

By providing **organizational change management** teams with details on the impacted resources and how they will be affected, they can develop stronger strategies and plans to successfully guide the transition of individuals, teams, and organizations. This alignment ensures that all key deliverables, such as communications, training, and monitoring, are tailored to the specific needs of those impacted, thereby increasing the chances of a successful transition. Furthermore, this alignment fosters better relatability between individuals and teams when leadership communicates their vision for the future.

The effectiveness of **project management** is enhanced by the traceability and transparency provided by the Process Inventory framework. Project plans and program roadmaps are supported by increased detail on impacts and the involved resources. Stakeholder engagement becomes clearer through the accountability that Process Inventory provides. Status reports offer enhanced clarity to leadership as they can communicate progress in business terms, such as the progress of processes or process areas toward the project goals. Figure 5-1 illustrates how traceability is accomplished throughout the life cycle of change delivery. As each output, from strategy through postproduction monitoring, is aligned to the process, it provides a business-oriented connection that stakeholders can understand when validating whether project objectives are being met.

Strategic Objectives   Scope   Requirements / User Stories   Design   Control Design   Code   Testing   Organizational Change Management   Production Deployment   Post-Production Monitoring

Figure 5-1. Change Process Traceability

Most deliverables in change initiatives are transitory, meaning they are created solely for a specific effort, are archived when that effort is complete, and are not typically leveraged in future initiatives. This is often due to the use of different organizing frameworks for each effort, making it challenging to correlate past deliverables to current project needs. Process Inventory, by providing a consistent framework, allows deliverables and the knowledge within them to be leveraged by subsequent efforts. This promotes **continuous improvement and optimization** of processes and documentation by capitalizing on the collective wisdom and lessons learned from previous initiatives. This means that initiatives will no longer begin with a "blank sheet of paper." Instead, teams can direct their energies toward improvements rather than spending significant effort on understanding how things work.

The Change Initiative Process

Figure 5-2 represents the change initiative process, which goes from developing a strategy through deployment and monitoring of changes. I will leverage this through the remainder of the chapter to detail various phases and to demonstrate how Process Inventory supports much greater effectiveness of the change process.

It's important to note that not all change initiatives will involve changes to processes as some may be focused on infrastructure or cosmetic user interface changes. However, understanding the impacts of these changes on processes is still important.

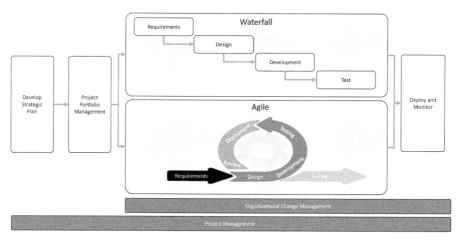

Figure 5-2. The Change Initiative Process

Develop Strategic Plans

Strategic planning is the organizational process of defining its strategy or direction and making decisions on allocating resources to achieve strategic goals [10]. By envisioning the desired future state and aligning strategies and actions accordingly, strategic planning shapes the plans and decisions of the organization. In many organizations, this is performed yearly, and it provides a roadmap that guides investments, goal setting, and performance evaluation, ensuring that the organization moves in a purposeful and coordinated manner toward its long-term objectives.

In many organizations, the primary goal of strategic planning is to identify the organization's direction and priorities for the next three to five years. Figure 5-3 illustrates a typical strategic planning process.

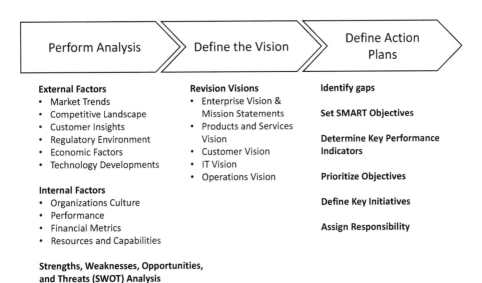

External Factors
- Market Trends
- Competitive Landscape
- Customer Insights
- Regulatory Environment
- Economic Factors
- Technology Developments

Internal Factors
- Organizations Culture
- Performance
- Financial Metrics
- Resources and Capabilities

Strengths, Weaknesses, Opportunities, and Threats (SWOT) Analysis

Revision Visions
- Enterprise Vision & Mission Statements
- Products and Services Vision
- Customer Vision
- IT Vision
- Operations Vision

Identify gaps

Set SMART Objectives

Determine Key Performance Indicators

Prioritize Objectives

Define Key Initiatives

Assign Responsibility

Figure 5-3. Strategic Planning Process

Perform Analysis

During this phase, various external inputs are gathered, including market trends, the competitive landscape, customer insights, changes in the regulatory environment, economic factors, technology developments, and other relevant external information. If the organization has a customer experience (CX) team that has been creating customer personas and customer journeys, this presents an excellent opportunity to incorporate their valuable insights.

In addition, internal inputs are gathered, including operational performance, financial performance, organizational culture, resources, and more. Process Inventory can support this process in two ways: Firstly, strategists can use it to identify each process area or capability as strategically important or foundational. Secondly, if the organization has aligned process performance metrics to the Process Inventory framework, this provides an opportunity to leverage this insight to identify important processes or capabilities that are underperforming.

These two inputs provide the basis for a SWOT analysis, which is a brainstorming tool to identify the organization's strengths, weaknesses, opportunities, and threats. This comprehensive analysis aids leaders in understanding the strategic changes required for the organization.

Define the Vision

A vision and mission statement represents the organization's purpose and value proposition, outlining its long-term aspirations and goals. Well-crafted vision and mission statements inspire and motivate employees, stakeholders, and customers by providing a clear sense of direction and purpose. While vision and mission statements are typically stable, they can be revisited and refined through this process. This can lead to changes in future state visions for other key aspects of the organization, such as products, services, customers, technology, and operations.

At this point, a vision for the future state of processes should be developed. Not all processes have the same importance as some are critical for customer interactions, profitability, or other reasons. Identifying which processes, through the Process Inventory framework, are of high strategic importance will help allocate initiative investment in subsequent steps.

Defining Action Plans

In this step, the organization's vision is compared to current capabilities to identify gaps that require investment. These gaps are converted into SMART objectives, which specify the objectives as specific, measurable, achievable, realistic, and timely. These objectives will be logically grouped based on how they will be implemented into change initiatives. Examples of these initiatives include mergers, acquisitions, divestitures, outsourcing process areas, new revenue streams, technology transformation, and more.

These initiatives will be mapped to the organization or organizations that are responsible for their implementation and will be impacted by them. By aligning them to the Process Inventory, this mapping can be done with precision and can lead to the identification of resources across all practitioner teams that will be responsible.

The output of the strategic planning process is typically reviewed and approved by the senior leaders of the organization and most likely the board.

Portfolio Planning Process

Portfolio planning is the process of evaluating initiatives to determine which, out of a finite amount of funding, provide maximum value to the business and are thus allocated funds. This process also enforces rigor to ensure that each project requesting funding creates a business case with the appropriate level of diligence in identifying scope, estimating costs and benefits, identifying risks, and addressing other factors that support the successful delivery of the project. Figure 5-4 illustrates the steps in the portfolio planning process.

US LIFE AND ANNUITY INSURANCE PROVIDER

A global insurance provider strategically determined that their US life and annuity business did not align with their future vision, leading them to decide to spin off this business segment.

The newly formed company embarked on a substantial transformation program to separate their people, processes, and technology from the global parent organization. They sought consulting assistance in defining the program, establishing priorities, and developing a multiyear roadmap.

Prior to initiating the program, the company established key principles that would guide their design decisions for the new organization. Their value proposition centered around being a low-cost insurance provider compared to their competitors. Consequently, they aimed to avoid inheriting any legacy systems, opting instead to build their infrastructure from scratch. Their vision included a cloud-based environment, leveraging vendor platforms, and outsourcing nonstrategic business processes. Essentially, they operated as a startup with substantial total assets and existing insurance policies.

When they approached us for a proposal, they expressed a desire to adopt a "City Plan" approach, where the program design would align with their functional areas. I was brought in to lead the proposal writing process, and upon winning the project, I assumed responsibility for building the engagement team.

Our initial step involved defining their project portfolio. We created a map of their functional areas, akin to a business capability model. The company's leadership then used this map to categorize each area as either "best in class," indicating a strategic differentiator requiring increased investment, or "best in cost," representing areas that needed to be efficient but didn't necessitate extensive investment.

Working closely with each functional area, we conducted sessions to define their inventory of processes and establish high-level requirements for each process. This information informed the development of request for proposal (RFP) requirements for vendors to support the initiative, as well as helped shape the portfolio of initiatives. We crafted a charter for each initiative, outlining the scope, effort and financial estimates, timelines, and key risks associated with each.

The culmination of these efforts resulted in an integrated roadmap for the program, taking a process-centric view. This roadmap served as a guide throughout the execution of the program, ultimately leading to its successful completion.

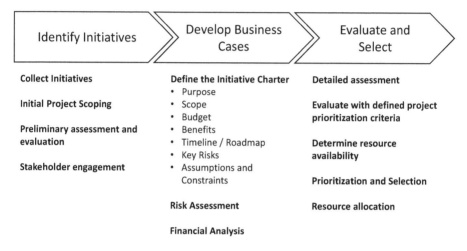

Figure 5-4. Project Portfolio Management

Identify Initiative

In this phase of the project portfolio process, all proposed initiatives are brought to light. While the strategic planning process contributes to some of these initiatives, it's important to note that each business unit or functional area may have its own proposed initiatives that align with its specific goals, which may include the continuation of funding for initiatives that have started in previous cycles.

During this phase, the project team engages with stakeholders from various areas and conducts initial scoping and evaluations based on the projected budget. The aim is to assess the feasibility and alignment of each proposal with the organization's strategic objectives. Through this process, some proposals are down selected and excluded, while others progress to the next step in the evaluation process.

Develop Business Cases

Initiatives that progress to this phase are required to develop a detailed business case, which is captured through an initiative charter. Initiative charters are applicable to both programs and projects. Programs generally encompass larger-scale initiatives that consist of multiple coordinated projects aimed at delivering significant value for the business. On the other hand, projects are scoped to deliver more focused changes, targeting specific objectives. The initiative charter serves as a formal document that outlines the goals, objectives, scope, resources, timelines, and expected outcomes of the proposed initiatives. It provides a comprehensive overview and foundation for effective planning and execution during the subsequent phases of the project portfolio process.

Figure 5-5 illustrates how Process Inventory can provide alignment for a change initiative.

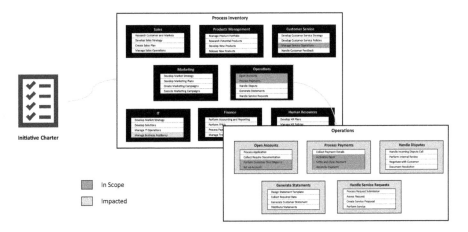

Figure 5-5. Define Initiative Scope

By leveraging Process Inventory, organizations can **define scope** with precision for programs or processes. This approach ensures that the boundaries of scope are clearly established using a business-oriented lens, enabling all stakeholders to understand and align with it. In addition, the preceding diagram distinguishes between processes that will change as part of the initiative and those that will be impacted. Impacted processes require regression testing to ensure that no errors are introduced due to changes in underlying resources.

Furthermore, Process Inventory enables programs to conduct detailed **impact analysis** by identifying process owners and understanding the resources associated with each process. This information facilitates more accurate effort, budget, and timeline estimation as it provides a comprehensive view of all required changes. Additionally, aligning performance metrics with Process Inventory allows for easier calculation of benefits derived from the initiative.

Risk assessments are completed with greater accuracy through the detailed information obtained via Process Inventory and its connection with risks and controls documented in the GRC (governance, risk, and compliance) repository. This comprehensive approach ensures that risks are properly identified, assessed, and managed, leveraging a thorough understanding of the underlying processes and associated controls. It highlights the value of leveraging Process Inventory to strengthen risk management practices and enhance the overall effectiveness of the organization's GRC framework.

Evaluation and Selection

Alignment of scope with business processes and improved precision in assessing impacts, dependencies, and cost estimates enable portfolio teams to make more objective assessments when selecting projects for funding. By prioritizing initiatives that align with the strategic importance of process areas, portfolio teams can enhance the efficiency of change funding, ensuring that necessary changes are effectively implemented.

Requirements

According to the Project Management Institute's (PMI) 2021 Pulse of the Profession report [11], 40% of project failures can primarily be attributed to poor requirements. The cost of addressing requirement defects in software rises exponentially as it progresses through the life cycle up to production deployment. In one estimate [12], requirements errors cost US businesses more than $30 billion per year.

MERGER OF REGIONAL BANKS

Two regional banks of approximately equal size had announced a merger and had set up a post-merger integration program to reach Client Day One, the day when the combined company operates as a single entity and serves its customer base under the new brand.

As part of their program, they recognized that future state process design was critical to a successful transition. They sought consulting help from a partner with expertise in large-scale process design.

I led the team that developed the request for proposal (RFP) response and ultimately in delivering the work. Our scope was to create future state designs for eight business units. Prior to our onboarding, the bank had already made decisions on the platforms and personnel they would leverage in their future state processes. Our engagement began with creating process inventories for each business unit and then process maps for high-priority processes.

This turned out to be a valuable input, providing clarity on the integration impacts and enabling better requirements for the system, personnel changes, and risk management.

Waterfall Business Requirements

Requirements are the needs of the system, typically expressed by business stakeholders, end users, and other subject matter experts. They encompass the functions, features, and behavior of the software system being delivered. Requirements provide traceability to the scope outlined in the charter, as well as to many deliverables in subsequent phases. They usually consist of high-level requirements that are then further detailed through low-level requirements. Final approval of requirements often rests with the business owner.

Requirements are completed upfront and remain relatively stable throughout the project life cycle. They form the basis for establishing the timeline and effort estimation. Most projects have a change control process in place, where proposed changes to requirements undergo evaluation for their impact on schedule and costs before being approved.

Agile User Stories

Agile is a different approach where requirements are not fully defined upfront but iterated on through the collaborative process of design, build, and test cycles called sprints in cross-functional scrum or feature teams.

User stories are short descriptions of functionality expressed from a user's perspective. They capture the "who," "what," and "why" of system requirements and are often documented in the format: "As a [type of user], I want [an action] so that [a benefit/value]." User stories are accompanied by acceptance criteria, which define the specific conditions that must be met for a user story to be considered complete. Agile teams commonly use story points to estimate the relative effort or complexity of user stories.

User stories are small, independent, and testable units of functionality that can be implemented within a sprint, which is typically two weeks but can vary in length. They are organized into epics, which are large customer-centric user stories encapsulating broad initiatives or features too large to develop in a single iteration. Epics can be part of themes that represent high-level business objectives or areas of focus. Themes and epics provide broad categories aligning with strategic goals, aiding in prioritization and work organization.

The product owner, working in the scrum team, takes the lead in developing user stories and adding them to a product backlog, which serves as the team's to-do list. Agile teams work in sprints to develop the product. Before each sprint, user stories are selected from the product backlog during the sprint planning process. At the end of the sprint, a demo is conducted to showcase completed features and gather feedback from business stakeholders.

User stories in the backlog undergo continual refinement throughout the iterative process as the scrum team and business stakeholders gain a better understanding of their requirements and preferences. Backlog grooming or refinement is an ongoing process where the product owner and development team regularly review and prioritize the product backlog, ensuring that user stories are up-to-date, well-defined, and aligned with the evolving needs of the project and stakeholders.

Top Challenges in Creating High-Quality Requirements

Regardless of the delivery methodology being followed, high-quality requirements or user stories are critical to successfully delivering change. Here are the top reasons for poor requirements:

- **Inadequate Stakeholder Involvement**: Various stakeholders, such as product managers, business owners, risk managers, subject matter experts, customers, users, and regulators, may have an interest in the project. While it may not be feasible to gather inputs from all stakeholders, it is crucial to identify the set of stakeholders that can cover all necessary perspectives.

- **Insufficient Domain Knowledge**: Insufficient or incomplete understanding of the business domain can lead to requirements that fail to address the business problem, are unrealistic, or do not align with regulatory needs. In large change initiatives, a lack of understanding of upstream and downstream connections can result in defects in the end-to-end process.

- **Ambiguous Language**: Requirements that are not clearly articulated can lead to misunderstandings and misinterpretations by implementation teams. However, this challenge is less pronounced in Agile methodologies due to the collaborative nature of the scrum team.

- **Insufficient Validation and Verification**: Failure to perform quality reviews to validate that the requirements meet stakeholder expectations and verify the accuracy and completeness of requirements during their creation can lead to undetected quality issues and conflicting requirements.

- **Lack of Requirements Documentation and Traceability**: Properly documenting requirements in a clear and accessible manner is important for other stakeholders to understand. Traceability involves establishing linkages to concepts in the project life cycle, such as scope, high-level requirements, and testing scripts. Failure to do so can result in confusion and gaps in requirements.

- **Poorly Defined Change Control Process**: In Waterfall projects with long durations, business needs or stakeholders' understanding of their needs may evolve, leading to requests for changes to requirements that have been locked down. Without a rigorous change control process that identifies the impacts of change requests on the timeline and budget, there is a risk of scope creep and the project becoming larger or spinning out of control due to frequent changes.

Some of these challenges may not apply to a single Agile team since they are built around what Amazon labeled the "Two Pizza Team," which means teams that are small enough to be fed with two pizzas. If the project or program is larger and requires coordination of multiple Agile scrum teams to deliver a larger set of functionalities, then these challenges do become relevant.

Benefits of Documenting Requirements After Processes

Process Inventory can address many of the challenges in business requirements by providing alignment as mentioned earlier. Figure 5-6 illustrates the correlation between the level of detail in business requirements for Waterfall and user stories for Agile and the depth of the Process Inventory. This enables leadership to express their requirements from their perspective and have project teams further detail them at lower levels.

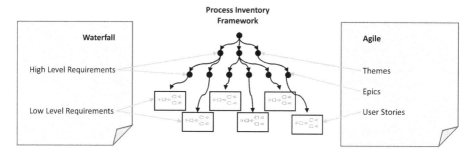

Figure 5-6. Alignment of Requirements to Process

The initial step in this model involves updating the Process Inventory to reflect any changes in the organization's processes. Processes may be added in response to new products, features, revenue streams, or acquisitions, while processes may be removed due to divestitures, outsourcing, product retirements, or process optimization. It is important to note that this list is not exhaustive as other factors can contribute to changes in the Process Inventory.

This step is crucial as it allows stakeholders to visualize the impact of the change on the organization's processes. It provides a comprehensive understanding of the business domain and scope, facilitating stronger collaboration among stakeholders. It also establishes a consistent structure that enables effective leveraging of existing knowledge.

Creating future state process models as the next step, prior to documenting requirements, enables product managers and process owners to align their understanding of strategic and project objectives with changes to how processes will be executed. It also ensures alignment from customer interactions through product design to underlying systems and behaviors. This step enables the identification of gaps and interdependencies, such as upstream and downstream connections, impacts on customers and employees, risks, and the use of third-party vendors and resources. By addressing these aspects, the resulting requirements comprehensively cover the necessary aspects of the project.

Furthermore, it serves as the foundation for traceability, a crucial aspect that can significantly enhance development projects. Research shows that traceability can accelerate project speed by 24% and improve project accuracy by 50% [13]. Traceability refers to the ability to track a requirement's life cycle across project deliverables, including software code, both forward and backward. The Process Inventory framework facilitates traceability from strategic objectives all the way to code deployment in production, as illustrated in Figure 5-1. By establishing traceability, organizations can effectively monitor and trace the origin of defects, enabling faster detection, analysis, and resolution of issues throughout the development process. As a result, there is a reduction in software defects and an improvement in the overall quality of software maintenance.

Taking a top-down approach by starting with future state process models yields higher quality and more complete requirements. Stronger validation and verification are achieved by enabling requirement teams to trace each requirement to its support of the future vision of processes. This approach also leads to process optimization by identifying and addressing redundancies, inefficiencies, and poor resource utilization during the implementation of change.

By building requirements from a complete set of impacted processes, this facilitates accountability by involving the process owner and business stakeholders in attesting to their completeness and accuracy. Communication with senior stakeholders becomes more effective as they can gain a rolled-up view to ensure that the requirements reflect their expectations.

Risk and Compliance Requirements

Managing risk and complying with regulatory obligations are critical for many industries and organizations. The change process, particularly for large transformational initiatives, can pose significant risks if essential controls are overlooked during deployment.

That's why it's crucial to integrate risk managers, including the first line of defense (business units or functions) and the second line of defense (risk oversight), into the requirements process. Implementing the solution outlined in Chapter 7, which involves aligning risks, controls, and regulatory obligations in the GRC (governance, risk, and compliance) repository with the processes identified in the Process Inventory, would enhance the effectiveness of the risk management teams in documenting risk requirements. They would be able to identify whether changes to existing processes introduce new risks or regulatory obligations and determine the need for new controls or updates to existing controls. In the case of implementing new processes, it allows them to review the processes defined in the future state Process Inventory and identify the additional controls required.

Risk managers are responsible for ensuring that requirements adequately cover the necessary controls, thereby collaborating more effectively with the project team to reduce risk during the solution's deployment.

Furthermore, involving the risk management team early in the process offers the valuable benefit of shaping the implementation of controls for enhanced effectiveness. Many organizations strive to automate controls, transitioning from manual and detective measures (after the risk is incurred) to proactive and preventative measures (before the risk is incurred). By including the risk management team from the outset, their expertise can contribute to optimizing control mechanisms and establishing a more efficient and robust risk management framework.

Testing

Testing plays a crucial role in the software development life cycle, serving as a vital step to prevent defects or quality issues from being released into production and impacting customers or damaging an organization's reputation.

There are two primary types of testing: functional testing and technical testing. Functional testing ensures that the software delivers the intended functionality as outlined in the requirements, while technical testing focuses on assessing the software's robustness and its adherence to necessary technical standards. This type of testing encompasses evaluating performance, security, scalability, and other technical aspects to ensure the software's overall soundness.

Within a project context, functional testing holds significant importance as it validates whether the project's original objectives and scope, as expressed through the requirements, have been successfully met. Figure 5-7 illustrates how this validation process aligns with the V-model framework.

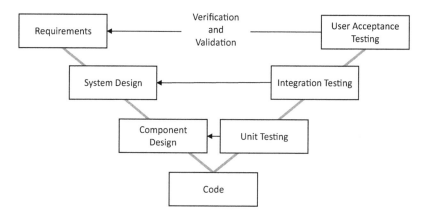

Figure 5-7. V-Model

As the model demonstrates on the left side, progressing downward, there are different levels of granularity involved in defining the solution, starting from requirements and extending to software code. On the right side, different levels of testing are depicted, each serving a specific purpose in terms of verifying and validating artifacts. The highest level of functional testing, user acceptance testing, plays a critical role in validating that the requirements have been satisfactorily met and that the solution effectively meets the needs and expectations of end users. This level of testing serves as a pivotal assurance to stakeholders that the software is ready for deployment and aligns with the defined business objectives.

While the V-model has traditionally been associated with Waterfall methodologies, adaptations have been made to accommodate Agile environments. The fundamental principle remains intact: the delivered software code must align with the Agile requirement artifacts, including themes, epics, and user stories. However, the key distinction lies in the iterative nature of Agile practices, where testing activities are integrated throughout the development process. This approach allows for continuous validation at each iteration or sprint, ensuring that the evolving software aligns with the desired objectives and meets the evolving needs of the stakeholders.

Benefits of Aligning Test Script to Process

If the alignment of requirements to processes, as defined through the Process Inventory framework, is adopted, it logically makes sense to align scripts in user acceptance testing with processes as well.

There are several benefits to this approach. The primary advantage is that it provides alignment across all stakeholders, such as the product manager, product owner, and risk manager, ensuring that requirements have been successfully met through testing. It also enables end-to-end testing from the customer's or end-user's perspective, validating that the system fulfills their needs.

Since the Process Inventory framework will outlive the project's duration, it offers an excellent structure for building a library of regression testing scripts. Regression testing involves executing test scripts at a later point in time to ensure that the systems continue to function as expected, even after changes such as defect fixes, software upgrades, or infrastructure modifications.

Furthermore, this consistent structure enables the development of an automated testing library, which reduces the time and cost associated with testing while improving accuracy and providing valuable insights.

Organizational Change Management

Organizational change management (OCM) is a discipline that focuses on effectively managing change to facilitate successful transitions of individuals and teams from the current state to the desired future state. While OCM encompasses technology-driven changes, such as those driven by Agile and Waterfall projects, it also extends to non-technology-driven changes, including strategy, organizational structure, culture, processes, and operations.

The primary objective of OCM is to maximize adoption, minimize resistance, and ensure the overall success of the change effort by employing structured methodologies, tools, and techniques. Central to OCM is the recognition of the importance of addressing the human aspects of change and gaining organizational buy-in to embrace new ways of working.

The adoption of digital technologies, especially artificial intelligence, will have a substantial impact on workforces. These technologies will act as productivity multipliers by reducing or eliminating repetitive tasks, affecting almost all roles and potentially making some obsolete. This level of disruption may induce fear and resistance among certain parts of the workforce who are inclined to defend the status quo. Resistance can be significant, as evidenced by a McKinsey study that found an average loss of 20% of a transformation's value after program completion [14], highlighting the importance of maintaining a long-term focus on OCM execution.

SOUTHWEST AIRLINES CULTURE FUELS ITS BUSINESS PERFORMANCE

Southwest Airlines' remarkable success can be attributed to its strong organizational culture, which has propelled the company to be profitable for more than 45 consecutive years and receive recognition as one of Fortune's Most Admired Companies for over 23 consecutive years [15].

Unlike many organizations that prioritize customer satisfaction, Southwest places a higher emphasis on the well-being of its employees. The company's hiring process revolves around selecting individuals who align with the company culture, focusing on attitude rather than solely on skills.

Furthermore, Southwest provides its employees with a unique and empowering work environment, fostering a sense of autonomy and offering ample opportunities for personal growth. This approach has led to a low employee turnover rate, with internal promotions being the norm within the company. Southwest's commitment to supporting and retaining top talent is well-known as the company openly states that employees will never be penalized for using good judgment and common sense in favor of providing exceptional customer experiences.

Former CEO and current chairman of Southwest, Gary Kelly, emphasizes the importance of the company's core values, known as the "Southwest Way," which include a warrior spirit, a servant's heart, and a fun-loving attitude. These values have been ingrained in the organization's culture for 36 years and continue to shape the company's operations and employee behavior. Southwest's dedication to maintaining its culture is evident through initiatives like the "Corporate Culture Committee," which promotes and sustains the "Southwest Way" by recognizing employees who deliver outstanding service.

Southwest Airlines' success story showcases how a strong organizational culture focused on employee well-being, customer service, and core values can drive business performance, foster employee engagement, and create a positive and enduring company reputation.

It's imperative that organizations develop a comprehensive workforce strategy to mitigate the downsides of digital disruption. However, this extends beyond digital as having a strong workforce strategy and a motivated, dedicated workforce is critical to business performance and long-term success. A well-defined workforce strategy ensures that an organization has the right people with the necessary skills and capabilities to meet its current and future needs. As illustrated by the Southwest Airlines example, by aligning the workforce strategy with business objectives, organizations can optimize performance, drive sustainable growth, and effectively navigate the challenges posed by digital disruption and other transformational changes.

Process Inventory plays a crucial role in achieving alignment and driving success in the organizational change management (OCM) process. Figure 5-8 provides a visual representation of this process, which can be executed independently for non-technology-driven changes or run parallel to technology-driven change.

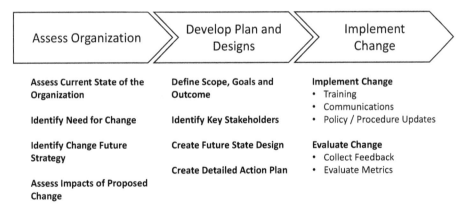

Figure 5-8. Organizational Change Management Process

Assess Organization

Process Inventory provides leaders with enhanced visibility into the organization's processes, allowing them to understand the current state and align their future state aspirations with the business objectives. This includes assessing the impacts of various types of change, including technology-driven change, to determine how teams and individual roles may be affected. This clarity enables leaders to proactively identify potential risks or challenges before launching the program.

Develop Plans and Designs

With its organizationally aligned structure, Process Inventory facilitates the identification and engagement of stakeholders. Detailed action plans can be created with precision by understanding all the artifacts, such as processes, training, policies, and procedures, that need to be updated or created to support the change. Plans can be refined with clear steps, milestones, and measures to determine success.

Implement Change

During the implementation phase, communications regarding the changes are conducted, procedure documentation is updated, and training is rolled out to individuals and teams. Stakeholders, adopting ownership and influencer roles, play a crucial part in championing the change to their managers and teams. Additionally, OCM teams remain engaged throughout the process, collecting feedback, evaluating metrics, and adjusting implementation strategies if necessary.

Project Management

The discipline of project management is critical to the success of implementing any change, and it is imperative for delivering complex transformation programs such as digital transformations. According to the Project Management Institute, projects that employ proven project management practices are 2.5 times more likely to succeed and waste 13 times less money [16].

Project and program managers play a pivotal role in guiding the delivery of change from initiation to production, utilizing proven techniques and tools to ensure accountability among team members and provide transparent communication to senior stakeholders. They are responsible for documenting and maintaining project scope, creating and managing delivery plans, providing comprehensive status reporting and effective communication to leadership, planning and allocating resources and finances, managing delivery risks, and conducting ongoing evaluations for continuous improvement. Their expertise and diligent management contribute significantly to the successful execution of projects, helping organizations achieve their desired outcomes with confidence.

Process Inventory Strengthen Project Management

Process Inventory bridges the gap between senior sponsors and execution teams, bringing clarity and alignment between those funding the project and those responsible for delivering on its objectives. As discussed earlier in this chapter, this process-driven approach enables clarity in defining scope, detailing impacts and plans, documenting requirements, aligning testing, and managing organizational change. In this section, we will explore how Process Inventory supports project managers in monitoring and controlling project delivery and facilitating transparent progress reporting to senior stakeholders.

Project Planning and Work Estimation

Delivering successful change requires effectively managing the constraints of scope, cost, and time. To achieve this, it is crucial to establish work packages that align with the scope defined in the Process Inventory. By framing the project scope in a business-oriented context understood by all stakeholders, work packages play a vital role in accurately estimating the cost and duration of implementing desired changes.

To illustrate this concept, let's consider a project with a scope consisting of five processes that require updates. Each process becomes a distinct work package, encompassing its specific set of requirements, design documents, software components, testing procedures, and other deliverables. This logical breakdown of the project into work packages provides clarity and assigns responsibility at the process level, ensuring accountability and ownership.

By breaking down deliverables into work packages, project managers can estimate the cost and duration associated with each package more precisely. Estimating each individual deliverable within a work package allows for better aggregation of the overall project cost and duration. This level of granularity enhances project planning and resource allocation, enabling effective constraint management.

Moreover, work packages contribute to aligning stakeholder expectations and understanding by providing a clear breakdown of responsibilities for each deliverable. Team members can easily identify their roles within specific work packages, promoting accountability and fostering collaboration throughout the project life cycle. This focused ownership facilitates efficient communication, streamlined decision-making, and effective coordination, ultimately driving successful project outcomes.

It is important to acknowledge that this approach has limitations, particularly when the change does not involve process changes, such as infrastructure-oriented changes or cosmetic updates to user interfaces. Additionally, while this level of granularity and structure may not be necessary for small agile projects, it becomes increasingly important when multiple scrum Agile teams need to coordinate and align their efforts to deliver transformative programs.

Monitoring Progress

By breaking down the work efforts associated with process-aligned work packages, this leads to the project management technique of measuring progress through earned value management (EVM). EVM provides a holistic view of the project's health by calculating the value of the work performed against the planned value, as determined by the initial estimate, and comparing it with the actual cost. This enables project managers to calculate the estimate-at-complete, providing them with a real-time understanding of the impacts on the planned budget and timeline.

The rigor of this approach enables project managers to calculate the cost and timeline implications of proposed scope changes through the change control process. This provides decision-makers with accurate information to determine the trade-offs associated with accepting changes to the project's scope.

Process Aligned Status Reporting

The Process Inventory approach leads to more transparent reporting of status for leadership. By framing progress through processes or process areas, which they can easily relate to, leadership gains a view of how progress aligns with the ultimate business objectives. This alignment provides clarity in terms of accountability for addressing delivery issues or risks, enabling leadership to make informed decisions and take necessary actions. Figure 5-9 showcases a process-aligned status dashboard, providing an illustrative view of how Process Inventory can be effectively presented.

Scope	Schedule	Budget	Requirements	Design	Development	Test
Process 1	●	●	100%	100%	25%	-
Process 2	○	●	75%	-	-	-
Process 3	○	○	100%	25%	-	-

Figure 5-9. Illustrative Process Aligned Status Dashboard

Tollgate to Production

An important mechanism that project managers use to control the delivery of projects is tollgates. Tollgates are checkpoints that occur typically after major phases, where project management and other critical stakeholders can review the quality of deliverables, assess delivery risks, review issues, and determine if the project has met its milestones and is on track to meet its business objectives. This gives senior sponsors and stakeholders the ability to determine if work can proceed to the next phase or if major issues need to be addressed before moving on.

The final tollgate before a change is implemented is the Go/No Go decision, where senior stakeholders can determine if the project will meet its business objectives and, most importantly, ensure that implementation won't incur unnecessary risk because a critical component isn't ready. For complex transformation programs, there may be many moving parts that must be coordinated to make this happen. New technology must not only be tested and defect-free, but the deployment plan, which may require complex sequencing and migration of data, must also be in place. Employees need to be properly trained and ready to operate in the new environment. Communications to customers will have to be completed to ensure a seamless experience. Risks must be understood, and the proper controls must be in place. There are many other items to be coordinated, and the Go/No Go tollgate gives leadership visibility that everything is ready, and the implementation can proceed.

Process Inventory promotes stronger tollgates through the alignment of deliverables, outcomes, and stakeholders with the impacted processes. This business-oriented perspective ensures that updates are presented in a way that stakeholders can understand. The framework's emphasis on accountability enables each stakeholder, including product managers, process owners, risk managers, and technical leaders, to verify that the change has met their expectations. This instills confidence in senior stakeholders, particularly during the final Go/No Go decision as they receive accurate and comprehensive information prior to making their decision. This structured approach enhances the success of change deployment.

Key Takeaways

- **Change process** is a broad term encompassing any change in organizational capability, regardless of size and scope.

- **Prominent change methodologies** include the strategy process, project portfolio management, Agile, Waterfall, organizational change management, and project management.

- **Process Inventory framework** can transform these methodologies by enabling alignment among all stakeholders and deliverables, ensuring that efforts remain focused on the strategic objectives of change.

- **Numerous benefits of this approach** include enhancing the strategy development process, streamlining project portfolio management, providing clarity in scope and impact analysis, improving the handling of requirements and user stories, facilitating rigorous testing, and empowering effective change management for people.

- **Project management** becomes more effective due to the transparency and traceability that the Process Inventory framework provides.

In the next chapter, we will delve into how the Process Inventory framework can enable stronger management and design of the technology environment.

The Technology Path to Digitization

We will explore how advancements in digital technologies are revolutionizing how organizations operate, necessitating the development of a strategy that outlines how these advancements will be leveraged to support the organizations' business strategy. Several trends will be examined, including intelligent process automation, data-centric AI, and business modular architectures.

We will also delve into the crucial role of Enterprise Architecture in defining and governing the IT strategy and roadmap, as well as their role in providing comprehensive system documentation and managing the portfolio of applications. Throughout, you'll gain an appreciation for how Process Inventory advances these trends by offering granular process information, enhanced data labeling, and alignment with business goals, enabling success in the digital age.

© Michael Schank 2023
M. Schank, *Digital Transformation Success*,
https://doi.org/10.1007/978-1-4842-9816-9_6

Netflix, Digital Leader

Netflix has emerged as a leader in embracing digital technologies to advance its mission, transform its business, and revolutionize the entertainment industry.

One of Netflix's most notable achievements is its successful transition from a DVD-by-mail sales and rental service to a streaming platform. Recognizing the increases in data speeds and the decreasing bandwidth costs, Netflix boldly disrupted its own business model by introducing a streaming service in 2007. This move allowed subscribers to access a vast catalog of movies and TV shows instantly over the Internet. By leveraging digital technologies, they eliminated the limitations and inconveniences associated with physical DVD rentals, paving the way for the streaming revolution [1].

A cornerstone of Netflix's success lies in its sophisticated use of machine learning algorithms to drive customer engagement. More than 80% of the shows people watch on Netflix are discovered through the platform's recommendation engine. Netflix has gathered hundreds of different attributes on each user based on their viewing behaviors [2] and categorizes them into different taste groups within their customer base. The recommendation engine not only personalizes title suggestions but also dynamically customizes the thumbnail of each show for each user to generate higher click-through rates. Additionally, Netflix extensively uses machine learning for other important use cases such as improving streaming quality, optimizing the show production process, and monitoring the quality of content.

Netflix has been a pioneer in transitioning to a cloud-based, loosely coupled, agile architecture. The company faced significant challenges due to the explosive growth of data and user information in its existing data centers. In 2009, they embarked on a transformation to break up their monolithic architecture into thousands of loosely coupled services, now known as microservices, deployed within a cloud infrastructure. The demand on their infrastructure is enormous, with Netflix apps consuming 15% of the Internet bandwidth worldwide and over six billion hours of collective viewership per day [3]. This microservices architecture has provided them with the ability to scale specific services on demand, accelerate software changes through an agile and continuous deployment model, and reinforce their environment with greater resiliency and fault tolerance. Since their success with this model, other prominent organizations have adopted this microservice architecture to address their own scaling challenges.

Through its strategic adoption of digital technologies, Netflix has achieved remarkable business success, growing from 857K subscribers and $152M in revenue in 2002 to 209M subscribers and $31.6B in revenue by 2022 [4]. As a digital pioneer, Netflix continues to push boundaries, redefine user expectations, and inspire organizations across industries to embrace the power of digital technologies to transform their business models and deliver exceptional customer experiences.

Embracing Digital Technologies

The pace of technological progress is nothing short of breathtaking. Every day, new advancements emerge that promise to revolutionize the way we work and live. From process automation to AI technologies and cloud-native design, the potential for operational excellence is limitless. This is not a fad or passing trend, these digital capabilities will continue to progress exponentially. Those who fail to adapt will be left behind, while those who embrace these changes will thrive in today's rapidly evolving business landscape.

These trends will also have significant implications on the future of the workforce. As automation and AI become more prevalent, organizations will need to reskill their employees to work alongside these technologies. These should be viewed as productivity multipliers that enable employees to focus less on mundane and repetitive tasks and focus more on strategic and customer-facing value, which if done correctly will increase employee engagement and satisfaction.

To prepare for this, organizations will need to prepare, which means defining a digital strategy that aligns to their mission, detailing the use cases that will drive business value, enhancing their enterprise IT and data architecture design, and investing in workforce change strategies.

An imperative to success is to focus on excellence in the business process environment as this represents the intersection between the workforce and technology. The Process Inventory framework by being a comprehensive and accurate inventory of all the processes that an organization performs is a perfect enabler to ensure that all impacts are considered and addressed while maintaining the lens of business value.

In this chapter, I will cover the state of each of these topics and discuss how the Process Inventory framework solves the challenges faced today.

Intelligent Process Automation (IPA)

Process automation is a universally acknowledged imperative in digital transformation programs. According to a survey of IT decision-makers, 97% agreed that process automation is vital to digital transformation [5]. Process automation involves using technology to automate complex business processes, eliminating or reducing the need for human interaction. The technologies involved in process automation include robotic process automation (RPA), workflow, and intelligent automation, which leverages AI technologies such as machine learning (ML), natural language processing (NLP), and computer vision.

When implemented correctly, process automation can be a game-changer that revolutionizes the way businesses operate with increased efficiency, reduced risk, and even revenue growth. According to a study conducted by McKinsey, two-thirds of the companies surveyed are actively pursuing process automation [6]. The market for intelligent process automation is forecasted to reach 30 billion US dollars by the end of 2024, with a compound annual growth rate (CAGR) of 16% [7].

However, it is estimated that 30%–50% [8] of automation projects fail. Here are the top reasons for failure:

- **Lack of Clear Goals and Integrated Governance**: Without clear alignment toward organizational goals and commitment from senior-level executives to sponsor the initiative, there can be challenges in securing sufficient funding and acquiring key subject matter resources. As a result, the program may struggle to gain traction, leading to subpar designs and incorrect results when implementing automation.

- **Incomplete Understanding of the Process Holistically**: Many efforts are focused on a task or part of a process within an organizational silos. The lack of understanding of the end-to-end process may lead to suboptimal design or challenges in handoffs from upstream or downstream processes.

- **Choosing the Wrong Process to Automate**: Processes that are too simple, too infrequent, or too changeable should not be automated as they may fail to have the desired impact needed to keep stakeholders engaged and may cause maintenance issues.

- **Choosing the Wrong Solution**: Automation teams can get locked into a single tool for all process automation needs. Choosing the wrong automation tool can lead to poor employee experiences or even codify a poor underlying system design.

- **Insufficient Training or Change Management**: Implementing automation can be disruptive to operational staff or create more issues if staff isn't properly trained and operating procedures aren't updated accordingly.

Defining the Intelligent Process Automation Program Charter

When embarking on an IPA program, it's important to have a clear strategy that outlines the goals and objectives of the program. A few key aspects of this strategy include the following:

A **business case** should be created to define how this effort will support the organization's strategy. It must identify the investment needed and the benefits to be gained. Since IPA is focused on improving human productivity, the benefits are usually stated in metrics such as increased productivity, reduced cost, improved process accuracy, improved customer experience, improved employee experience, and improved risk management. Part of the business case should include the design of a reporting dashboard and a plan for quantitatively capturing the resulting metrics.

The strategy should have clear details on the **scope of the effort and the selection criteria used to prioritize** automation opportunities. Factors such as complexity, repetitiveness, volume, error rate, cost savings, and risk ratings should be considered in a systematic manner. It's important to think through these details so that leaders have clarity when weighing different opportunities.

An **IT architecture strategy** is needed to provide clarity on which IPA tools will be available and for which use cases each should be leveraged (see Table 6-1). This should include a data management plan since intelligent automation requires quality data to be effective.

Table 6-1. Intelligent Process Automation Tools and Their Use Cases

Tool	Appropriate Use Cases
Robotic Process Automation (RPA)	RPA "bot" mimics human interactions with user interfaces to automate repetitive, rule-based tasks.
Workflow Automation	Workflow automation focuses on streamlining and automating the flow of tasks and activities within a business process. It ensures that tasks are assigned, executed, and monitored efficiently, often using a workflow management tool.
Artificial Intelligence	AI technologies enabling automation systems to perform cognitive tasks that traditionally require human intelligence. AI technologies used in IPA include machine learning, natural language processing, and computer vision.

These tools can be implemented stand-alone or combined depending on the complexity and the goals of each use case being addressed.

Several **operational model** considerations need to be addressed. First and foremost, senior-level sponsorship is critical. This leader or leaders need to understand the benefits and be passionate about the potential to be a champion. This sponsorship is important in securing necessary resources, gaining organizational buy-in, and clearing any hurdles.

The operating model for the program will have to be defined. There are options such as a centralized Automation Center of Excellence (COE) that performs all design and implementation work, or there are federated models where methods and standards are published, but each business unit or functional area performs their own automation. A methodology should be built that details the series of activities and deliverables, as well as business sign-off, to show how an automation opportunity goes from concept to implementation. Since many of these technologies are new, a plan will have to be identified on how to upskill existing staff or acquire skilled resources.

Overall, these steps and considerations can pave the way for a successful intelligent process automation program, driving efficiency and transformation within the organization.

Discovery and Assessment

Many Automation Centers of Excellence (COEs) typically reside in the IT organization, presenting a challenge as they may have expertise in automation tools but struggle to understand the process landscape.

Process documentation, as exemplified in Figure 6-1, plays a crucial role in supporting intelligent process automation efforts by providing a clear summary of existing business processes and serving as a foundation for automation scoping, analysis, and design.

It ensures that automation initiatives are built upon accurate and comprehensive knowledge not only of individual processes but also the context of those processes within the business, including upstream or downstream process dependencies. Process metadata offers rich information, such as the resources leveraged in process execution.

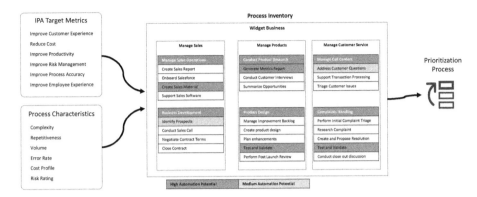

Figure 6-1. IPA Discovery and Assessment Process

The Process Inventory framework enables a **top-down identification of candidates**, which can start with interviewing the business unit or functional area leaders. They possess insights into their processes, particularly those causing the most pain, and can help align potential scope to their executive-level performance goals and metrics.

The assessment team can then collaborate with process owners and other key stakeholders identified in the Process Inventory framework to assess each opportunity. This involves conducting a deep dive into current performance metrics, process characteristics, and the details of process execution as captured in the Integrated Operational Repository. Based on this analysis, the teams can form hypotheses regarding the root causes of challenges, benefits, potential IPA solutions, and the required effort to implement an IPA solution.

The outcome of this assessment is a score reflecting the cost-benefits of each opportunity. A common summary, depicted in Figure 6-1 as a heatmap of opportunities, serves as a visual tool for engaging senior business leaders and stakeholders to gain consensus on which processes should be prioritized for automation.

Process Design and Optimization

Once a process is identified for automation, it is essential to redesign the process to fully leverage the capabilities of the automation technology.

During this phase, the design team builds upon the hypothesis developed during the assessment phase to determine the future state design. If a current state process model does not exist, one should be created, outlining the people, process steps, technologies, and controls that may be impacted by the design changes.

Using the principles of design thinking, the design team collaborates with process owners and other users to gain a detailed understanding of their pain points and challenges. By empathizing with the users, the team can select the most suitable IPA tool and create a future state process model, along with the necessary technical design documents.

At this stage, there is a comprehensive understanding of how the process redesign will impact the users. It is crucial to develop a change management plan that addresses potential disruptions. This plan may include training programs, updates to procedure documents, and communication strategies to ensure a smooth transition.

Furthermore, the business case should be refined to incorporate updated cost and benefit projections, as well as an updated implementation timeline. This ensures that the business case remains aligned with the evolving project requirements and goals.

Development and Testing

In this phase, developers take the future state designs to create the solution. Following an iterative development approach, the solution is developed in incremental stages, allowing for early feedback and adjustments based on user input. This iterative approach ensures a more user-centric and effective solution by actively involving end users in the development process.

Quality assurance and testing play a critical role in ensuring the reliability and functionality of the developed solution. Rigorous testing methodologies are employed to identify and resolve any issues or bugs. This includes various testing levels (which are covered more extensively in Chapter 5), such as unit testing, integration testing, and user acceptance testing. Unit testing focuses on testing individual components or modules of the solution, while integration testing verifies the interaction between different components. User acceptance testing involves end users validating the solution against predefined criteria to ensure it meets their requirements.

Additionally, a pilot implementation is conducted with a subset of users to validate the expected benefits and gather further feedback. This real-world testing provides an opportunity to fine-tune the solution, validate its performance, and make any necessary refinements before rolling it out to the entire user base.

As part of the development and testing phase, it is essential to update documentation to reflect the changes introduced by the automation solution. This includes updating the Process Inventory, creating a new process model, revising control documentation, and updating procedure documentation to reflect any changes in tasks or responsibilities resulting from the automation implementation.

Data-Centric AI

The advancement that holds the greatest potential for disruption is machine learning models, a branch of artificial intelligence that utilizes data to enhance computer performance by enabling machines to "learn." In modern-day machine learning, there are two primary objectives. The first is to classify data based on developed models, while the second is to make predictions for future outcomes using these models [9]. Machine learning has been a concept since the 1950s but has recently gained significant attention with the release of ChatGPT in November 2022 and its impressive capabilities in natural language processing and conversation generation. ChatGPT, which is a generative AI technology that leverages machine learning models, is generating excitement for what it can mean for productivity.

The potential for this technology to drive business performance is enormous. According to a McKinsey report [10], generative AI has the potential to contribute an estimated $2.6 trillion to $4.4 trillion annually across the 63 use cases they analyzed. Machine learning models have been successfully deployed in various use cases, including customer service chatbots, personalized marketing, and more. However, the level of success with this technology varies, with digitally native technology companies leading the pack, while traditional companies are investing to catch up.

Even for leaders in this field, the full potential of AI technology has not yet been fully realized, indicating that there is still a long way to go. The true value of AI emerges when it is operationalized at scale. Business leaders seeking to maximize the benefits of AI understand that scale refers to the deep and wide integration of AI into an organization's core products, services, and business processes [11].

Renowned computer scientist and entrepreneur Andrew Ng has championed a movement called data-centric AI, which he believes is the key to unlocking additional value [12]. According to Mr. Ng, the recent focus in AI has primarily been on advancing machine learning models and software code, which have now reached a mature stage. However, the limiting factor in realizing added value lies in the quality of data.

Data is the fuel for a machine learning system as it relies on data for analysis and pattern recognition. To illustrate its importance, ChatGPT 4, for instance, boasts an estimated 100 trillion parameters [13], with parameters being mathematical relationships that connect words through numbers and algorithms. In the emerging field of MLOps (machine learning operations), which involves operationalizing machine learning models, up to 80% of the effort is dedicated to ensuring data quality [14].

According to Ng, a data-centric approach involves systematically engineering high-quality data for these models to consume. High-quality data is characterized by consistent labeling. Data labeling involves adding one or more informative labels to provide context for machine learning models to learn from. For example, if different groups within an organization use diverse terms like "Payment," "Wire Payment," and "Move Money" to describe the same process, although none of these terms are inherently incorrect, the lack of consistency poses a challenge for the models to establish connections between events, ultimately leading to limited insights.

State of Data Quality

According to a study conducted by KPMG, 84% of CEOs are concerned about the quality of the data they're basing decisions on. Gartner measures that the average financial impact of poor data on businesses at $9.7 million per year [15]. Trust is key; if business leaders can't trust the insights from these models because the underlying data is flawed, then efforts to more broadly adopt machine learning may struggle.

Data governance is the function that is responsible for ensuring data quality through all its life cycle stages. The problem is that large-scale data governance programs that live up to this mandate are rare. According to a study conducted by Gartner, only 42% of organizations are succeeding in optimizing data for business processes and productivity [16]. This statistic just underscores that leaders can't wait for data governance programs alone to address this situation.

Even if data quality could be addressed through effective data governance, there are more challenges. A typical data environment consists of heterogeneous and unconnected data sources and unstructured data which are managed in organizational silos. When data is siloed within individual departments—an all-too-common occurrence—companies will struggle to realize generative AI's true potential [17].

Process Inventory Provides an Enterprise Labeling Schema

In order to fully leverage the potential of machine learning, which involves integrating it deeply and extensively into an organization's core products, services, and business processes, resulting in operational excellence characterized by optimized efficiency and maximized resource utilization, it is essential to have a consistent labeling schema across the entire enterprise and all AI use cases.

Process Inventory serves as the foundation for this consistent labeling schema. As explained in Chapter 2, an organization's comprehensive knowledge is captured through an ontology, which in this case is a polycategorical ontology due to the integration of multiple concepts with their respective taxonomies.

The fundamental taxonomy in this context is the Process Inventory as all concepts, except for strategy, rely on processes for their existence. Therefore, the Process Inventory acts as the unified language that connects all concepts together coherently.

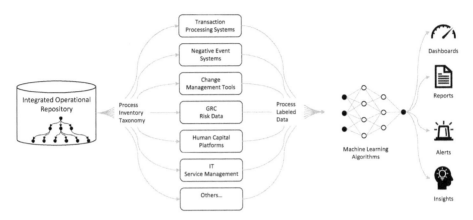

Figure 6-2. Process Inventory Enterprise Labeling Schema

Figure 6-2 illustrates a solution to this problem. The Process Inventory taxonomy is published to multiple systems responsible for generating and managing data related to the organization's core products, services, and business processes. These systems align their data with the corresponding processes in the Process Inventory taxonomy. For instance, GRC systems would label risks based on the associated processes (as described in Chapter 7), while transaction processing systems would label customer behavior data according to the process that drove the interaction.

Using a consistent labeling schema promotes transfer learning, which is where knowledge learned from one use case can be applied to other use cases. This enables improved performance of models by reusing labeled data. By applying knowledge from one use case to the next can uncover hidden patterns that might have been overlooked otherwise. For instance, data collected to identify emerging risks in order to identify and strengthen controls can detect patterns of resource usage which can lead to optimization of costs for certain processes.

This will fundamentally change how businesses are run and the relationship between humans and machines within organizations. Competitive advantages will go to the early movers who define their strategy and move toward creating the data environment required for success.

Use Cases for Operational Excellence

The potential impact of AI on transforming business operations cannot be overstated. Through the implementation of an enterprise labeling schema, machine learning models can gain access to all aspects of a business within a single, comprehensive indexed framework. This framework enables a holistic understanding of the organization, empowering the models to make informed decisions and provide valuable insights across various business functions.

The **strategic decisions** leaders make can be transformed as AI can process vast amounts of internal and external intelligence to provide a thorough assessment of threats and opportunities. It can simulate multiple scenarios to assess potential outcomes of strategic decisions. This capability gives organizations a competitive edge in strategy formulation and decision-making.

Customer experience can undergo a transformation, not only through customized and personalized content that leverages a 360-degree view of the customer but also with predictive customer service. This involves anticipating potential issues or needs and proactively addressing them. Continual monitoring of sentiment analysis and customer feedback allows for the identification of opportunities to enhance the customer experience and pinpoint the root causes, enabling teams to address them promptly.

A new level of **operational efficiency** can be achieved by monitoring near-real-time performance data to identify where business processes and the use of resources can be optimized. By including information on upstream and downstream partners, the supply chain can be optimized to streamline logistics, refine inventory levels, and reduce lead times.

Change management investments become more effective as discretionary change dollars are allocated to the highest level of strategic need. Impact analysis for proposed changes becomes precise in terms of identifying what needs to change and how. This improvement leads to more accurate budget and timeline estimates, as well as driving new levels of accountability for implementation. Additionally, personalized communication and training can be delivered to employees who are impacted by the change, facilitating a smooth change deployment. This can include targeted communication campaigns, training modules tailored to specific roles, and change management support to address employee concerns.

Risk management efforts create a more comprehensive and quantifiable picture of the risk landscape, providing senior leaders and the board with increased confidence in making strategic decisions. AI can analyze vast amounts of data related to each process, enabling the identification of emerging risks and the evaluation of the effectiveness of existing controls. Compliance becomes more accurate as changes to laws and regulations are monitored, allowing for the identification of necessary adjustments to compliance processes and controls. AI-powered calculations of financial risks are enhanced, potentially eliminating or significantly mitigating substantial losses. For example, AI algorithms can analyze financial market data, identify patterns, and assess the likelihood of potential losses, enabling proactive risk management measures.

Engagement in the workforce rises significantly as repetitive and mundane work gets replaced by more strategic and value-added activities. Knowledge and training become more readily accessible and personalized to the role and needs of each employee.

It's imperative that organizations formally create strategies for adopting these new technologies. This includes identifying a prioritized set of use cases, defining a new operating model, creating policies to address the risks these platforms pose, establishing quality guidelines, and designing an architecture and vision for safely integrating this technology into their environment.

AI technologies are here to stay! The urgency lies in establishing a strategy and tactics to adopt this technology to stay competitive or even thrive in this new world.

Business-Led Modular Architectures

Traditionally, IT has often relied on a monolithic architecture paradigm in which all the logic for a broad set of functionalities is contained within a single, often large code base. In monolithic architectures, the application's components, including the user interface, business logic, and data storage, are tightly interconnected and interdependent. Consequently, making changes to functionality requires extensive coordination among various stakeholders and rigorous regression testing to prevent unintended impacts on other processes. Even minor changes could take months to deploy, while major changes often require years of effort and significant costs before reaching production.

In today's fast-paced digital world, the ability to respond quickly to customer expectations and competitive pressures is paramount. This necessitates an agile IT architecture that allows businesses to adapt rapidly and deploy changes within much shorter timelines. Given the significant dependence on IT systems for business functionality, a new paradigm has emerged: a business-led, modular, and loosely coupled IT architecture. "Business-led" means that IT services directly align with the goals and processes of the business, enabling greater involvement of business stakeholders in shaping system functionality to meet their needs. "Modular and loosely coupled" means that software is deployed in independent and decoupled components or modules, allowing for flexibility, scalability, and easy maintenance. Additionally, organizations are increasingly migrating their systems to the cloud and adopting cloud-native architectures, which enhance scalability, fault tolerance, flexibility, security, and cost savings.

The trend in IT architectures toward modular architectures dates to the advent of service-oriented architectures (SOA) which gained popularity in the 1990s. The concept was to break apart large monolithic systems into smaller components, which would be accessed through API-based interfaces that represented the business function being requested. SOA was a huge success if you measure it by adoption, which was widespread. It certainly was a step in the right direction as SOA services would be aligned to the business functionality that was accessed, which increased reuse, interoperability, and in some cases, agility. But this had limitations as SOA services, in many cases, were facilitated by middleware applications, but the underlying architecture remained monolithic, so some of the underlying challenges remain.

The next evolution of this paradigm, increasingly popular in many scenarios, is the microservices architecture. This was popularized when Netflix, driven by the increasing data and user information which was difficult to manage in their current data center infrastructure, was driven to this new architecture. Since then, Google, Amazon, Twitter, and others just to name a few have embraced this concept.

Microservices [18] are an architectural and organizational approach to software development where software is composed of small independent services that communicate over well-defined APIs. This means that large monolithic systems, in this new style, would be replaced by many small-grained microservice applications which are independent. At the current estimate, Netflix has over 1,000 microservices [19] each managing a different part of their site.

Here are some characteristics of the microservices architecture:

- **Loosely Based Autonomous Services**: Each service is stand-alone, meaning that each has its own business and data access logic and only communicates with other microservices via well-defined interfaces.

- **Independently Deployable**: Each microservice can be built, tested, and deployed independent of other microservices.

- **Aligned to Business Capabilities**: Microservices are designed with the single-responsibility principle, meaning they are to have one responsibility and do that responsibility well. A business capability model is employed to define and rationalize these responsibilities across the business and to establish the bounded context for each microservice.

This has revolutionized how software is developed. Since services are independently deployable and cover a small-bounded context of business functionality, that means that they can be **owned by small cross-functional feature teams.** Ownership means everything from development, deployment, and maintenance for that specific business functionality. Cross-functional teams include developers, testers, process, and product owners.

This removes the significant amount of coordination across a large set of stakeholders that comes through monolithic architectures. This has led to the integration of the development teams with the IT operations teams through DevOps which has enabled software development to be truly Agile. This is accomplished through continuous integration and continuous delivery (CI/CD) which is a set of practices, tools, and methodologies to automate the building, testing, and deployment of software. This has enabled Amazon, one of the most technically complex companies around, to average a deploy of software every second to the development, testing, and production environments [20].

Microservices are designed to be cloud native which gives them all the benefits of the cloud such as scalability on demand, resiliency, flexibility, and security.

Anchoring Microservice Design to Process Inventory

According to a survey conducted by Camuda [21], the top challenges in implementing microservices include the lack of visibility into end-to-end business processes spanning multiple microservices (59%), error handling issues at the boundary of two or more microservices (50%), and communication between teams (46%).

While aligning designs to a business capability model has been beneficial for the microservices community, the characteristics of a business capability model being organizationally agnostic and not linking to business processes have proven limiting. This presents challenges in demonstrating the processing idiosyncrasies across business units and capturing the necessary level of detail for showcasing end-to-end processes.

Process Inventory equips design teams with comprehensive details to enhance their designs. By combining the Process Inventory with customer journeys or value stream maps, teams gain an **end-to-end view** of how processes support customers or internal stakeholders, fostering seamless integration and interoperability between microservices.

As a top-down derived taxonomy, the Process Inventory establishes clear boundaries for **defining the bounded context** of microservices, ensuring a focused and well-defined scope, leading to a rationalized and optimal set of services.

The **metadata associated with processes**, including intricate data details, aids in designing precise API interfaces for microservices. Additionally, events identified in process models play a crucial role in microservices design. Events serve as triggers that call a microservice interface, facilitating communication between microservices. They also signify state changes for data entities. For example, when the event "LoanApproved" occurs, the data table storing the loan data will transition from "In Process" to "Approved." Moreover, microservices are complementary to event-driven architectures as a process-aligned service can publish events upon completing its work, thereby triggering other microservices.

Process ownership, as specified in the Process Inventory, establishes accountability, incorporating valuable business stakeholder input and approval. This also helps in defining feature teams to ensure they have the appropriate ownership composition.

Furthermore, this structured approach facilitates microservice reuse as the Process Inventory and business capability models enable teams to identify and integrate requirements from similar processes across diverse business units.

Figure 6-3 illustrates this approach with a Process Inventory for a retail bank. The processes detailed in the diagram form the basis for microservice design as each process will have its own activities and processing requirements from the underlying IT systems.

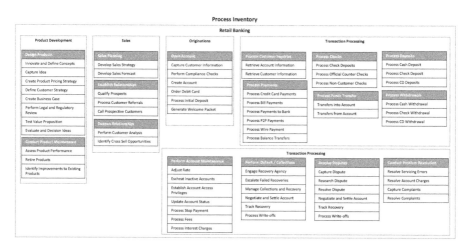

Figure 6-3. Banking Process Inventory

Enabling Enterprise Architecture Design

Prior to investing in any of the aforementioned technologies, it's imperative for an organization to create an IT strategy, target state vision, and roadmap that supports the business's ambitions. This responsibility typically falls under the mandate of an Enterprise Architecture organization, which reports to the Chief Information Officer (CIO). Enterprise Architecture is the process by which organizations standardize and organize their IT environment to align with business goals. These strategies support digital transformation, IT growth, and the modernization of IT [22]. Among their responsibilities are building and governing the journey to the target state vision.

This task is not an easy one. Enterprise Architecture often faces a natural tension with business leaders who are confronted with immediate business needs and cannot afford the cost or timelines associated with implementing technology solutions that align with the long-term IT vision. I have witnessed this scenario play out multiple times during mergers, where the communicated timeline to investors did not allow for the rationalization of redundant applications. As a result, end users had to work with different systems depending on the customer base they were servicing.

Other pressures, such as a poorly conceived IT vision, inadequate business requirements, insufficient technical documentation, and a tightly coupled IT architecture, contribute to the challenges. These factors lead to the accumulation of technical debt, which refers to the implied cost of reworking suboptimal solutions at a later stage. According to a recent McKinsey survey, CIOs reported that 10%–20% of the technology budget allocated to new products is diverted to resolving issues related to tech debt.

Consequently, many organizations end up with a complex and fragmented IT landscape characterized by redundant systems, poor interoperability, legacy technology platforms, and variations in architectures. The proliferation of end-user computing, which involves the development and management of applications outside the central IT organization, further exacerbates this complexity and fragmentation.

These environments become a web of dependencies that stifle innovation, reduce agility, increase security vulnerabilities, undermine resiliency, and hinder the organization's ability to meet customer and market expectations. In severe cases, complexity can degrade customer experience and pose significant risks to the organization, which are contrary to the requirements for successful digital transformation initiatives.

Enterprise Architecture Frameworks

There are many different Enterprise Architecture frameworks such as The Open Group Architecture Framework (TOGAF), Zachman Framework, Federal Enterprise Architecture Framework, and more. These frameworks help structure architects' thinking by identifying subdomains from which they can align organizational objectives. These domains are consistent across these frameworks, which include [24]

- **Business architecture** defines the business strategy, governance, organization, and key business processes of the organization.

- **Information/data architecture** describes the structure of an organization's logical and physical data assets and the associated data management resources.

- **Application architecture** provides a blueprint for the individual systems to be deployed, the interactions between the application systems, and their relationships to the core business processes of the organization with the frameworks for services to be exposed as business functions for integration.

- **Technical architecture** describes the hardware, software, and network infrastructure needed to support the deployment of core, mission-critical applications.

The value and understanding of the business architecture domain will be enhanced through the incorporation of the Process Inventory, which complements existing artifacts like the business capability model by providing additional details on business processes.

In the following sections, I'll cover key Enterprise Architecture responsibilities and how Process Inventory supports the effectiveness of their efforts.

Translate Business Strategy into IT Strategy

A business strategy defines the initiatives an organization will undertake to fulfill its purpose and create value for the organization and its stakeholders. The business strategy incorporates components that an IT strategy should anchor to, such as product differentiation, customer strategy, critical business capabilities, metrics goals, and in a digital context, how the organization plans to maximize the capabilities of digital technology.

The IT strategy, on the other hand, should focus on how IT will enable business success. During the development of the strategy, the Enterprise Architecture team will need to make a series of trade-off decisions, such as buy vs. build, insource vs. outsource, tactics for agility, data integration style, and more. These decisions are typically formalized through IT principles, which are widely distributed to guide teams in making design decisions. The IT strategy should also outline operational considerations, including governance and financial management structures required to achieve the strategic vision. Additionally, the strategy should identify success metrics that align with the business strategy.

Process Inventory plays a crucial role in bridging these two strategies by providing a comprehensive view of an organization's business processes. It enables a deeper understanding of how technology can align with and support those processes. This understanding is essential for aligning success metrics, ensuring that the IT organization aligns its goals and performance measures with the strategic objectives of the business.

Create Transparency

In my experience, many IT organizations have inadequate documentation on their systems and the interactions between systems that support business process activities or serve other purposes. This lack of transparency results in numerous inefficiencies as the reliance on a few key subject matter experts becomes necessary for troubleshooting issues, identifying risks, analyzing the impact of changes, and performing other tasks. Additionally, this situation creates a key person risk as the departure of these experts could lead to a loss of critical knowledge.

The challenge has been the absence of consistent standards for modeling and governing these interaction models and mapping them to the business context. Solution architects often create diagrams during the design phase of a project, but once the project is deployed, these diagrams are rarely updated.

Since Process Inventory provides a complete and accurate inventory of all business processes in the organization, it delivers a comprehensive organizing framework for aligning IT assets to the business processes they support. It goes further: process models are created to illustrate how business processes are executed, providing a platform to demonstrate the flow of data through underlying systems.

CAPITAL MARKETS ORGANIZATION

This Capital Markets Organization had become concerned about the extensive use of legacy mainframe COBOL for executing high-volume critical transactions. The potential consequences of system failure were deemed catastrophic, highlighting the resiliency risk associated with relying on a limited number of subject matter experts. Their objective was to map these transactions with the goal of migrating the functionality to a modern cloud infrastructure.

To address this challenge from a business perspective, the organization established a business architecture team. They sought a partner who could support their new team in adopting an appropriate approach.

The project spanned 16 weeks and focused on the following areas: creating a Playbook with detailed standards and methods, documenting the Process Inventory across the enterprise, identifying requirements for a modeling tool, and executing proof of concepts to map the rules within the COBOL transactions.

Within this timeframe, we successfully mapped the Process Inventory and proceeded to decompose one set of processes to illustrate how human activities in a business process triggered interactions and business rules within the COBOL platform. This accomplishment provided the necessary foundation for the team to continue with the remaining key processes and define requirements for their cloud solution.

A component of the Unified Modeling Language, **system sequence diagrams** (SSD) are not a new concept. What is new is linking them to the inventory of processes in the organization. Linking process models to SSDs provides traceability between activities of the business and actions of the underlying systems, which is critical for business alignment. It provides a structure for maintaining these diagrams over time which will drive efficiency in all processes related to the IT ecosystem.

Figure 6-4 shows an example of how an activity in a business process can trigger a system event to be captured in a system sequence diagram.

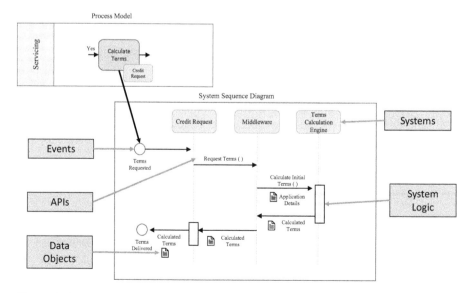

Figure 6-4. System Sequence Diagram Example

All actions within an organization, including those in the IT environment, start with a triggering event. For the purpose of categorization, events can be broadly classified as business events, which are triggered during the fulfillment of a business process, or system events, which are triggered by system actions such as scheduled batch jobs. Business events are represented in process models, and since these processes are documented in the Process Inventory, it provides an ideal mechanism for alignment with the business context.

Each activity performed on a system within a business process represents a system event that initiates the system sequence diagram (SSD). In the given example, an activity called "Calculate Terms" triggers an event called "Terms Requested," which in turn kicks off the SSD. Swimlanes in SSDs represent systems, and each line entering a system represents an API for that action. The blocks within each lane depict the logic performed by each system. In cases where the logic is complex or supports a critical process, details on business rules or logic can be detailed. Data objects are also represented to demonstrate the flow of data and data lineage.

The creation and maintenance of these diagrams can be facilitated using an Enterprise Architecture modeling tool. Several vendor tools provide business process and Enterprise Architecture modeling capabilities within the same tool. These tools treat everything as objects, which is important for reporting and impact analysis purposes. Establishing a new team within Enterprise Architecture to build and maintain these models, mirroring the roles and responsibilities of the Process COE, will be required.

The power of this structure cannot be emphasized enough. Integrating business and technology models allows the organization to be viewed from a top-level C-suite perspective and drilled down to the granular level of logic within a system. This alignment ensures that everything within the IT ecosystem is directly tied to the business activities they support.

Building and maintaining these models will require investment and commitment, but the payoff in terms of increased efficiency, reduced risk, decreased security vulnerabilities, and enhanced innovation will be substantial.

Application Portfolio Management

One of the important roles of an Enterprise Architecture team is managing the portfolio of applications or systems within an organization. As complexity grows, organizations may end up with multiple systems that perform similar or redundant functions. This complexity increases the costs and risks associated with IT.

APM is a governance activity that involves building and maintaining an accurate inventory of systems. Each system is assessed based on its functional fit, which determines how well it serves the business, and its technical fit, which assesses how the system aligns with the IT strategy. The outcome of this assessment is typically a determination of the organization's position on the system, which could be categorized as buy (to expand the use of existing systems), sell (to explore opportunities for retiring or divesting systems), or hold (to maintain the system without significant changes).

By conducting application rationalization projects through application portfolio management (APM), organizations can effectively reduce redundancy, streamline their application portfolio, and align their IT investments with business objectives. This process not only optimizes costs but also mitigates risks and enhances the overall efficiency and effectiveness of the IT landscape.

During the functional fit assessment, applications are labeled according to the business capabilities they serve. This labeling helps identify overlaps and redundancies within the application portfolio. Additionally, aligning systems based on business processes, as documented in the Process Inventory, adds a level of granularity that aids the assessment team in governance and decision-making processes. The inclusion of business process alignment allows for a more detailed analysis of system dependencies and impacts, facilitating thorough impact analysis when retiring or decommissioning a platform. This level of granularity also assists in documenting detailed requirements for application rationalization projects.

By integrating the information from the Process Inventory and the functional fit assessment, organizations can make well-informed decisions about retiring, consolidating, or modernizing applications. This holistic approach to application rationalization helps ensure that the resulting portfolio of applications aligns with business processes and requirements, enabling organizations to achieve their strategic objectives more effectively.

Define Target State Vision and Roadmap

After the creation of the IT strategy, the Enterprise Architecture team will collaboratively develop a target state vision that aligns with the organization's business strategy and objectives. This vision provides a forward-looking perspective, typically spanning three to five years, and encompasses various aspects such as changes to the integration architecture, adoption of emerging technologies, new methods or frameworks, reengineering of key process areas, and modifications to the IT operating model.

To ensure the target state vision is well-aligned with the business, the Enterprise Architecture team actively engages key stakeholders, including business leaders, process owners, and IT teams. This collaborative approach facilitates a deeper understanding of business needs, challenges, and priorities. By involving stakeholders in the process, the team can incorporate their insights and ensure the target state vision reflects the organization's strategic direction.

As part of the target state vision development, the Enterprise Architecture team conducts a comprehensive gap analysis to identify the initiatives necessary to bridge the current state and the desired future state. While these initiatives are defined at a conceptual level rather than detailed requirements, the availability of Process Inventory enhances the precision in identifying impacts, costs, and benefits. The granular view provided by Process Inventory enables the team to assess the implications of proposed changes on specific processes, identify potential overlaps or gaps, and estimate the resources required.

Moreover, the Process Inventory remains foundational throughout the refinement of estimates, prioritization of initiatives, and the construction of business cases to secure funding. By continuously leveraging Process Inventory, the Enterprise Architecture team can refine and validate their understanding of the processes, identify further optimization opportunities, and ensure that the initiatives align with the overall business strategy.

Through a collaborative and iterative approach, the target state vision, supported by the insights gained from Process Inventory, enables organizations to align their IT initiatives with business objectives, gain stakeholder buy-in, and pave the way for successful execution.

Key Takeaways

- **Digital technologies** are advancing at a rapid pace and revolutionizing how organizations operate. It's imperative for organizations to define a strategy for leveraging these advancements to further their business goals.

- **Key digital technologies** that organizations are deriving business value from include intelligent process automation, data-centric AI, and business-led modular architectures.

- **Enterprise architecture** plays a pivotal role in defining and governing the IT strategy and roadmap. Additionally, it is responsible for overseeing system documentation and managing the application portfolio.

- **Process Inventory** is a critical enabler for all these efforts, providing alignment across business goals and IT designs at the granular process level.

In the next chapter, we will delve into how the Process Inventory framework can enable stronger risk management.

Strengthening Risk Management

In this chapter, we will explore the growing importance of risk management in today's complex business landscape. We'll discuss the factors driving this importance, including increasing complexity, regulatory requirements, and the evolving role of risk oversight in boards.

Throughout the chapter, you will gain insights into the components of an Enterprise Risk Management program. We'll delve into various opportunities to enhance risk management, such as the adoption of quantitative measurements, minimizing human bias in risk assessments, improving cross-organizational coordination through end-to-end process awareness, enhancing risk data quality, and clarifying the risk accountability model.

Furthermore, we will examine how Process Inventory can play a pivotal role in strengthening risk management by aligning all risk-related activities with processes. This approach has the potential to elevate the quality of risk data, strengthen the risk operating model, and leverage emerging technologies to

© Michael Schank 2023

M. Schank, *Digital Transformation Success*,

https://doi.org/10.1007/978-1-4842-9816-9_7

elevate risk intelligence. We will review examples in the areas of business continuity, compliance, and operational risk to illustrate how these concepts work in practice.

Deepwater Horizon Oil Spill

At 7:45 p.m. CDT on April 20, 2010 [1], high-pressure methane gas from a well that the Deepwater Horizon was drilling expanded into the marine riser and rose into the drilling rig, igniting and causing an explosion that engulfed the platform. Eleven workers went missing and were never found, while 94 other crew members were rescued by lifeboat or helicopter. The Deepwater Horizon drilling rig, located approximately 50 miles off the Louisiana coast, sank on the morning of April 22. The rig wouldn't be declared sealed until September 19 of that year.

Approximately 210 million gallons of oil were spilled into the Gulf of Mexico [2]. According to satellite images, the spill directly affected 70,000 square miles of ocean, which is comparable to the size of Oklahoma. The incident disrupted the coastal economy and devastated the ecosystem, resulting in the deaths of as many as 105,400 seabirds, 7,600 adult sea turtles, and 160,000 juvenile sea turtles, as well as up to a 51% decrease in dolphins in Louisiana's Barataria Bay [3].

The fallout for British Petroleum (BP) was significant. In November 2012, BP and the US Department of Justice settled criminal charges, with BP pleading guilty to 11 counts of manslaughter, two misdemeanors, and a felony count of lying to Congress. BP and the DOJ agreed to a record-setting $4.5 billion in fines and other payments [4]. BP was also responsible for the cost of the cleanup, which was estimated to be more than $65 billion [5]. In September 2014, a US district court judge primarily held BP responsible for the oil spill due to gross negligence and reckless conduct, leading BP to agree to pay $20.8 billion in fines [6].

The Deepwater Horizon incident represents a failure of risk management within BP. A quote from BP's Accident Investigation Report stated the following: "Through a review of rig audit findings and maintenance records, the investigation team found indications of potential weaknesses in the testing regime and maintenance management system for the blowout preventer (BOP)" [7].

Importance of Risk Management

This is one of several recent high-profile failures in risk management, including the 2008 financial crash, the Boeing 737 crashes, the Fukushima nuclear disaster, and the Enron accounting scandal, to name a few prominent ones. It underscores the need for strong risk management, especially when customer, market, or environmental concerns are at stake.

In today's digital age, there are several factors driving organizations to implement a formal risk management program. The environments in which organizations operate are increasingly complex, with interconnected supply chains, globalization, and technological advancements. Emerging risks, such as cyber threats, ESG mandates, geopolitical instability, natural/weather events, and most recently, a global pandemic, are present. Regulatory requirements have been growing exponentially. According to the US Chamber of Commerce, "Over the last 60 years, the U.S population has increased by 98 percent, while the federal regulatory code has increased by 850 percent" [8].

Beyond surviving and managing the downside of risk, organizations increasingly view risk management as strategically important and critical in decision-making. According to a Deloitte survey [9], companies with a compound annual growth rate (CAGR) of 5% or more were twice as likely to consider risk management key to achieving strategic goals compared to those with a CAGR under 5% (40% vs. 20%).

Risk management is vital in corporate governance. The US Securities and Exchange Commission (SEC) requires boards of publicly traded companies to provide risk oversight. The SEC emphasizes the importance of effective risk management and expects boards to fulfill their responsibilities in overseeing the company's risk management processes.

Shareholders are increasingly holding board directors accountable for their role in risk oversight, as highlighted by examples from a speech by the former director of the SEC, Luis A. Aguilar [10]:

> In early 2014, in the wake of a coal-ash spill, the California Public Employees' Retirement System ("CalPERS") and the New York City Comptroller urged shareholders to vote against four independent directors to Duke Energy Corp.'s board, accusing them of having "failed to fulfill their obligations of risk oversight as members of a committee overseeing health, safety and environmental compliance at the company." Separately, in 2013, a prominent shareholder advisory firm recommended that shareholders withhold support for three directors of the board of JPMorgan Chase and Co., accusing them of "material failures of stewardship and risk oversight" after the bank suffered a multibillion-dollar loss as a result of the "London Whale" trading scandal.

With the board, shareholders, and other stakeholders taking an increasing interest in how risk is managed, it is important to establish a formal risk program that provides a comprehensive view. This enables strategic and tactical decisions to be informed appropriately, prompting many organizations to develop a formal Enterprise Risk Management program.

Enterprise Risk Management

The Committee on Sponsoring Organizations of the Treadway Commission (COSO), a prominent risk management standards organization, defines Enterprise Risk Management (ERM) as a process, effected by an entity's board of directors, management, and other personnel, applied in strategy setting and across the enterprise, designed to identify potential events that may affect the entity, and manage risk to be within its risk appetite, to provide reasonable assurance regarding the achievement of entity objectives [11].

The primary goal of ERM is to enable organizations to effectively anticipate and respond to risks in a holistic manner, considering internal and external factors that may influence desired outcomes. Risks come in various types, which will be covered in the following section "Risk Taxonomy," and may require specific approaches in the risk management process. Additionally, nearly every part of the organization can be involved in identifying and mitigating risk, making a holistic approach a significant undertaking.

COSO and the International Organization for Standardization (ISO) 31000 Risk Management Process are two leading sources of risk management guidance. According to a 2020 ERM Benchmarking Study conducted by the Risk & Insurance Management Society (RIMS) with 288 organizations, 37% of organizations have custom-built their own frameworks based on various sources [12], including these two organizations.

Figure 7-1 presents an ERM framework that incorporates standards from COSO, ISO 31000 Risk Management Process, and Management of Risk: Guidance for Practitioners (Orange Book). This framework serves as a reference point to discuss the structure of a robust ERM program, address current challenges, and illustrate how the Process Inventory framework can enhance the effectiveness of these efforts.

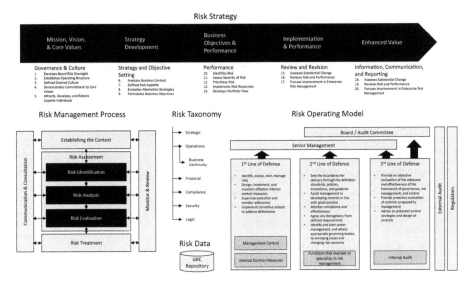

Figure 7-1. Enterprise Risk Management Framework

A strong ERM program typically exhibits the following characteristics:

- **Integrated Approach**: Risk management should be seamlessly integrated into the organization's culture, operations, and governance structure. It should be an inherent part of strategic planning and decision-making processes.

- **Governance**: Various stakeholders within the organization should have defined roles, responsibilities, separation of duties, and accountability for risk management. Senior management and the board must prioritize their oversight role and ensure clear documentation of their responsibilities.

- **Risk Assessment**: Risks should be systematically identified, assessed, and prioritized across the organization. Since different types of risks exist, each may require a unique assessment approach. This typically involves rating the likelihood and impact of risks using a risk matrix.

- **Risk Appetite**: Organizations need to define their tolerance for risk in alignment with their strategic objectives. This establishes a framework for prioritization and strategic decision-making processes.

- **Risk Treatment**: Effective risk response strategies should be developed to adequately control and manage identified risks.

- **Communications and Consultation**: Accurate and timely reporting on risks is crucial, especially for the board and senior leaders. Key stakeholders should receive appropriate risk information, and risk managers should be available to provide guidance and consultation in decision-making processes.

- **Monitor and Review**: Continuous monitoring and review of risks are essential to validate accurate risk identification and assess the effectiveness of implemented controls in mitigating risks.

- **Continuous Improvement**: The organization should foster a culture of innovation by regularly evaluating the performance of the risk management program and identifying opportunities for improvement.

Opportunities in Enterprise Risk Management

The history of risk management dates to ancient practices. Merchants in Babylon would distribute their goods across different ships to reduce the risk of losing everything in a single event [13]. Much of the history is tied to insurance, where in maritime cities such as Genoa and Venice, merchants and shipowners started pooling their resources to protect against the risks of shipwrecks, piracy, and other perils of the sea.

The emergence of life insurance and the need for assessing mortality risks in the eighteenth century led to the origins of actuarial science, applying mathematical principles to analyze life expectancy and mortality rates. In the mid-nineteenth century, actuaries became an established profession with accreditation requirements, earning the title of actuarial science.

In the 1970s and 1980s, financial institutions began focusing on risks that were not insurable, such as credit risk, market risk, and liquidity risk. In the 1990s, after a series of corporate failures resulting in significant losses, the UK Financial Reporting Council (FRC) established a commission that led to the Cadbury Report (1992) [14]. Subsequently, the London Stock Exchange and the Institute of Directors (IoD) set up another commission that resulted in the Turnbull Report (1998) [15]. These reports identified recommendations for corporate governance and internal control systems, influencing changes in the UK Corporate Governance Code and listing requirements. Executives now needed a holistic view of the risk landscape, leading to a change in approach toward qualitative scoring and the concept of Enterprise Risk Management (ERM). In 2004, the Committee of Sponsoring Organizations of the Treadway Commission (COSO) released its Enterprise Risk Management—Integrated Framework, providing a comprehensive structure for implementing ERM within organizations.

It has been over 20 years since Enterprise Risk Management became a framework and methodology. It is remarkable to see the widespread adoption of formal ERM programs, particularly among large organizations. ERM has become a substantial industry with significant resources dedicated to services, software, and efforts within organizations.

While the evolution of this concept has been remarkable, there are still opportunities for further development. According to an EY Global Board Risk Survey, 84% of boards do not believe their organizations have a highly effective risk management strategy [16]. As consistent with the theme of this book, the ERM profession will be influenced by the same technological enhancements and innovations driving the digital transformation movement.

Having spent a significant number of years consulting in the banking industry, advising clients and executives on strategies to address their major risk management challenges, I have identified the biggest opportunities, supported by other industry research I will reference.

Moving Beyond Qualitative Risk Assessments

In his book *The Failure of Risk Management: Why It's Broken and How to Fix It* [13], author Douglas Hubbard highlights the shortcomings of the qualification approach to measuring risk.

According to Hubbard, many risk management surveys, including the EY Global Board Risk Survey mentioned earlier, often rely on questions like "How do you rate your risk management strategy?" The problem with such surveys is that the responses are subjective opinions that lack empirical evidence to support them. This raises concerns for senior leaders and boards as they question whether their risk management programs truly have a grasp on all major and emerging risks. There is a prevailing perception that ERM is effective in addressing past issues but struggles to proactively address emerging risks.

THE 2008 FINANCIAL CRISIS

The 2008 financial crisis serves as a prime example of a failure that can be attributed to a lack of quantification. The root cause of the crisis was the relaxation of underwriting standards, with approximately one-third of all mortgages in 2006 being subprime or no documentation loans, accounting for 17% of home purchases that year [17].

Numerous actors played a role in the crisis, including government-sponsored entities like Fannie Mae and Freddie Mac, regulators, mortgage lenders, credit rating agencies, rating institutions, and financial institutions. Any of these actors could have assessed the sensitivity of those lower-quality mortgages to a potential housing bubble, but none of them did so or took appropriate action, potentially due to their self-interest. The resulting failure had catastrophic consequences for various stakeholders, including the global economy, homeowners, taxpayers, investors, and others.

The basis for assessing risk is the risk matrix. Figure 7-2 provides an example of a risk matrix, where risk assessors plot the likelihood and impact of a risk. In this example, each axis of the matrix is assigned a value from 1 to 5. An aggregate score is calculated by multiplying the likelihood and impact, resulting in a risk designation ranging from low to high. This process helps translate a qualitative model into a semiquantitative model, facilitating the prioritization of different risks for mitigation.

Superimposed on the risk matrix are three distinct risk level designations commonly used to evaluate control effectiveness. Inherent risk refers to the risk level before implementing any mitigation measures. Residual risk represents the risk level considering the current controls in place. Target risk represents the desired risk level to be achieved through further mitigation efforts.

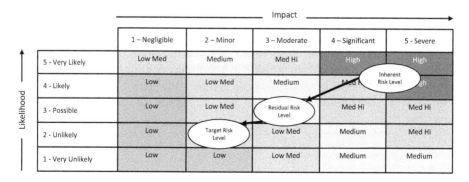

Figure 7-2. Risk Matrix

Given the need for Enterprise Risk Management (ERM) to provide a comprehensive summary of the risk landscape for executive consumption and the reality that it is not feasible to create a quantifiable model for every risk, it is unlikely that the risk matrix will be eliminated anytime soon. However, to identify opportunities for improving ERM, we must have an honest understanding of its limitations.

The current method of assessing risk is a subjective process carried out by humans, who are prone to various biases. Here are some of the biases that may impact scoring:

- **Confirmation Bias**: This refers to our tendency to interpret the world in a way that confirms our existing beliefs or values. An example of this is the 2008 financial crisis, where individuals within different actor groups could have recognized the impending disaster, but their cognitive biases only allowed them to see what aligned with their financial success.

- **Interpretation Bias**: This bias involves interpreting information or situations in a way that is influenced by preexisting beliefs, expectations, or emotions. Since the assignment of likelihood and impact is based on subjective judgment, scoring may have been interpreted differently across organizational boundaries, hindering consistency, prioritization, and decision-making.

- **Groupthink Bias**: Groupthink occurs when a group of people, aiming for consensus and cohesion, prioritize agreement and harmony over critical thinking and independent evaluation of ideas. This can lead to overconfidence and downplay certain risks while suppressing important dissenting points of view.

By acknowledging and addressing these biases, organizations can strive for a more objective and robust risk assessment process within their ERM frameworks.

Midsize and large corporations are typically complex systems in which various parts of the organization collaborate to serve customers or fulfill important purposes. Often, assessments are conducted within business or functional units without a comprehensive consideration of upstream or downstream processes. When assessments are performed across organizational boundaries, a lack of common language and understanding of individual processes hinders the ability to grasp their interdependencies. This challenge is particularly pronounced for teams lacking functional expertise, such as internal audit. Consequently, risks that are deemed low at the component level may result in high failure when combined. Analyzing the correlation of events along the value chain can provide valuable insights and impact risk ratings along the end-to-end process.

Similarly, there is the challenge of risk aggregation. While scoring in the risk matrix is performed for individual risks, it may fail to capture the compounding effect in which a certain number of medium risks can lead to a high-risk situation. Ultimately, when presenting a report for executive consumption, it is crucial that the view represents an accurate depiction of overall risk.

The lack of granularity in process and contextual information, including the definition of processes, process boundaries, and historical negative events such as risks and operational losses, can contribute to an incomplete identification of potential failures.

The opportunity lies in defining and implementing strategies that instill confidence in senior leaders, providing them with an accurate assessment of the risk landscape and enabling better-informed strategic decisions. This entails quantifying risk to a greater extent and equipping risk assessment teams with more granular information and robust methods to enhance accuracy and mitigate human bias.

Need to Improve Risk Data

Unfortunately, poor data quality is prevalent in most large organizations. According to the Forbes Insights and KPMG study [18], "84% of CEOs are concerned about the quality of the data they're basing their decisions on." This statement is concerning as it not only affects the ability to effectively manage risks such as operational losses and regulatory fines, but it also hinders the organization's risk manager from having a seat at the table in strategic decision-making.

CITIBANK CONSENT ORDER

In August 2020, Citibank intended to make an interest payment to lenders on behalf of Revlon, a company for which Citibank served as the loan agent. However, due to a combination of human error and a lack of adequate safeguards in the payment system, the full principal amount of the loans, totaling nearly $900 million, was transferred to the lenders.

As a fallout of this incident, the US Office of the Comptroller of the Currency (OCC) issued a Consent Order [19]. A Consent Order is essentially a directive from a regulatory body to a company to address its compliance shortcomings, which in this case included deficiencies in Citibank's risk management practices and internal controls, particularly in operational risk. A significant aspect of the Consent Order was related to data issues, particularly in relation to risk data, which prevented Citibank from identifying this risk and implementing mitigating controls. Article II of the Consent Order specifically addressed concerns regarding data quality issues.

The OCC has identified the following deficiencies, noncompliance with 12 C.F.R. Part 30, Appendix D, or unsafe or unsound practices with respect to the Bank's data quality and data governance, including risk data aggregation and management and regulatory reporting:

(b) inability to develop and execute on a comprehensive plan to address data governance deficiencies, including data quality errors and failure to produce timely and accurate management and regulatory reporting; and

(c) inadequate reporting to the Board on the status of data quality and progress in remediating identified deficiencies.

This Citibank example is a great illustration of a **nonfinancial risk** failure. Nonfinancial risks are the risks that occur in the normal course of doing business. To safeguard against these risks, it's imperative to have a detailed understanding of all the business-as-usual activities so that an accurate assessment of risk can occur and effective controls can be implemented.

In the case mentioned earlier, Citibank did not have controls in place to guard against such a massive errant payment. It is fair to say that their risk assessment process was flawed as this payment process should have scored high in both its inherent and residual risk ratings, considering its capacity for such a massive payment. This would have made it a high priority, demanding focused efforts to implement stronger mitigating controls. The root cause of this failure seems to be that their risk management program literally lost sight of the existence of this processes. This is not uncommon in an enterprise as large and complex as Citibank, where there are hundreds or thousands of processes that can pose similar risks. That is why it is imperative to build and maintain high-quality risk data so that the highest risks are addressed with the necessary urgency. According to the text of the Consent Order, it appears that poor data quality was at the heart of this issue.

In a recent Deloitte Global Risk Management Survey, it was reported that "most respondents said their institutions found certain issues to be extremely or very challenging: maintaining reliable data to quantify nonfinancial risk and drive risk-based decisions (74%) and the ability to leverage and source alternative data, such as unstructured data (74%)" [20]. Only about one-quarter of respondents believed their institutions are extremely or very effective at managing data quality (26%) for nonfinancial risks. Only about one-quarter of respondents believed their institutions are extremely or very effective at managing data quality (26%) for nonfinancial risks. This means that this issue is pervasive across institutions.

Since an organization can have a significant quantity of risks, risk stakeholders, and the need for accurate risk reporting, organizations must create and maintain a repository of information from which to manage and report on the risk landscape.

For organizations that are maturing their risk management capability, this may mean a risk registry spreadsheet that is built and maintained in each organizational unit. The challenges with this are obvious: spreadsheets are prone to quality issues. Additionally, aggregating information across the enterprise for senior-level decision-making would be a time-intensive activity to reconcile each unique structure into a coherent story.

A common tool for mature ERM programs is a governance, risk, and compliance (GRC) platform. GRC tools encompass the systems, processes, and practices that enable an organization to achieve its risk objectives while effectively managing risks and complying with applicable laws, regulations, and internal policies. GRC tools can be built in-house, but there are also vendor software platforms. The global vendor market is expected to reach $134 billion by 2030, with a compound annual growth rate (CAGR) of 13.8% [21]. Adoption is continuing at a healthy pace.

Here are the capabilities of these platforms that will aid an ERM program:

Governance refers to the capabilities of leadership to provide oversight and control of the ERM program to ensure it aligns with business goals. These platforms enable management to document and manage policies and procedures and track compliance from the stakeholders involved. Stronger decision-making is promoted by aggregating risk information through reporting into actionable items for senior leadership and board consumption.

Through that, it connects the dots between strategic decision-makers and risk practitioners across the organization by facilitating accountability and stronger coordination across internal stakeholders since all teams would work off the single source of truth. Integration with external stakeholders, such as external auditors and regulators, would benefit from reports generated from this single source.

Risk capabilities provide a structured approach to managing risk. They support all steps in the risk management process, such as identification, assessment, prioritization, and documentation of mitigating controls. They provide monitoring and reporting capabilities by aggregating data from multiple sources. The platform can model scenarios so risk practitioners can assess the impact across these scenarios. It promotes the risk culture by documenting ownership of the various risk concepts. Workflow capabilities track activities in risk processes, send out reminder emails, track responses, and provide an audit trail.

Compliance capabilities help organizations comply with regulatory requirements, standards, and industry guidelines by providing a repository to map regulations, the resulting obligations for the organization, and the policies, procedures, and controls put in place. These platforms can monitor changes in regulations so that changes can be implemented. Compliance reporting and dashboards facilitate productive conversations with regulators.

A foundational feature of GRC platforms is providing a centralized repository for risk information. I've provided a partial and illustrative GRC data model in Figure 7-3. As you can see from the diagram, this is more than just a registry of risk; it also stores many other data subjects, such as processes, controls, regulations, and monitors. Each data subject may have distinct stakeholders that provide input and leverage this data in their roles. It's critical that this data and the associations across the concepts are governed to maintain their fidelity.

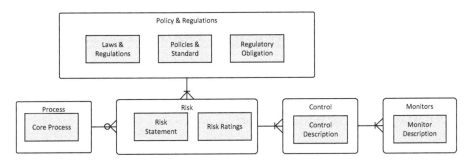

Figure 7-3. Illustrative GRC Data Model

A process can have zero to many risks. Every risk must be associated with a process as internal risks do not occur without some action trigger, which is represented by a process. This association also provides business context and accountability if process owners have been designated. Every risk has one or more controls, and each control should have one or more monitors. I will cover regulatory obligations a bit later in this chapter.

In my experience, a prominent root cause of nonfinancial risk failures is poorly managed data. Since the activities that an organization performs are the source of risk, I cannot stress enough the importance of having an accurate inventory of those activities, specifically processes, as a key component of this data structure.

Unfortunately, I have yet to come across an organization that has mastered this aspect. Much of the standard ERM literature refers to aligning with "core processes," but this term is vague and subject to different perceptions among stakeholders. Other organizations may adopt a standard process framework such as APQC's Process Classification Framework. However, the challenge with this approach, especially within organizations with disparate business units, is that these standard models rarely reflect the granularity of business activities due to their unique idiosyncrasies. As a result, risk assessors and business stakeholders must interpret the activities performed by the business and map them to the standard model for storage, which often leads to data quality issues.

There are new GRC platforms emerging called Cognitive GRC, which integrate traditional GRC platforms with the capabilities of artificial intelligence and machine learning. This integration significantly enhances the capabilities of these platforms.

From a GRC perspective, I still believe that high-quality data is the key to an effective ERM program. Prior to undertaking a GRC implementation, it is critical to carefully consider the ontology of risk concepts and identify the appropriate data model for your organization.

2012 JPMORGAN CHASE TRADING LOSS

In April and May of 2012, JPMorgan Chase's Synthetic Credit Portfolio (SCP) group, which traded credit default swaps (CDSs), suffered substantial losses, initially estimated at $2 billion but later revised to $6.2 billion [22]. This incident represented one of the largest losses in financial history.

There were several control breakdowns that contributed to this incident. The SCP relied on financial models built into spreadsheets that assumed a correlation between short-term and long-term hedges, which had become invalid. Value-at-risk (VAR) limits were breached over 300 times, and traders were given the freedom to choose their preferred daily intraday price range, effectively marking their own positions.

However, one significant failure was the lack of comprehensive position reports on the portfolio provided to the chief investment officer, who was responsible for overseeing the SCP. As a result, senior executives lacked a complete understanding of the risks until it was too late.

The preceding JPMorgan Chase example highlights a failure in **financial risk** management. Financial risk refers to the possibility of losing money in an investment or business venture. This category encompasses

- **Credit Risk**: The risk of financial loss resulting from counterparties failing to meet their obligations, such as defaulting on loans or credit.

- **Market Risk**: The risk of financial loss resulting from adverse events in market prices, such as interest rates, exchange rates, commodity prices, or stock prices.

- **Liquidity Risk**: The risk of not being able to meet financial obligations as they become due because of insufficient liquid assets or the inability to quickly sell assets without significant loss. Liquidity risk can arise from cash flow mismatches, reduced marketability of assets, or disruptions in funding sources.

Assessing and quantifying financial risk involves building models to quantify financial positions. This is also true for some regulatory compliance reports such as capital adequacy reports. These models require high-quality, accurate, granular data with auditable data lineage. This extends beyond GRC as the data needs to be sourced from multiple transactions, asset portfolios, or finance systems, emphasizing the need for data quality beyond just risk purposes.

Effective financial risk management means that senior leaders, and in some cases regulators, trust the reports guiding their decision-making in mitigating risks. There is ample opportunity through data governance and data architecture to increase confidence in risk management data, providing senior leaders with assurance that their decisions are based on solid factual foundations.

Risk Operating Model Opportunities

A standard model for identifying accountabilities and delineating responsibilities within an Enterprise Risk Management program is the Three Lines of Defense (3LoD) model. The exact origin of this model is unclear; its roots seem to be in the banking industry, with the Basel Committee on Banking Supervision (BCBS) publishing a position paper titled "Sound Practices for the Management and Supervision of Operational Risk" [23] in 2003. Although the paper did not explicitly name the 3LoD model, it outlined many principles for effective risk management and supervision that have since become associated with the model. The 3LoD model has expanded beyond banking and is now commonly practiced in many industries, especially after the Institute of Internal Auditors (IIA) formally adopted the model in 2013. However, the level of adoption varies based on the level of regulatory scrutiny as it is a model that regulators expect.

Risk Operating Model

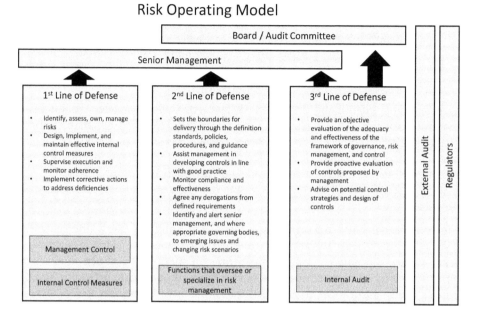

Figure 7-4. Three Lines of Defense Model

The 3LoD model is highlighted in Figure 7-4, which was sourced from The Orange Book Management of Risk – Principles and Concepts [24]. The roles of each line of defense are as follows:

The **first line of defense** is embedded within the business units or supporting functions (such as technology, finance, etc.). The business units have direct responsibility for delivering products and services to clients while supporting functions directly support the goals of the business unit or enterprise. This group possesses in-depth knowledge of their processes and takes the lead in risk assessments and control designs. The first line executes controls in their business unit or function which are not technology-based, and they are accountable for the performance of those controls. Control steps, for manual controls, are typically outlined in process procedure manuals for staff.

The **second line of defense** is responsible for monitoring and overseeing risks. In many organizations, the second line is organized around the risk taxonomy, such as operational risk, compliance risk, cybersecurity risk, etc. They bring domain expertise and establish policies, procedures, and standards that guide the first line in the risk process. They monitor and review the work of the first line to gain assurance of the effectiveness of controls. They also prepare reports and dashboards for management and board review, providing an aggregated view of the risk landscape across business units and functions.

In some smaller organizations or those with lower regulatory requirements, the first and second lines may be combined in the organizational structure.

The **third line of defense** is the independent internal audit function. They perform objective evaluations to assess the adequacy and effectiveness of internal controls and provide recommendations on improving risk management and governance. They provide assurance directly to senior leadership and the board that the risk management processes are operating effectively. While they can provide feedback and advice to the first and second lines of defense, they cannot design controls, which is essential to maintaining their independence.

Although the Three Lines of Defense model has been around for over 20 years and is pervasive in many industries, significant challenges exist in its implementation. In a recent Deloitte Global Risk Management [25] Survey of 57 financial service institutions worldwide, the following concerns were highlighted:

The most frequently cited challenges concerned the responsibilities and capabilities of the first line, including

- 44% gaining buy-in from the first line
- 50% defining the roles and responsibilities between the first line and the second line
- 33% executing first-line responsibilities
- 39% having a sufficient number of skilled personnel in the first line

These results are not shocking as they align with my experiences in various financial services organizations. I also assume this is not limited just to financial services and that other nonfinancial service organizations are experiencing similar challenges.

The opportunities to improve this model lie in defining and adopting stronger leadership and governance, implementing a stronger accountability model, and enhancing collaboration among the three lines.

Leadership for each line of defense can be strengthened by improving how they govern their teams. This involves cascading goals down the organization and enhancing risk management reporting with more quantifiable metrics to drive a culture of continuous improvement.

To enhance accountability, it is crucial to provide clarity on individual accountabilities. These accountabilities should be formalized in yearly performance goals, and performance based on these accountabilities should be integrated into the annual review process. While documenting accountabilities is important, measuring individuals' performance and aligning financial incentives can further reinforce the desired behaviors.

These accountabilities should also be reflected in the risk data mentioned earlier. I worked with a marketing team at a Global Financial Services organization, and I observed that their risk data did not even include the name of the accountable first-line business owner for each risk and control. Without such clarity, things are bound to fall through the cracks as no one takes ownership of individual controls.

Lastly, it is essential to establish clear areas of collaboration between the lines. Tensions are inevitable between the lines as the first line is often focused on revenue generation and business results, while the second line tends to be risk-averse. Recognizing potential points of conflict and fostering collaboration between teams, with the involvement of their leaders, are crucial for negotiating solutions that meet the needs of the business. This is the path to breaking down silos in the ERM program.

The Future of ERM Fueled by Process Inventory

The first part of this chapter was dedicated to the history of Enterprise Risk Management and the challenges faced by those programs. The remaining part of this chapter will focus on a vision for the future of ERM, fueled by the Process Inventory framework. It will include a summary of that vision as well as some practical examples of how the future of ERM would work.

There are several trends influencing the future of ERM, many of which are driving the overall digital transformation. Here are some of the most pressing drivers that I would like to highlight.

Technology poses the biggest disruption while also offering opportunities for the future. To illustrate this disruption, let's consider regulatory compliance. Previously, legal and compliance teams had to engage in manual and intensive efforts to understand changes in laws and regulations. Now, machine learning can accomplish this task in a fraction of that time with a high degree of accuracy. This productivity multiplier allows resources to focus on other high-value tasks. Furthermore, machine learning can continuously process internal and external signals to validate existing controls and detect patterns that point to new threats. However, this opportunity is only available to organizations that recognize **data as an asset**. The proliferation of data in recent years necessitates a data management approach to organize and ensure the quality of the data, enabling the extraction of valuable insights for better business decisions.

We are currently experiencing an era of significant change, where **competition** from disruptors could pose a threat to established players, particularly in highly regulated industries where regulatory requirements act as entry barriers. Innovation, not only in risk management but across all aspects, is increasingly critical for organizations that want to survive and thrive.

The **regulatory** landscape is becoming increasingly complex. The winners of the future will establish strong operating models with clear processes to ensure that compliance doesn't create unnecessary complexity within their organizations. Lastly, globalization and the risk of interconnected global **supply chains** will persist. Organizations must not only understand their own risks but also have mitigation measures in place in case of a failure by upstream or downstream partners.

Here are three strategies to succeed in the future:

Strategy 1—Reconstructing the Risk and Control Framework

The current state of complexity in risk data needs to adapt not only to address the challenges mentioned earlier but also to become agile in the face of a continually changing landscape. This cannot be emphasized strongly enough: without accurate risk data, the complexity of the operating model will persist, and the quality of information on which leaders base their decisions will always be questioned.

This means orienting the framework toward processes. Logically speaking, an internal risk cannot be incurred without some trigger taking place. For internal triggers, that means an action, or in other words, a process. Anchoring the framework to a single truth for processes, Process Inventory is foundational to getting the business context right and complete, thus ensuring high-quality risk data.

Aligning with processes brings **clarity and alignment** to the risk management environment. The root of the challenges is not the complexity of the business itself, but rather the different levels of understanding across the practitioner teams. These disparate levels of understanding result in gaps in interpretations, which cause inefficiencies and errors. This approach effectively breaks down silos as everyone will have a common and detailed language to work from.

This alignment results in **faster root cause analysis** of issues as the resources that support the process, such as technology systems, are directly aligned. Getting technology resources on the same page of understanding can facilitate the shift from manual and reactive controls to automated and preventative controls, which are less susceptible to human error. This has the side benefit of freeing up resources for higher value activities.

With the Process Inventory providing an accurate and comprehensive inventory of all processes, it gives risk teams a denominator from which to evaluate the **completeness** of their efforts. The outcome would provide a higher confidence in the periodic assessment of risk, as each process area would have to be reviewed, or a conscious decision made not to review an area. Regardless, nothing will fall through the cracks.

This structure empowers risk teams to extend risk ratings beyond the risk itself and aggregate a measure for rating the riskiness of processes. This puts it in a language that business leaders understand and gives them insights into which processes require investment to strengthen.

This structure becomes the anchor point within the GRC data structure, mapping all the data concepts, such as regulatory obligations, business continuity events, etc., to the processes impacted. As Figure 7-5 illustrates, this model brings frontline execution teams as process owners, ensuring **higher data quality**, as they can validate the accuracy of process information.

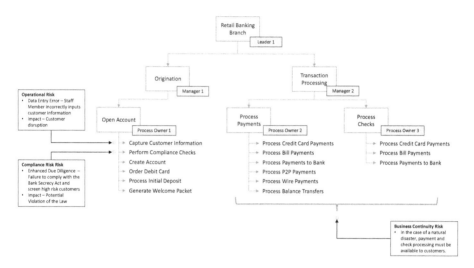

Figure 7-5. Process Inventory Risk Alignment Example

Strategy 2—Strengthen the Risk Management Operating Model

Accountability is the key to driving a high-performance culture. Many ERM programs place a significant emphasis on culture, which is critical, but it must be accompanied by setting clear expectations, establishing goals that cascade throughout the organization, and holding everyone accountable to those goals.

As illustrated in Figure 7-5, each process in the Process Inventory is designated with ownership throughout the structure. Process owners, who are part of the first line of defense, are key since they attest to the accuracy of the inventory and have the best understanding of the process details. Process owners must play an active role in the risk assessment process and sign off on the controls for which they have accountability. Since the Process Inventory aligns with the organizational structure, a control for which a process owner is responsible is also a measurement for their leader and that leader's leader. This means accountability is cascaded at all levels of the organization. Through this model, risk management is perceived not as a burden that distracts from their day job but as a core part of their responsibilities.

There are many second-line defense functions that currently operate in silos and compete for the limited attention of first-line leaders and process owners. As depicted in Figure 7-5, processes in the inventory can have risks of almost any type. Aligning them to a single source of process truth will break down silos and foster better coordination through the process lens. Second-line functions will be accountable for reviewing the accuracy of risk assessments and ensuring that controls align with their policies. This overlap of goals will lead to better collaboration.

For the third line of defense, this approach should make their job much easier. In my experience, internal audit teams have struggled to understand how the business operates, and I've seen many of them establish process teams in an attempt to gain clarity. Since this structure provides them with clarity on the business's operations, they can focus their energies on testing controls and evaluating the overall control environment. Having near real-time data on control performance will assist them in identifying areas of focus when they construct their audit plan.

Strategy 3—Exploit Technology Advancements to Achieve a New Level of Risk Intelligence

Machine learning can analyze processing events to identify patterns, make predictions, and provide risk managers with insights into the strength of existing controls, as well as alert them to emerging risks. To capitalize on this potential, machine learning will have to be given labeled data [26] to understand the boundaries between these events and to correlate data from disparate sources. Training machine learning with labeled data powers data-centric artificial intelligence and facilitates effective supervised learning.

The Process Inventory is the structure for demarcating processing events and provides the perfect structure for labeling data. The data sets for machine learning to learn from include transactional data, control performance data, negative event data (such as issues, complaints, operational losses, etc.), system data, and performance data. To fully leverage the potential of these sources, organizations must align their data with a consistent data structure, which is provided by Process Inventory.

Machine learning technologies will also be useful for horizon scanning of the external environment to identify emerging trends, events, and potential risks that may impact an organization. These include economic trends, regulatory and compliance changes, geopolitical risks, natural environmental risks, and even social media trends that may point to emerging risks. Many organizations already perform horizon scanning, but with machine learning technologies, the efficiency and level of insights will result in stronger response plans.

This would provide leadership with a dashboard framed in a business context to understand the health of the control environment. This is demonstrated in Figure 7-6; this example dashboard would give leadership and other risk professionals the ability to drill down into the performance of any individual process area or process. Moreover, it would provide machine learning with a rich set of quality data to identify emerging patterns and mitigate human bias in the risk assessment process.

Machine learning provides the ability to analyze data and run mathematical models, which can move the needle from qualitative measurement of risk to quantitative. For instance, the Monte Carlo simulation incorporates input variables, each with a range of possible values or probability distributions based on available data or assumptions. It then runs simulations using the distribution of these variables to provide a range of possible outcomes with their probabilities. This approach applies not just to a single process or risk but to the larger ecosystem of interconnected processes and risks, uncovering risks that may otherwise go unidentified using traditional methods. This provides teams with richer insights to identify and design stronger controls.

The result of these enhancements is that senior leaders will have assurance that they are getting an accurate picture of the risk landscape to aid them in strategic decision-making. Near real-time dashboards will provide all leaders with the state of the control environment in the appropriate business context, which is viewed through the lens of the Process Inventory. All of this would be achieved while driving better performance in risk processes and being efficient with resources.

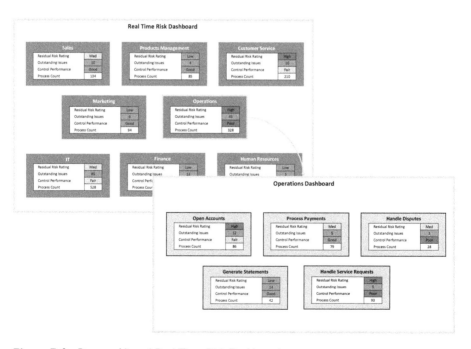

Figure 7-6. Process Aligned Real-Time Risk Dashboard

Defining the Enterprise Risk Management Framework

Enterprise Risk Management Framework

Mission, Vision, & Core Values	Strategy Development	Business Objectives & Performance	Implementation & Performance	Enhanced Value
Governance & Culture	**Strategy and Objective Setting**	**Performance**	**Review and Revision**	**Information, Communication, and Reporting**
1. Exercises Board Risk Oversight		10. Identifies Risk	15. Assesses Substantial Change	
2. Establishes Operating Structure	6. Analyzes Business Context	11. Assess Severity of Risk	16. Reviews Risk and Performance	18. Assesses Substantial Change
3. Defined Desired Culture	7. Defined Risk Appetite	12. Prioritizes Risk	17. Pursues improvement in Enterprise	19. Reviews Risk and Performance
4. Demonstrates Commitment to Core Values	8. Evaluates Alternative Strategies	13. Implements Risk Responses	Risk Management	20. Pursues improvement in Enterprise Risk Management
5. Attracts, Develops, and Retains Capable Individuals	9. Formulates Business Objectives	14. Develops Portfolio View		

Figure 7-7. COSO Enterprise Risk Management Framework—Integrating with Strategy and Performance

Figure 7-7 represents *COSO's Enterprise Risk Management—Integrating with Strategy and Performance Framework*, which provides guidance to the board and management in defining risk strategy.

As mentioned earlier, the US Securities and Exchange Commission (SEC) mandates that boards of publicly traded companies ensure risk oversight, indicating that the tone for risk management begins at the top. Boards may establish dedicated risk committees or assign primary risk oversight to the audit committee. According to the Deloitte Global Risk Management Survey, regulators increasingly expect risk committees to include independent directors with risk management expertise, and this expectation has influenced board compositions. Seventy percent of respondents stated that their board's risk committee comprises either entirely or mostly independent directors [25].

Boards have several oversight responsibilities. They review the organization's formal risk governance framework, which outlines the structure, processes, and responsibilities of risk management within the organization. They also review the risk policy, which outlines the organization's approach to identifying, assessing, and managing risk. Boards are involved in defining the enterprise-level risk appetite statement, which represents the level of risk that the organization is willing to accept in pursuit of its business objectives. Additionally, they regularly review risk management reports and provide guidance, leveraging their expertise, on the top risks facing the organization.

The management of risks falls under the responsibility of the organization's leadership, starting with the CEO. CEOs often appoint a senior risk manager, which may be designated with the title of chief risk officer, to oversee the risk management program. In many cases, the risk managers report directly to the CEO and provide reports to the board.

The primary role of the risk manager is to establish the framework, processes, and policies of the Enterprise Risk Management (ERM) program. Increasingly, risk managers are involved in strategic decision-making, requiring them to possess not only risk management skills but also a deep understanding of the business. This enables them to integrate a risk perspective into strategic decision-making processes.

The CEO and the risk manager must work together to foster a risk-aware culture throughout the organization. This culture begins with accountability. They need to define a clear operating structure with well-defined accountabilities and goals that cascade throughout the organization. It should be evident to everyone how risk management contributes to their performance evaluations. The culture must strike a balance between risk management, innovation, and business growth.

Risk managers take the lead in risk governance efforts and are responsible for producing comprehensive reports for the CEO and the board. These reports provide a holistic and accurate summary of the risk landscape, highlighting key risks that require attention and guidance from the leadership.

The Process Inventory framework is a valuable tool for these leaders. It offers a holistic view of processes and provides a structured approach to aggregate and quantify risks, ensuring a comprehensive understanding of the risk landscape. The framework strengthens the operating model by establishing a hierarchy of processes with clear ownership, enabling the cascading of goals throughout the organization, and reporting the status of controls.

Ignite ERM of the Future with Data Excellence

Data has presented challenges for organizations, but when managed properly, it can serve as a robust foundation for enhancing the effectiveness of risk management programs. In this section, we will explore how the Process Inventory can contribute to high-quality GRC risk data and how it provides a framework for unlocking valuable insights. By harnessing the potential of the Process Inventory, organizations can elevate their risk management practices and leverage the transformative power of data-driven decision-making.

High-Quality GRC Risk Data

Risk data, stored within a GRC repository, serves as the critical foundation for effective risk management practices. This data plays a pivotal role in facilitating informed risk identification during the risk assessment process. Moreover, it forms the basis for comprehensive reporting on the organization's risk landscape, enabling strategic decision-making based on accurate and timely insights. Additionally, risk data serves as tangible evidence of the organization's compliance with relevant laws and regulations, providing assurance to regulators.

Since Process Inventory is constructed by following the organizational hierarchy and each point in the Process Inventory taxonomy has an identified owner, it fosters a culture of accountability and strengthens the organization's risk management framework. Identified process owners become the core of the first line of defense. Data quality is achieved by periodically requiring process owners to attest to not only the processes in their inventory but also the associated risk data.

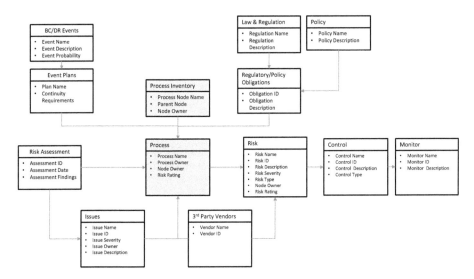

Figure 7-8. Illustrative Target State GRC Data Model

Figure 7-8 illustrates the GRC data model with Process Inventory as the grounding truth for business context. Process Inventory and the processes are highlighted in blue. These data would be built and maintained in the Integrated Operational Repository. This data would be exported to the GRC repository. Since process owners would be active participants in the risk assessment process, they would be required to attest to the accuracy of the process information for which they are an owner as part of the assessment process. This would ensure that assessments are performed on accurate process information.

Here are some of the relationships that are key in this model:

- **Risk** is associated with a process, as risk must be triggered by an activity, which for internal risks is a process. Each risk can have one or more controls, and each control can have one or more monitors.

- **Laws, regulations, and policies** have obligations which are the interpretation of those rules and the requirements that it places on processes. Those obligations need to be placed on processes so process owners can design the appropriate controls needed to comply.

- **Third-party vendors** can provide a wide range of services to an organization such as being a business process outsourcer, providing software platforms, and providing professional services. For business process outsourcers, it's important to remember that even if the process is outsourced to a vendor, the accountability remains with the organization. Due to that, Process Inventory should contain an inventory of processes that the vendor is performing so that risk management teams can have clarity on which controls that vendor is required to implement. For software platforms, it's important to know which processes are served by those platforms for root cause and monitoring purposes.

- **Issues** are associated with the processes that incur them. This relationship provides the triage and resolutions team with access to not only the controls associated with those processes but also all the resources that are leveraged.

- **Risk assessments** are performed on processes so that relationship must be maintained in this data model. Findings are placed on individual processes which place accountability for the resolution on the process owner.

- **Business continuity/disaster recovery events** are predominantly external events that can cause disruption to operations. Continuity plans are created for each scenario which includes which processes must be maintained, even at a degraded level. This also enables the design team to look for points of weakness in processes, such as a single data center in a hurricane zone, and remediate those weaknesses before the event occurs.

Data-Driven Risk Insights

Risk intelligence is a term that has been around since the 1980s. David Apgar defines it in his book *Risk Intelligence: Learning to Manage What We Don't Know* as "experience, any and all experience, past and future, that can help us solve problems requiring an understanding of risk" [27].

Organizations generate a massive amount of data related to the experiences of their business processes. This data holds valuable insights into better performance, especially in terms of risk management. However, most organizations lack a structured approach to extracting these insights and applying them to the risk management process.

The core challenge is that we are missing a single language for correlating data across these disparate platforms and for demarcating process signals. With the power of machine learning, addressing this challenge has become more urgent. Machine learning technology enables us to process information, detect patterns, and test our current risk assumptions, helping us identify weaknesses that were previously unknown.

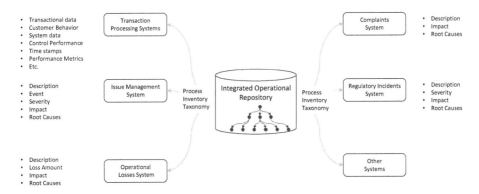

Figure 7-9. Publishing Process Inventory Taxonomy

The Process Inventory serves as a unified language for consistently categorizing data in various systems with the appropriate business context. Numerous systems generate and manage data on process performance, encompassing both positive and negative aspects. The key opportunity lies in establishing a common language among these systems.

Figure 7-9 depicts how the Process Inventory taxonomy is disseminated from the Integrated Operating Repository to these systems. Transaction processing systems would need to align their data with this standardized language through coding or configuration. On the other hand, systems like issue tracking or operational loss systems, which rely more on manual processes, would benefit from the Process Inventory's classification system. It allows triage teams to categorize each record based on the process that generated the incident.

The data derived from these systems, combined with the insights generated by machine learning, would enhance the work of risk management teams during risk assessments. It strengthens their risk inventory and aids in designing effective controls. Moreover, this data serves as input for mathematical models that quantify risk, enhancing the precision of their output.

Risk Assessment Examples

According to a Deloitte article, "Organizations can struggle with how they consolidate multiple risk assessments and reduce the duplication of efforts across assurance functions, which can lead to gaps in risk coverage and inconsistent approaches to managing risks" [28]. This underscores some of the previously mentioned challenges in the risk operating model between the first and second lines of defense.

In this section, I will demonstrate how risk assessment across different risk types in the risk taxonomy can be coordinated through the lens of process and how this will lead to much better coordination and clarity in roles and responsibilities.

Risk Taxonomy

A robust ERM program relies on a well-developed risk taxonomy as its foundation. A risk taxonomy establishes a standardized language for identifying, assessing, and managing the diverse range of risks faced by an organization across its business units and functions. It takes the form of a hierarchical structure, with higher levels encompassing broader risk categories and lower levels offering more precise definitions. By utilizing a risk taxonomy, organizations can benchmark risks, detect trends, ensure consistent aggregation and reporting, define risk appetite, and effectively allocate resources. The risk taxonomy has implications for the risk operating model as it provides the structure for how an organization manages risks, which often defines the framework of the second line of defense.

While several risk standards organizations provide a basic framework for classifying risks, an effective risk taxonomy must be comprehensive and tailored to an organization's unique risk landscape. Industry-specific reference risk taxonomies can serve as valuable starting points as they address common risks arising from shared markets, regulatory requirements, and operational complexities. However, organizations must customize and refine the risk taxonomy to align with their specific circumstances, accurately reflecting the risks they encounter.

By employing a well-designed and comprehensive risk taxonomy, organizations can enhance their risk management practices, promote consistent understanding and communication of risks, and make informed decisions to mitigate and address potential threats.

Integrated Risk Assessment

To demonstrate the benefits of Process Inventory, let's focus on an integrated risk assessment process. This approach involves assessing all risk types that impact a business unit or function in a single assessment, providing a comprehensive view of risks and enabling better prioritization and resource allocation. This stands in contrast to organizations that assess different risk types in isolation, aligned to specific second-line functions. Given that a single process can have multiple risk types, Process Inventory serves as a coordination point across the second-line functions. Additionally, it facilitates accountability for the design and performance of mitigating controls through the identification of process owners.

To illustrate this concept, let's focus on the integrated risk assessment approach, which is used to coordinate the assessment of business continuity, compliance, and operational risks. This approach involves conducting research before engaging the first line to define the risk landscapes and requirements associated with business continuity and compliance. By doing so, a comprehensive understanding of the risks impacting processes can be achieved.

Recertification of Process Inventory

Since the Process Inventory serves as the foundation for risk assessment across various risk types, it is imperative that the inventory accurately and comprehensively represents the processes within the business unit or function. The first-line PMO resource should collaborate with the Process COE team to conduct a review of the inventory with process owners, incorporating any necessary changes and collecting Process Owner attestation. This proactive approach will help ensure that risk assessments are not hindered by quality issues.

Business Continuity Risk

US PROPERTY AND CASUALTY INSURANCE PROVIDER

In February 2021, after a series of severe winter storms, more than 4.5 million homes and businesses in Texas were without power for several days. These storms brought the coldest temperatures to North Texas in over 72 years. Homes in Texas, lacking proper insulation for such frigid conditions, relied on inefficient electric heaters, leading to a significant surge in electricity demand. Unfortunately, the Texas power grid, which was not adequately winterized, experienced a failure. Federal regulators had previously warned about the potential failure of power plants under extremely cold conditions, but the necessary actions were not taken [29].

Due to the power grid failure, there was a substantial increase in insurance claims for property and other damages, with over 456,000 claims reported and an expected payout of $8.2 billion [30].

Later that summer, in my role as a consultant, I became involved in a project for this organization. This event exposed that their claims systems were exclusively hosted in Texas data centers. This situation required agents to capture claim details offline in spreadsheets and enter the information into the system once it was back online. This introduced a significant risk of missing claims or inaccurately entering claim data.

To address these issues and prevent similar disruptions in the future, the client initiated the project to create a comprehensive inventory of their processes. The goal was to identify similar critical processes and discover additional points of failure and implement measures to mitigate risks in the event of similar disruptive incidents.

Business continuity is the ability of an organization to maintain critical business processes during a disruptive event such as natural disasters, technological failures, cyberattacks, supply chain disruptions, pandemics, or other unforeseen circumstances. The goal of Business Continuity Risk Management is to identify potential disruptive events, defining the minimal level of operations, implementing risk mitigation measures, and developing business continuity plans.

Figure 7-10. Business Continuity Risk Assessment Approach

Identify Potential Disruptive Events phase is an accountability of the second line of defense as these events may impact business units or functions across the enterprise. The second-line team should gather internal data, such as historical failures, and leverage external sources, such as industry or regulatory reports, to be as comprehensive as possible to the potential event scenarios and to estimate the likelihood of each occurrence. In this phase, a draft Business Impact Analysis document will be created, capturing details related to the impact on business operations, minimum level of operations, mission-critical operations, and disaster recovery procedures.

Analyze Likelihood and Impact to Business phase focuses on refining the assessment of the likelihood and impact of potential disruptive events on the business. The impacts should be mapped to specific processes in the Process Inventory, providing the assessment team with access to the resources those processes leverage in execution and the procedures that staff follows. The second-line team is accountable but collaborates with the first-line team, which helps identify the processes that may be affected.

Evaluate Current Exposure phase involves reviewing these potential events with existing controls in relation to the organization's risk tolerance to identify any weaknesses or gaps. The goal of this phase is to strengthen the resilience of processes, identify recovery mechanisms, and determine contingency plans. The findings are captured and maintained in the Business Impact Analysis document. The second line is accountable for this phase, but process owners play a key role in designing and implementing controls identified during this exercise.

Compliance Risk

A GLOBAL FINANCIAL INSTITUTION

This institution has faced several regulatory findings related to weaknesses in their operational and compliance control environment throughout their enterprise. In response, they have embarked on a multiyear program to address these concerns, with a focus on establishing a robust process framework.

Given this context, I was brought on to lead the Process Excellence team for the US Personal Bank. Since joining, I worked closely with the business unit leaders and their staff to create a comprehensive Process Inventory. Despite having a relatively small team, this was on track to complete the inventory by the end of a year, which is an impressive achievement.

During the process, we mapped data from their GRC repository to the Process Inventory in key business units. This exercise has helped identify opportunities to address risk data quality issues and improve overall data management practices. Furthermore, the introduction of Process Ownership has fostered a stronger culture of accountability within the first line of defense units.

Overall, this effort was aimed at enhancing operational and compliance controls, and the progress made thus far demonstrates that this framework can be effective in these complex risk challenges.

Compliance risk is the potential for organizations to violate laws, regulations, industry standards, or internal policies and procedures. Failure to effectively manage compliance risk can result in penalties, fines, legal actions, damaged reputation, and loss of customer trust.

Figure 7-11. Compliance Risk Assessment Approach

Identify Applicable Laws and Regulations is the accountability of the Compliance team within the second line, usually in partnership with the legal organization. There are a finite number of rules that govern the organization. The objective is to have a complete inventory to report to leadership and regulators, highlighting any potential gaps. This process must be led by the second line as these rules cut across organizational boundaries, especially in heavily regulated industries.

Assess Compliance Requirements and Risks begins with interpreting the regulatory rules and translating them into specific requirements or duties that business units or functions must fulfill. The second-line teams will identify and document the risks associated with noncompliance of these obligations through the risk matrix. This step is the accountability of the second-line team with support from the first-line teams.

Map Regulatory Obligations to Process involves taking the identified regulatory obligations and mapping them to specific processes within the Process Inventory. This alignment ensures Process Owners are accountable for the design and implementation of controls. This work is a collaborative effort between the first- and second-line teams.

Evaluate Existing Controls and Prioritize Mitigations focuses on reviewing the existing controls, relative to the identified regulatory obligations, for those specific processes to determine their adequacy in meeting those obligations. If any gaps or weaknesses are identified, they are prioritized for mitigation.

Operational Risk

Operational risk is the risk of doing business; it's the risk of loss resulting from inadequate or failed internal processes, people, systems, or external events. It is the potential for negative consequences arising from the day-to-day operations and activities of an organization. Operational risk includes a wide range of risks such as human error, system failures, fraud, supply chain disruptions, and other operational issues that can impact the organization's reputation, financial stability, and ability to achieve its objectives.

Figure 7-12. Operational Risk Assessment Approach

Review relevant monitoring information is focused on reviewing monitoring data, process performance data, issues, complaints, etc., to gain deeper insights into the performance of controls and identify emerging risks. If machine learning has been deployed to identify patterns, this would be a great opportunity to review its observations. The first-line team and the process owner must take the lead on this since they have the greatest expertise in the processes. The second-line teams should collaborate as effective challenge partners to mitigate biases that may arise from the owners being too close to the details.

Identify and Assess Potential Risks is typically conducted through collaborative workshops and focuses on a business process or group of processes identified in the Process Inventory to identify and qualify risks. The workshop participants usually include the process owners, second-line representatives for all subtypes of operational risk, technology representatives, product owners, and anyone else with expertise in these processes or who can act as an outside challenger. Risks are scored in the risk matrix, and any other pertinent information such as potential losses is captured. The first line is accountable for running this process and documenting the output.

Evaluate Existing Controls and Prioritize Mitigations is the responsibility of the first line with second-line review. In this phase, the risks identified in the previous workshops are reviewed against the existing controls in the GRC risk data repository to identify gaps or weaknesses in the current controls. Updates to existing controls or the implementation of new controls are prioritized.

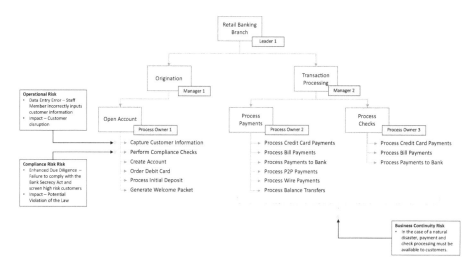

Figure 7-13. Process Inventory Risk Alignment Example

Outcome of the Integrated Risk Assessment Approach

The common theme across the risk assessment approaches for these risk types is the focus on business processes and clear accountability of the first line, the process owner, and the second line. As shown in Figure 8-5, each risk is aligned with the processes or process groups identified in the Process Inventory. At the end of these assessments, the process owner should formally attest, with the second line concurring, that these risks are valid and that they accept accountability for the implementation and performance of the controls. Once attestation has been captured, these records are entered into the GRC risk data repository.

This structured approach ensures that each process is evaluated through these assessments which means nothing will fall through the cracks. It also enables risk ratings to be aggregated to report on the risk of processes and process areas, which will focus business leaders on processes that fall outside of risk appetite to prioritize investments more effectively for mitigating actions.

This addresses the previously mentioned challenges of risk data quality issues and role clarity in the risk operating model.

Key Takeaways

- **The importance of risk management** is driven by various factors, including increasing complexity, regulatory requirements, and the evolving role of risk oversight on boards.

- **Enterprise Risk Management** is a standard methodology designed to identify potential events that may affect the entity and manage risk to be within its risk appetite to provide reasonable assurance regarding the achievement of entity objectives.

- **Opportunities to enhance risk management** include the adoption of quantitative measurements, minimizing human bias in risk assessments, improving cross-organizational coordination through end-to-end process awareness, enhancing risk data quality, and clarifying the risk accountability model.

- **Process Inventory can enable strong risk management** by aligning all risk-related activities with organizational processes. This approach has the potential to enhance the quality of risk data, strengthen the risk operating model, and leverage emerging technologies to improve risk intelligence.

In Part 3 of this book, we'll explore how to implement the Process Inventory framework. This exploration begins with the next chapter, which focuses on roles and accountabilities within the Process Inventory Operation Model.

Implementing the Process Inventory Framework

The Process Inventory Accountability Model

In this chapter, we will start by emphasizing the importance of establishing clear roles and accountability throughout the organization when implementing the Process Inventory framework. This will provide you with a comprehensive understanding of the pivotal roles played across the organization in developing comprehensive and accurate models, which will ultimately result in significant organizational benefits.

We will also explore the significance of creating a centralized Process Center of Excellence (COE) team, offering valuable insights into the specific processes they undertake to develop and maintain the models and data necessary for this strategic approach.

© Michael Schank 2023
M. Schank, *Digital Transformation Success*,
https://doi.org/10.1007/978-1-4842-9816-9_8

Furthermore, we will delve into key collaboration points across organizational units, including business, technology, customer experience, and risk management. This exploration will help you grasp the integral roles these domains play in driving the success of this strategy.

Driving Employee Engagement at Spotify: Balancing Autonomy and Accountability

Spotify, with a revenue of €11.7 billion and a workforce of 9,473, is a prime example of a company that strategically leverages its organizational structure to enhance employee engagement and drive business performance [1]. Spotify's business model and strategies require rapid growth to optimize operational effectiveness and maximize competitive advantages. This growth involves innovation, such as new product development for enhancing customers' mobile listening experiences [2].

Their growth is in part powered by how they balance autonomy and accountability within their organizational culture, creating an environment where innovation thrives and employees are motivated to contribute their best efforts. This approach has led the company to secure the top spot in Newsweek's "America's Most Loved Workplaces" in 2021 [3].

The heart of Spotify's culture lies in its "controlled chaos" philosophy, embodied by its band manifesto [4]. Like a band, they're dependent on each other to create the best audio experience, they need to be in sync, and like any successful band, they have a set of rules, a band manifesto, that keeps them focused on where they want to go and guides how they get there.

This analogy emphasizes the interdependence and synchronization among employees, fostering a sense of shared purpose. The core values of innovation, collaboration, sincerity, passion, and playfulness further define Spotify's culture, setting the stage for an environment where employees are encouraged to explore and innovate.

Spotify's model underscores the need for alignment to effectively enable autonomy while balancing controls [5]. The company had to make explicit choices in its operating model, ways of working, and culture that address the three core tensions between individual autonomy and organizational goals.

Leadership's role is in reinforcing alignment. Prior to launching projects, leadership emphasizes establishing alignment on objectives and goals. This shared understanding provides the anchor for autonomous decision-making, exemplifying how strong alignment among teams can drive collaboration.

Central to Spotify's approach is the organization of employees into autonomous, self-organizing units known as "squads." These squads, comprising cross-functional teams, are accountable for a discrete aspect of the product and own it from cradle to grave. These squads, which are no more than eight people, possess the authority to decide what to build, how to build it, and with whom to work with to make the product interoperable. They are organized into a light matrix called a tribe. Tribes comprise several squads linked together through a chapter, which is a horizontal grouping that helps support specific competencies such as quality assistance, agile coaching, and web development. The chapter's primary role is to facilitate learning and competency development throughout the squads.

This autonomy empowers employees to take ownership of their work, experiment with innovative ideas, and foster a heightened sense of accountability as they directly impact project outcomes. The company values the speed of iteration over the pursuit of perfection, fostering a culture where experimentation is encouraged, and failure is embraced as a learning opportunity. To enable this, they supported this strategy with measurable objectives, consistent measurement of progress toward those goals, feedback systems to monitor activities along the way, and appropriate consequences for reaching or failing to reach the goals. Results are visible both through internal reviews and customer feedback, and squads are expected to fully understand successes and failures. Squads go through postmortem analyses of failures to ensure learning. Every few weeks, squads conduct retrospectives to evaluate what is going well and what needs to improve.

The Spotify model, which integrates autonomy with accountability, serves as a blueprint for driving employee engagement through a culture of innovation. By encouraging ownership, enabling learning, and fostering alignment, Spotify creates an environment where employees are motivated to contribute creatively and collaboratively. This dynamic model serves as an inspiration to organizations seeking to maximize engagement while maintaining focus on strategic goals.

Establishing a Culture of Accountability

The culture of an organization largely determines business performance. As with the Spotify example, this includes many factors but especially alignment to organizational goals, accountability, and culture of innovation. According to a recent Gallup poll [6], accountability is an area that needs some improvement as they report that only 14% of employees feel their performance is managed in a way that motives them, only 21% feel their performance metrics are within their control, and that 70% of employees feel their managers aren't objective in how they evaluate their performance.

Defining a clear accountability framework is particularly crucial for the success of implementing the Process Inventory framework to drive digital transformation or other high-priority business goals. This chapter focuses on the human side of implementing this framework. As you'll see, implementation will require coordination across a wide set of stakeholders and organizational units.

When defining the Process Inventory strategy, in addition to detailing the short- and long-term ambitions of the framework and its use cases, it's critical to include an **operating model design** that outlines the necessary processes, roles, accountabilities, governance, and culture required to facilitate its implementation.

This operating model needs to explicitly **define goals and metrics** that cascade throughout the organization, ensuring that individual and team objectives align with the organization's goals and are harmonized with the aspirations of implementing this framework.

A substantial aspect of achieving a clear accountability framework is being meticulous in **setting expectations**. Employees need to have a clear understanding of what's expected of them and how their performance will be measured. Managers will need to gain commitment from team members regarding these expectations, providing them with the opportunity to ask clarifying questions and ultimately take ownership of these accountabilities.

Leadership plays a pivotal role, as any cultural changes must be reinforced from the top. They must articulate in their communications the compelling change story that motivates the organization. They also need to demonstrate in their actions that this is a strategic endeavor and that they, along with the rest of the management team, are committed to the transition and will support employees along the way.

A critical aspect of this blueprint is a **comprehensive assessment** of the prevailing organizational culture and human resources. This evaluation enables strategic decisions related to hiring, outsourcing, training, and other initiatives to be identified and effectively planned.

Process Inventory Framework Operating Model

As mentioned earlier, a key to success in this initiative is to detail the operating model, define processes and roles, and set clear expectations for this framework to reach its potential. To highlight what that looks like in practice, the remainder of this chapter will be dedicated to going through the roles in Figure 8-1 for delivering and maintaining the models and data in this framework.

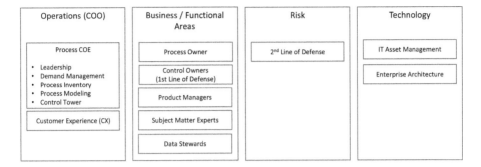

Figure 8-1. Process Inventory Partial Operating Model

It's important to note a couple of points relative to this model:

- **Illustrative Model**: Each organization has a unique organizational structure, which the following model may not be aligned with. It's important to leverage these illustrative insights and define the model in the context of your organization.

- **Delivering and Maintaining Models and Data Only**: The use cases covered in Chapters 4–7 and the Transformation Management Office covered in Chapter 3 are excluded from this discussion as many of the roles and accountabilities were covered in those chapters. This chapter will be focused on the core roles in creating and maintaining quality models and data.

- **Not Exhaustive**: This model can extend significantly to other parts of the organization, especially as it relates to the management and integration of metadata from other sources. The purpose here is to give a representative sample to extend from.

This model has been deployed in numerous large organizations, through which this approach has been continually refined to increase effectiveness. The processes, roles, and accountabilities have been proven to scale and sustain the Process Inventory framework, positioning it to deliver value to the organization.

Process Center of Excellence (COE)

At the core of an effective Process Inventory strategy is the Process COE. This organization is responsible for defining the strategy, facilitating model creation through engagement with stakeholders, managing the platform and data infrastructure, sustaining the models through governance to remain reflective of the organization, and more. In this section, we'll delve into the details of the role this group performs.

Organizational Structure

Figure 8-2 is an illustrative organizational structure that is meant to showcase the roles and reporting structures, rather than the headcount, as that will depend on factors such as the ambition of the strategy and the size of the organization.

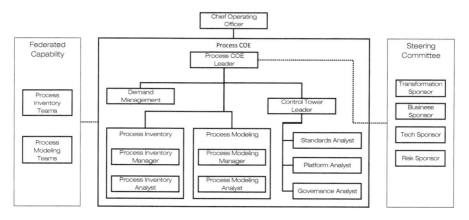

Figure 8-2. Process COE Organizational Chart

A couple of items to highlight here include

- **Placement Within the Organization**: In this illustration, the group reports to the chief operational officer, which makes logical sense as the goal of this effort is to streamline operations by adopting digital technologies. I have also seen this group roll up at other organizations to technology, risk, and transformation offices. I believe any of these options will work if this team isn't hindered in their purview or focus and is able to accomplish their vision.

- **Steering Committee**: Building and maintaining a diverse set of senior stakeholders is a best practice as they can provide you with their insights on the organization's highest priorities, ensuring that the team is focused on what's most important.

- **Federation**: In some large organizations, business units may want to create their own Process Inventory and process models. This is perfectly acceptable as long as they comply with all modeling standards and quality review practices, ensuring that the models across the organization remain consistent. A close and collaborative relationship across these federated teams and the Process COE should be maintained.

Process COE Process Inventory

Figure 8-3 represents the Process Inventory for the organization. I'll leverage this to cover the details of the accountabilities, processes, and skills for each part of the organization.

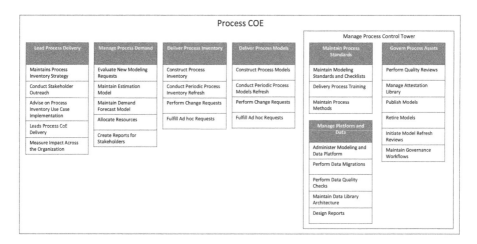

Figure 8-3. Process COE Process Inventory

Lead Process Delivery

Accountabilities

The leader of this group is accountable for the success of the effort. They must build and maintain relationships with senior stakeholders to define the Process Inventory strategy and ensure alignment with the organization's goals. This leader must also consult with other stakeholders on leveraging the team's assets to drive value through the implemented use cases. Additionally, the person is responsible for guiding the team to deliver quantifiable benefits, through a commitment to this framework, for the organization. They are accountable for execuing the processes in Table 8-1.

Processes

Table 8-1. Lead Process Delivery Processes

Process Name	Process Description
Maintains Process Inventory Strategy	Works with a broad set of stakeholders to document the organization's goals and then define the Process Inventory strategy, which includes scope, processes, tools, and model types. The strategy should be continually revisited as the organization's strategy and priorities change.
Conduct Stakeholder Outreach	Maintains an ongoing relationship with key stakeholders to identify their needs and critical priorities. Works with them on solutions for how this framework can address their challenges.
Advise on Process Inventory Use Case Implementation	Advises stakeholders to define use case methodologies for leveraging process modeling assets to achieve their goals. This leader actively champions the use of this framework to ensure maximum value is derived from it.
Leads Process COE Delivery	Sets direction for the team, guides them to deliver high quality, hires/trains their team, reviews critical deliverables, and addresses critical issues.
Measure Impact Across the Organization	Defines metrics to measure impact and maintains a scorecard to share with key stakeholders to demonstrate the business value this framework is having.

Required Competencies

The ideal candidate for this role should exhibit a genuine passion for the subject matter, driven by a desire to create a meaningful impact throughout the organization. They should possess extensive experience in successfully implementing process management frameworks, methodologies, and tools. With strong leadership skills, they should have the ability to guide and motivate their team while also exerting influence across various levels of the organization.

Their strategic mindset should enable them to connect the dots and proactively identify opportunities to deliver value. Furthermore, a solid understanding of the business landscape coupled with broad experience across diverse functional areas will contribute to their effectiveness in this crucial role.

Manage Process Demand

Accountabilities

This team is accountable for managing a consistent level of demand for the modeling teams. This includes evaluating, prioritizing, and sizing incoming modeling requests to ensure alignment with organizational goals and resource availability. They work closely with managers within the Process COE to confirm resource availability and schedule the work appropriately to maintain a steady flow of effort. They continuously monitor and adjust demand to optimize resource allocation. Ultimately, their role contributes to keeping key stakeholders satisfied that their priorities are being effectively addressed. They are accountable for execuing the processes in Table 8-2.

Processes

Table 8-2. Manage Process Demand Processes

Process Name	Process Description
Evaluate New Modeling Requests	Establish a standard process and intake form for assessing new work requests. This team must deep dive into the proposed scope, align it with the framework to quantify resource needs, and perform prioritization.
Maintain Estimation Model	Construct and maintain an estimation model that assists in accurately determining the necessary duration and resource effort, anchored in estimation criteria such as the organization's scale and the quantity of process areas. After work efforts are completed, document the actual effort expended, and continuously analyze and refine the model to further enhance accuracy.
Maintain Demand Forecast Model	Implement a model that accurately forecasts demand and supply for every week in the future. This approach will greatly improve visibility into capacity constraints and resource availability.
Allocate Resources	Collaborate with managers within the Process COE to confirm resource assignments for upcoming projects. Allocate resources to these efforts and schedule kickoff calls with key stakeholders.
Create Reports for Stakeholders	Maintain an aggregated status of all modeling efforts, including overall color status, progress toward committed milestone dates, percent completion for deliverables, and identification of critical issues. Distribute these reports to key stakeholders.

Required Competencies

The demand management team plays a critical role and requires strong project management skills for assessing and prioritizing initiatives, as well as efficiently allocating resources to meet stated goals. Proficiency in data analysis and reporting is crucial to maintain an accurate effort estimation model and demand forecast. Effective communication and collaboration abilities are essential as they act as a bridge between initiative stakeholders and the modeling teams. Additionally, strong stakeholder management skills are vital for crafting status reports that effectively address the needs and expectations of various stakeholders.

Deliver Process Inventory and Deliver Process Models

These teams are focused on building and maintaining their respective models. I'm combining them into a single section as their work is similar while focused on different model types.

Accountabilities

These teams are accountable for the delivery of accurate and comprehensive Process Inventory documentation and process models, respectively, for the scope that they are assigned. Adhering to established quality practices and complying with modeling standards are imperative aspects of their role. Their accountability extends to collaborating with stakeholders across various organizational levels, ensuring that the final work products are satisfactory to all and that required attestations are collected. They are accountable for facilitating effective sessions to make efficient use of stakeholders' time. These teams are accountable for execuing the processes in Table 8-3.

Processes

Table 8-3. Deliver Process Inventory and Deliver Process Models Processes

Process Name	Process Description
Construct Process Inventory	This involves collaborating with an organizational unit for the first time to inventory their processes, identify process owners, align metadata, and collect attestations.
Construct Process Models	This is focused on working with process owners to model how the process is executed, with all required metadata aligned. These models must comply with quality standards and receive attestations.
Conduct Periodic Process Inventory Refresh	This involves engaging with the organizational unit periodically, as the timing defined by policy, to review the Process Inventory and adjust based on any process or process owner changes.
Conduct Periodic Process Models Refresh	The focus is on engaging with process owners periodically, as the timing defined by policy, to review and update process models to reflect any changes in the environment.
Perform Change Requests	The business or other stakeholders may request changes to the Process Inventory or process models based on new initiatives, organizational changes, or other drivers. This team will engage with stakeholders to make the necessary adjustments and collect attestations.
Fulfill Ad Hoc Requests	As these assets become an anchor point for use cases throughout the organization, stakeholders may need clarification or data from the completed models. This is focused on supporting those requests.

Required Competencies

Modelers must possess a strong command of process modeling techniques and industry standards, demonstrating proficiency in utilizing process modeling tools. Effective communication skills are essential, enabling them to lead sessions with stakeholders, pose clarifying questions, and ensure the accuracy of models while optimizing the use of time. A comprehensive grasp of cross-functional domains, encompassing business, technology, risk, and other areas, empowers them to fully comprehend and critically question the subject being modeled. Their attention to detail and commitment to delivering high-quality work products are crucial for maintaining the integrity of the models. Their appreciation for governance principles and adherence to standard methodologies further enhance their ability to contribute effectively to the modeling process.

Control Tower

Accountabilities

The control tower team is accountable for defining and maintaining documented standards and ensuring that the assets published in the Integrated Operational Repository adhere to strict quality standards. They achieve this by conducting training for modeling teams, maintaining and distributing quality checklists, and serving as the last line of defense for quality by conducting reviews on models and data assets. This team is also responsible for architecting, administering, and configuring features in the Business Process Analysis platform, as well as managing the migration and quality of data in the platform. Additionally, they facilitate governance processes to ensure that accuracy and quality are sustained over time. They are accountable for execuing the processes in Table 8-4.

Processes

Table 8-4. Control Tower Processes

Process Name	Process Description
Maintain Process Standards	
Maintain Modeling Standards and Checklists	The focus is on building and maintaining the standards for Process Inventory, process models, and the associated metadata, which are based on industry norms and the needs of the organization. These standards are translated into quality checklists so that modeling resources can conduct quality reviews on their own and others' models.
Delivery Process Training	Training is essential for new modelers in the Process COE and federated modeling teams. This process is dedicated to delivering comprehensive training to ensure that these resources possess a deep understanding of how to effectively create models.
Maintain Process Methods	Methods outline how modeling should be conducted, encompassing activities, templates, quality checkpoints, and more. This team continuously learns from completed endeavors to enhance the methods, making them more effective over time.
Manage Platform and Data	
Administer Modeling and Data Platform	This group is responsible for all administrative tasks, such as user entitlements, configurations, performance monitoring, license management, and more. This is a higher-level process that further breaks down into many subprocesses.
Perform Data Migrations	Data from authoritative data sources needs to be migrated and periodically refreshed on the platform. This process handles the refreshes and addresses any data conflicts that arise.

(continued)

Table 8-4. (*continued*)

Process Name	Process Description
Perform Data Quality Checks	Periodically, reports must be executed to highlight any data inconsistencies or conflicts in the models and data libraries. These processes not only identify issues but also work to resolve them.
Maintain Data Library Architecture	Migrated data from authoritative sources needs to be stored in libraries for modelers to perform associations within their models. This process designs these libraries and updates them as required.
Design Reports	This team collaborates with stakeholders to capture their reporting requirements and then configures custom-built reports in the Business Process Analysis platforms.
Govern Process Assets	
Perform Quality Reviews	As part of the processes to construct Process Inventory and process models, this quality team will conduct a final quality review of the models.
Manage Attestation Library	A library for storing attestations needs to be maintained so that each artifact can be traced back to the owner who approved it. This process is focused on managing this library for completeness and accessibility.
Publish Models	Once models have completed the necessary quality checks and obtained all required attestations, they can be published to the production environment within the Business Process Analysis platform.
Retire Models	There are several reasons models may need to be retired, such as changes to the process, elimination, business reorganization, or outdated content. This process is focused on removing these models from the production environment and archiving them.
Initiate Model Refresh Reviews	To maintain the accuracy of models, they need to be periodically re-attested. This group is responsible for maintaining accurate date information on models that require re-evaluation. They will collaborate with the modeling teams to conduct stakeholder reviews, update model content, and obtain necessary approvals.
Maintain Governance Workflows	Many of the governance processes require facilitation through workflows, either within the Business Process Analysis platform or using external tools. These workflows play a critical role in coordinating and monitoring governance activities. The primary focus of this process is to establish and maintain these workflows, implementing ongoing enhancement as governance processes are refined.

Required Competencies

This team must possess meticulous attention to detail and a commitment to quality. They need the courage to reject poor quality, even if it means challenging individuals with higher seniority. They must be experts in modeling standards and possess critical thinking skills to define standards that are tailored to the organization. Additionally, they should be capable of designing and executing rigorous governance processes to ensure nothing is overlooked.

The team must also have the technical acumen to architect and configure the structure of models and data within the Business Process Analysis platform. They require data management competencies for performing data migrations and executing data quality processes. Moreover, they need to be dedicated to customer service, innovation, and continuous learning from past efforts to enhance methods and standards going forward.

Furthermore, this team requires strong communication and stakeholder management skills to effectively design and deploy training as well as other communications about the platform.

Business/Functional Areas

Business units, which are profit-generating segments of the organization, and functional areas that support the business both play a critical role in the success of these frameworks as they are ultimately accountable for the content of the models. To be successful, these accountabilities need to be detailed clearly and broadly communicated, especially in large organizations where many individuals will perform these duties. The most important roles are the following.

Process Owner

Process owners hold the accountability of providing precise process information to modeling teams, ensuring an accurate representation of the inventory of processes and their execution details. Their responsibility extends to formally attesting to the accuracy of completed models.

As the Process Inventory is derived from the organizational structure, a distinct hierarchy of ownership can be traced to senior leadership. Process owners and their teams, actively involved in the day-to-day execution of these processes, inherently possess deep knowledge, eliminating the need for extensive training to be effective. Their responsibility lies in upholding the clarity and precision of the models and promptly notifying the Process COE of significant changes, ensuring timely updates to the models.

Risk Owner

Assuming that risk management is a prioritized use case within the organization, as defined in the Process Inventory strategy, the role of the risk owner becomes significant in identifying risks in processes and defining appropriate controls. A risk owner may be the same individual as the process owner, or in some organizational units, a central risk management team may fulfill this role. Regardless, risk owners need to identify risks and ensure that they are appropriately aligned in the Process Inventory taxonomy and accurately represented in process models.

Product Manager

Product managers hold the responsibility for steering the strategy and success of a product throughout its life cycle. Through market research and understanding of customer expectations, they establish business goals and are accountable for delivering results for each product they own. They manage a product roadmap, which details new features and functionalities to drive the product's objectives.

Since products are supported with numerous processes across the organization, the features and functionalities directly correlate with how processes are designed. Product managers and their teams frequently play a key role in defining the behavior of future state processes that are being implemented through change initiatives. It's important that they understand the landscape of processes which support their products so they can provide direction for improvement or optimization.

Subject Matter Experts

Subject matter experts play a critical role within the Process Inventory framework, bringing deep knowledge and insights that contribute to accurate process models. Beyond that, they can provide valuable coaching to modeling teams navigating organizational units, offering effective challenges to what process owners are describing. They typically possess a perspective on how to enhance the process environment and can identify opportunities for improvement or optimization.

Data Stewards

In certain organizations, the role of data stewards is employed within specific business or functional units. This role holds the responsibility of identifying and documenting crucial data elements, including definitions, rules, governance processes, linkage to data models, ownership, custodianship, and more, utilized by those organizational units [7]. Serving as a bridge between the organization's data users and technical teams, data stewards facilitate the alignment of business needs with technical requirements.

If your organization features this role and data management is a prioritized use case for leveraging the Process Inventory framework, data stewards assume a pivotal role in modeling the process environment. When processes are modeled, they contribute to identifying data attributes leveraged during process execution. These attributes are captured in the data objects of the process models, and within the Business Process Analysis platform, they can be mapped to the enterprise glossary or data model. This practice delivers a clearer depiction of how data is utilized across processes, fostering enhancements in data governance, data controls, data quality, data architecture, ownership, accountability, and more.

Technology

The intersection between processes and technology, combined with the adoption of a digital agenda, necessitates a strong partnership between the Process COE and various segments of the technology organization, where alignment on goals is key. IT Asset Management and Enterprise Architecture represent a subset of those partnerships.

IT Asset Management

The IT Asset Management team is accountable for tracking, monitoring, and optimizing the entire life cycle of IT assets within the organization, encompassing hardware, software, licenses, and other technology-related resources. The Process Inventory initiative relies heavily on the accuracy of this data as it must be migrated to the Business Process Analysis platform to facilitate mapping between IT assets and activities within processes. While this holds true for any metadata integrated into process libraries, given the paramount role of this relationship in digital transformation, the quality of this information becomes critically significant. This necessity underscores the need for a close collaboration across groups.

Enterprise Architecture

Enterprise Architecture is the discipline by which organizations standardize and organize their IT environment to align with business goals. Chapter 6 covered several ways in which the Process Inventory framework can enable Enterprise Architecture designs. When designing the accountability model for the Process Inventory framework, leaders from the Process COE and the

Enterprise Architecture organization should closely work together to define areas of close collaboration which will be dictated by their respective strategies.

Many Enterprise Architecture organizations are responsible for modeling the technology environment. An Enterprise Architecture platform, which has similar capabilities as the Business Process Analysis platform, can be used to document the architecture framework, define IT blueprints, document solution architectures, and more. The models across both environments need to harmonize so that stakeholders can clearly understand how the technology architecture supports business processes. Processes within each organization must include collaboration points to ensure integrity.

In addition, if Enterprise Architecture adopts system sequence diagrams at scale with a goal of sustaining these assets, then an operating model very similar to the Process COE outlined earlier in this chapter would be needed to build and maintain the connection between process activity and interactions across downstream systems. Maintaining integrity across both environments can deliver powerful benefits for streamlining and making the IT environment cost-efficient.

Customer Experience (CX)

In the realm of digital adoption, enhancing customer experience and engagement emerges as a significant driver. This concept gains validation from a survey that shows 70% of senior executives consider CX a top priority [8]. Consequently, numerous organizations are creating dedicated customer experience teams to advance the customer agenda. These teams focus on customer research, identifying opportunities, and crafting solutions to elevate the overall customer experience.

As described in Chapter 2, these teams will create models, specifically customer personas and customer journeys, to replicate and study the current and desired experience of customers. To enhance root cause analysis for opportunities, it's crucial to link interaction points in a customer journey to specific processes within the Process Inventory that are executed during those interactions.

Close collaboration between the CX and the Process COE is needed to identify those linkages. The CX team should consider building and maintaining their models in the Business Process Analysis platform to gain many of the benefits the platform brings such as dynamic impact analysis, reporting, and transparency to processes directly supporting customers. If so, then collaboration with the Process COE control team is needed to harmonize how model governance is implemented.

Risk

Second Line of Defense

I extensively covered the significant opportunities for Process Inventory to contribute to a robust risk management environment in Chapter 7. If prioritized within the organization's strategy, this goal necessitates the definition of multiple collaboration points across the organization.

In this section, I would like to highlight a couple of areas within the second line of defense, which holds the responsibility for overseeing and monitoring risks. The second line encompasses various suborganizations, typically aligned with the risk taxonomy such as operational risk, compliance risk, cybersecurity risk, etc.

If the Process Inventory taxonomy is integrated into the governance, risk, and compliance (GRC) tool—a platform for risk data and process management—a tight collaboration between the governance teams within process and the second-line function that manages the platform becomes paramount. This collaboration ensures the integrity and quality of data sets are upheld. Additionally, the second-line risk functions should conduct reviews of risks and controls aligned with processes to validate their accuracy and alignment with policy.

Key Takeaways

- **Establishing clear accountabilities** is critical to drive business value leveraging this framework, which will require collaboration across many diverse organizational units. Designing explicit processes, roles, accountabilities, governance, and a unified culture across organizational boundaries is essential for success.

- **Process COE** is a central body that articulates strategy, defines standards, builds process models, and governs assets. Establishing this COE with clear roles and processes is crucial for delivering comprehensive and accurate models that contribute to business value over time.

- **Defining partnerships and collaborations** across diverse domains, such as technology, customer experience, and risk, and aligning on objectives are crucial for crafting a comprehensive end-to-end model for success.

In the next chapter, we will delve into the methods and modeling rules required to create high-quality models that deliver business value.

Process Methods and Modeling Rules

In this chapter, you will gain a deep understanding of why modeling the processes of an organization through Process Inventory and process models is of paramount importance. We will delve into the guiding principles that maximize the value an organization can derive from these models.

We will introduce you to an industrialized approach for creating models, one that not only produces high-quality output but also optimizes the use of valuable resources, such as process owners and other stakeholders. This will include best practices for conducting modeling workshops, whether for current state or future state processes.

You will learn best practices and industry standards for creating clear and consistent models, which include the significance of maintaining the integrity of the relationship between Process Inventory and process models.

Finally, we will cover the role of peer reviews and final quality checks in the delivering model that are accurate and comply with modeling standards.

© Michael Schank 2023
M. Schank, *Digital Transformation Success*,
https://doi.org/10.1007/978-1-4842-9816-9_9

Unilever's Digital Transformation of Supply Chain Through Modeling Processes

Unilever plc, a British multinational consumer packaged goods company founded in 1929, has established itself as a global leader with a portfolio of renowned brands including Axe, Ben & Jerry's, Dove, Knorr, and more. Operating in over 190 countries, Unilever delivers high-quality products to more than 2.5 billion consumers daily, underscoring the significance of an integrated and connected supply chain in managing an impressive array of 77,000 stock keeping units (SKUs) across the globe [1].

As challenges within the consumer goods sector mount—ranging from inflation-driven pricing surges to material and labor shortages—Unilever embarked on a digital transformation journey to maintain a competitive edge [2]. With a market value of $55 billion, the company recognized the power of data insights in predicting the future and responding to evolving consumer demands [3].

One of Unilever's key objectives was to harness the capabilities of digital technology to revolutionize its supply chain. This task is further complicated by the fact that they oversee more than 220 owned factories, manage over 3,300 discrete product lines, and maintain more than 900 partnerships [1].

Customers now expect customization, on-demand products, and brands with a clear purpose. This vision compelled Unilever to commit to digital transformation, underscoring the significance of becoming data-driven to meet evolving customer expectations.

At the heart of Unilever's transformation lies the concept of the "digital twin." A digital twin is a next-generation digital model of a physical environment. In Unilever's case, it's a digital replica of their factories. This digital twin, powered by the Internet of Things (IoT) and intelligent edge services within the Azure IoT platform, captures data from sensor-equipped machines and processes. The digital twin models the physical plant, providing real-time insights into operations [3].

By creating this digital twin, Unilever gains unprecedented visibility into its supply chain. The digital model simulates all aspects of the plant, from individual machines to entire processes. Advanced analytics and machine learning algorithms are applied to the collected data to predict outcomes based on historical patterns. This empowers Unilever to readily anticipate and respond to various challenges, ensuring optimal efficiency, resiliency, and flexibility. The strategy aligns with the growing trend of utilizing data streams from the Internet of Things to drive operational enhancements across various industries [4].

Through the modeling of processes and the harnessing of advanced technologies, Unilever has not only optimized its supply chain operations but also gained the ability to predict and respond to market dynamics. This approach has facilitated cost reduction, improved efficiency, and enhanced decision-making, positioning Unilever as an industry trailblazer at the forefront of digital innovation.

The impact of this digital transformation has already become tangible. Unilever's digital twin empowered operators to exercise meticulous control over soap-making machine moisture levels, resulting in enhanced consistency. Furthermore, by analyzing data on production times for liquid batches, such as shampoo and detergent, the digital twin optimizes the order of processes to maximize production capacity [3].

The Importance of Models

Organizations are complex systems; in fact, they are systems made up of complex systems. A complex system is defined as being made of many interacting components that exhibit emergent behavior, meaning that the behavior of the system cannot be explained solely by the behavior of its individual components. As organizations grow, they don't just get bigger, but they get more complex from specialized resources and tight integration internally and with external parties. Each component is and should be working toward the corporate strategy, but in many cases, they adopt a goal of sustaining itself.

The study of complex systems is prominent in many different fields such as biology, ecology, economics, sociology, and computer science. These fields create models to predict behavior, apply control, and optimize systems. The overarching goal is to make these systems understandable to humans, and increasingly machines, so that pressing problems can be triaged and informed business decisions can be made.

As demonstrated in the Unilever case study, modeling the environment through processes is necessary to maximize the utilization of digital technologies to achieve operational excellence and competitive business value.

This chapter is focused on creating models, through the Process Inventory framework, within organizations to achieve a deeper level of transparency. As I highlighted in Chapter 2, there are multiple models that come together to fully describe an organization. Detailed in the following include the approach for creating the models, standards to adhere to a high level of quality, best practices, and guiding principles.

Guiding Principles for Success

Prior to delving into the specifics of individual creation processes, it's essential to establish a bedrock of crucial guiding principles. These principles are pivotal in enhancing the likelihood of achieving success:

- **Alignment with Strategic Goals**: The models generated by this process should seamlessly integrate with the organization's requirements, as highlighted in the digital strategy covered in Chapter 3. The documentation and aligned metadata need to support the digital aspirations, use cases, and overarching vision of the organization.

- **Prioritizing Quality**: Quality takes center stage—these models come together to form a repository of information, offering a comprehensive view of the organization. As stakeholders begin to utilize this repository within their roles, encountering significant quality discrepancies could undermine their confidence in the initiative. Overcoming negative perceptions of inadequate quality presents a considerable challenge. For each model, I will outline a construction approach. Within these methodologies, I will demonstrate multiple stages for quality reviews and stakeholder attestation. Adhering to these quality checkpoints is of utmost importance to prevent potentially costly or detrimental errors. A best practice involves conducting internal quality reviews before seeking stakeholders' validation. This approach avoids the need for repeated validations if quality issues emerge.

- **Clarity and Consistency**: Models must be documented with a level of clarity that even individuals unfamiliar with the process or its domain can grasp the depicted actions. Furthermore, these models should adhere to consistent standards, ensuring uniformity across diverse organizational units. Accomplishing this entails the establishment and upkeep of comprehensive standards and checklists that seamlessly integrate into the quality assurance processes.

- **Ownership and Formal Attestations**: Every model requires a designated owner who can vouch for the accuracy and comprehensiveness of the models. As individuals transition between roles or depart, it is crucial to establish clear ownership within the organizational hierarchy, ensuring that a replacement owner can be designated, if necessary. The process of attestation should be conducted formally and documented for audit purposes. Capturing attestations can range from straightforward email confirmations stored on a shared drive to utilizing a workflow tool. In case concerns about quality arise, maintaining a traceable record of the attestation provider's identity becomes indispensable.

- **Balancing Excellence and Practicality**: This sentiment underscores the necessity for efficiency. The stakeholders with whom the Process COE team engages have full-time day jobs. Hence, optimizing their time is paramount. I've witnessed endeavors of this nature stagnate in prolonged analysis without any substantial progress. Therefore, it's essential to strike a balance between aiming for perfection and achieving practical results.

- **Progressive Strengthening Through Adoption**: Although the models may not achieve perfection upon their initial creation, their refinement will evolve with time as broader stakeholders embrace and integrate them into their operations.

- **Sustaining Model Relevance**: Organizations are dynamic entities, undergoing frequent changes. An inevitable question raised when presenting this concept to new stakeholders revolves around the models' ability to maintain accuracy over time. The concise response entails implementing a periodic attestation process, which at a minimum should be done annually. This process entails presenting the model to its owner(s), who identify alterations and subsequently revalidate its accuracy. However, I regard this as the baseline approach. Ideally, if these models are leveraged across a broad set of use cases, the organization's vested interest in accuracy simplifies the integration of updates.

- **Fostering Continuous Enhancement**: Maintain a culture of continuous enhancements by reviewing lessons learned to refine and elevate the methodology for constructing models. Actively solicit feedback from users and stakeholders, channeling their insights to iteratively elevate the efficiency and efficacy in documenting the process environment.

Process Inventory

The main objective of creating the Process Inventory is to identify all the processes within the specified scope of the organization. This forms the fundamental basis for the alignment of resources and operating information. In this section, I will delve deeper into the approach of engaging with the business to create this model while also emphasizing the importance of standards and best practices for success.

For well-established business domains, this task is typically carried out based on the current state. This approach is highly efficient as it involves interviewing stakeholders about the processes they currently execute. This shouldn't require additional research as stakeholders are expected to have expertise in their respective processes. However, in situations where the business area is new or undergoing a redesign, the focus can shift toward the future state. This might take more time, especially if the leaders haven't fully conceptualized their future processes. When interacting with leaders, you'll need to ensure clarity on the focus, which will help you create accurate timelines and resource estimates as needed.

Construct Process Inventory

When creating the Process Inventory, the following approach as depicted in Figure 9-1, which has been demonstrated in multiple organizations, has been proven to be efficient and to produce high-quality output due to the rigor of multiple quality checkpoints.

Figure 9-1. Construct Process Inventory

Engage Business Leaders to Plan Effort

This step assumes that you have already secured broad leadership buy-in, from the chief transformation officer and other equivalent senior leaders, for this initiative. The purpose of this phase is to connect with organizational unit leaders, who might not possess a comprehensive understanding of this work. The aim is to educate them about the effort and formulate a plan outlining the timeline and the precise resource requirements from their respective departments. The objective is to gain their authorization to involve their teams in this initiative. The activities in this phase are outlined in Table 9-1.

Table 9-1. Engage Business Leaders to Plan Effort Activities

Activities	Outcome(s)
• **Prepare the Benefits Case**: If this leader is not entirely familiar with this effort, it's crucial to educate them on the rationale and benefits behind this exercise. Whenever possible, align the case with their priorities.	• Permission to Engage with Resources • Agreed Upon Timeline
• **Develop an Estimated Timeline and Resource Hours**: Excess capacity is in short supply for business stakeholders. Creating and maintaining an estimation model is important, enabling you to calculate the effort needed and be efficient in the use of your time.	
• **Validate Engaged Resources**: While the organizational chart can largely provide this, confirming the appropriate resources for engagement is important. Identify any resource scheduling limitations that need to be navigated.	
• **Identify Assets for Prework**: In many instances, process details can be gleaned from existing documentation. To conserve valuable stakeholder time, request a list of resources that can provide a robust initial draft. This may include organizational charts, roles and responsibility documents, procedure manuals, and more.	

Best Practices

- **Strive for Precision in Estimating Timelines and Resource Commitments**: Given the scale of large enterprises, Process Inventory collection may involve numerous organizational units. Construct and maintain an estimation model that assists in precisely determining the necessary duration and resource effort, anchored in estimation criteria like the organization's scale and the quantity of process areas. After completing each area, document the actual effort expended, and continuously analyze and refine your model to further enhance accuracy.

- **Tailor the Benefits Case to Organizational Priorities**: Depending on the group's specific dynamics, customize the benefits case to align with their priorities. It might be beneficial to seek guidance from a coach who possesses insights into the group. Emphasize the significance of this endeavor in terms that resonate with them, and illustrate how the resulting output can be harnessed to deliver value for their business. Aligning with their priorities enhances the likelihood of a more receptive response to this effort.

Perform Prep Work

When you request information that is readily available, there's a potential risk of giving the impression of squandering their time, leading to stakeholder frustration, and jeopardizing the entire initiative. Certain assets can detail many of the organization's activities. Investing the necessary time in this prep work is essential to prevent entering sessions with a blank sheet of paper. It's possible that a portion of this prep material might be outdated, which is fine as it will focus the interview sessions on making necessary updates. Demonstrating this level of preparation will be greatly appreciated by your stakeholders, showcasing your commitment to both their efficiency and time savings. The activities in this phase are outlined in Table 9-2.

Table 9-2. Perform Prep Work Activities

Activities	Outcome(s)
• **Review Gathered Material**: Carefully review all the gathered material, paying particular attention to verbs that indicate actions. If there's a substantial amount of material, there's a chance of identifying gaps or even conflicts among them. In such cases, prepare a list of clarifying questions for engagement with process owners.	• Draft Process Inventory
• **Draft the Process Inventory**: Utilize the collected material to draft the Process Inventory. Take note of areas where gaps exist, requiring further clarity from stakeholders.	

Best Practices

- **Engage a Coach**: The Process COE team leading this effort may not possess expertise in every organizational unit, potentially making it difficult to interpret the prep materials. Identify a coach within the organizational unit who can assist in navigating these documents and addressing any clarifying questions. Collaborating with a coach will yield substantial value from this step.

Standards

This is the initial step in creating the Process Inventory model for an organizational unit. It's crucial to ensure compliance with modeling standards before presenting the draft to organizational unit stakeholders.

- **Organizational Structure Alignment**: The key to being comprehensively exhaustive in the Process Inventory is to construct it following the organizational structure. This should be the case in your initial draft as this will facilitate productive discussions when you are interviewing stakeholders.

- **Identify Process Owners**: Each identified process must have an owner. When crafting this draft, make an effort to pinpoint owners, with adherence to the organizational structure being crucial. Stakeholders in the subsequent phase can then validate or refine your draft.

- **Mutually Exclusive**: Each identified process should be uniquely defined and distinctly differentiated from others.

- **Identify All Unique Processes**: It's not uncommon for various areas within an organizational unit to carry out similar processes, such as project management and issue management. While the instinct might be to group them together under a common category in the Process Inventory, it's important to resist this inclination. Each of these seemingly similar processes may be executed and managed differently. Giving into this urge to group them could limit the potential of various use cases, including uncovering organizational inefficiencies, identifying overlaps, and effectively managing risks.

- **Determining the Process Level**: Establishing the appropriate level of process decomposition is more of an art than a precise science. Deciding when the Process Inventory has been adequately broken down and it's time to proceed with process modeling is a nuanced task. Process can be modeled at multiple levels if their activities follow a logical and continuous sequence. The Process COE team overseeing this effort must possess the expertise to discern the suitable level for initiating process modeling.

- **In Taxonomies, a Child Can Only Have One Parent**: This further underscores the point of uniqueness of processes. A single process cannot be mapped to multiple points in the Process Inventory taxonomy.

- **Use Verb + Noun Naming Convention**: Having consistent and clear naming is critical for any stakeholder to leverage this asset. This naming convention provides that as the verb specifies the action and the noun represents the entity on which the action is performed on.

- **Avoid Vague Verbs**: The focus should be on avoiding verbs that are vague in process names, which don't clarify the action such as manage or support. For the upper levels of the taxonomy, these work fine, but for a process, it's hard to understand what is exactly happening.

- **Spell Out Uncommon Acronyms**: To achieve clarity for individuals unfamiliar with the process or its domain, spell out uncommon acronyms that are only familiar to those with expertise in the domain.

- **Capture Process Descriptions**: Ensure the process descriptions are concise, spanning approximately two to four sentences, to offer enhanced clarity regarding the process actions.

- **Decompose to No More Than 15**: When a parent in the taxonomy has more than 15 children, the decomposition becomes increasingly unreadable. In such cases, consider defining additional categories and appropriately grouping the processes or process levels within them.

- **Minimum Decomposition**: To decompose a top-level node of the Process Inventory taxonomy to the next level, it's best practice to have a minimum of three at that next level. Decomposing 1:1 just means that you are renaming the top level.

- **External Vendors**: When processes are outsourced to an external vendor, it's still important to collect an inventory of *what* that vendor is performing as your organization is still accountable for those processes. Depending on the contract, you may not have the ability to perform detailed process modeling, but having an inventory of processes will enable proper oversight of the vendors' performance and compliance with your policies.

Conduct Interview Sessions

In this step of the process, interview sessions are conducted with owners within the organizational unit. These sessions initiate at the top of the organizational hierarchy, often starting with the organizational unit's leader, to establish the structure of the Process Inventory taxonomy for the organizational unit. Sequentially, iterative sessions are carried out at progressively lower levels, culminating in a comprehensive inventory of processes. This iterative approach serves to validate the process structure while also confirming the accurate identification of process owners.

During these sessions, drafts created in the previous step serve as the starting point. Process and process area owners actively participate, leveraging their expertise to refine the draft to become accurate and comprehensive.

Table 9-3. Conduct Interview Sessions Activities

Activities	Outcome(s)
• **Set Up Working Sessions**: Collaborate with leadership and a designated champion within the organizational unit to determine the most suitable meeting times. Typically lasting around one to two hours although the duration may vary based on the group's size and complexity.	• Process Inventory • Process Owner Names • Improvement Opportunities
• **Conduct Interviews**: Focus on comprehensively inventorying the processes undertaken by the organization. If the need arises to delve deeper within the organization, confirm the involvement of relevant attendees for subsequent follow-up sessions.	
• **Identify Opportunities for Improvement**: Although not the primary focus of these sessions, it's possible that the team may recognize opportunities for enhancement. Formally capture these observations and present them to leadership during the final review as potential avenues for improvement.	
• **Take Detailed Meeting Minutes**: Capture comprehensive meeting minutes, record the session, and share them with the attendees after the discussion, expressing appreciation for their active participation.	

Best Practices

- **Prioritize the Process Owner**: While inviting additional functional experts like technology and risk specialists to the sessions might be beneficial, it's crucial to emphasize the central role of the process owner. In cases of disagreement, the authority of the process owner should be recognized as final. This approach not only reinforces the significance of the process owner role but also prevents extended debates that could extend the effort's duration.

- **Generate Work Product in the Sessions**: The most efficient approach to compiling the inventory is to craft the work product during the session itself. This method allows attendees to rectify errors on the spot and avoids the need for subsequent offline exchanges, which inevitably leads to misinterpretations, to make corrections.

- **Cultivate Curiosity**: When engaging with stakeholders, they might not remember every aspect of their work. Use open-ended questions with sincere curiosity to prompt them. This approach is effective for uncovering valuable details necessary for a comprehensive representation.

- **Effective Challenge Resource(s)**: Especially in situations where the organization deals with complex tasks, it's worth considering the participation of a subject matter expert(s). This expert(s) can attend the sessions to ask clarifying questions and fulfill the role of an effective challenger(s), leveraging their domain knowledge to prompt discussions and ensure accuracy.

Align Metadata and Perform Reviews

To obtain the final Process Owner attestation of the Process Inventory for an organizational unit, the final package needs to be refined with all required metadata and undergo a rigorous review to ensure compliance with documented standards. This step is crucial to ensuring that the package accurately represents the real-world environment and can be leveraged in various use cases for business value.

Table 9-4. Align Metadata and Perform Reviews Activities

Activities	Outcome(s)
• **Confirm Process Descriptions**: Ask process owners to review and confirm the written descriptions of each process. • **Align Metadata**: Identify and align the required metadata according to the documented process standards. This may involve discussions with additional functional stakeholders such as risk, technology, and others, as well as validation from process owners to ensure alignment. • **Conduct Quality Reviews**: This involves ensuring that the Process Inventory is clear and complies with documented standards. • **Review with Process Owners**: Conduct a review with process owners to validate the accuracy of the complete product. • **Obtain Process Owner Attestation**: Request process owners to provide formal attestation to validate the accuracy and completeness of the work product.	• Metadata Alignment • Quality Review Acceptance • Process Owner Attestation

Best Practices

- **Standards Checklist**: Standards for Process Inventory and process models should be documented and distributed broadly in the form of a checklist. This ensures that process team members have a clear understanding of what constitutes a quality work product and enables them to self-assess their work.

- **Levels of Reviews**: Typically, there are multiple levels of review. Initially, the individual creating the models should review their own work against the standards checklist. Subsequently, a peer review is conducted by a team member not involved in this specific effort. Finally, an independent review is carried out by a member of the Process COE control tower team. This multilevel review approach ensures high quality and reinforces the importance of quality throughout the team.

- **Review Workflow**: Utilizing a workflow, preferably available within the Business Process Analysis tool, is the preferred method for effectively organizing, tracking, and documenting both quality reviews and Process Owner attestations.

- **Leverage Metadata Libraries**: It's essential to use metadata from these libraries, where applicable, to maintain traceability to authoritative sources and enable impact analysis and reporting. Chapter 10 will explain how to set up metadata libraries in Business Process Analysis tools.

- **Types of Metadata**: At this stage, any applicable metadata can be aligned. Typically, metadata that doesn't require detailed process modeling is aligned. The following list, while not exhaustive, provides examples of metadata mapping that may be required.

Table 9-5. Sample Metadata to Align

Meta Data	Description
Process Description	A concise description consisting of two to four sentences, aimed at being comprehensible to individuals outside of this specific business area.
Process Owner	This is the designated individual who holds ownership of this process within the organizational unit. As the Process Inventory follows a hierarchical structure, the complete lineage of owners is traced throughout the taxonomy.
Product(s)	These are the product(s) that this process supports. In shared service organizations, it's not uncommon for a process to support multiple products. Additionally, certain support processes might not directly relate to any specific products.
Channel(s)	For customer-facing processes, especially those supported across various channels, this approach offers a valuable means of comprehending this relationship. This understanding enables the creation of a consistent omnichannel experience for customers.
Business Capability Model and Standard Process Model Alignment	This involves matching each process identified through the Process Inventory exercise to the corresponding capability or process identified in the enterprise's adopted model.
Risk and Controls	This typically requires the support of the first line of defense risk managers. Extracting risk and controls from the GRC or risk repository will position the team to conduct more robust risk assessments and design more effective controls.

- **Attestation Template**: Before engaging with a business area, make sure to clarify the expectations that you'll be asking them to confirm the accuracy and completeness of the information. Create a standardized template that will be used with all process owners and stored for future reference.

Conduct Readout with Leadership

This step is crucial within the approach, offering leadership the chance to review the final product for their organizational unit and provide any feedback before concluding this effort. It also serves as an excellent occasion to discuss how the Process Inventory can contribute to their future goals.

Table 9-6. Conduct Readout with Leadership Activities

Activities	Outcome(s)
• **Prepare the Final Readout Packet**: This should include the completed Process Inventory, the list of attestations collected, identified opportunities, and suggested next steps.	• Final Read Out Packet
	• Organizational Unit Leader Attestation
• **Conduct the Readout Session**: Review the information packet and adjust based on their feedback.	• Prioritize List of Opportunities and Next Steps
• **Discuss Opportunities and Next Steps**: Particularly highlight any high-priority areas the team should address in a subsequent effort.	

Best Practices

- **Gain Alignment Prior to the Meeting**: These readouts go smoothly when all stakeholders within the organizational unit are aligned with the content of the final readout packet prior to the discussion with leadership. Take the time to review the packet with key stakeholders before the final discussion.

Process Models

Process models are a natural extension of Process Inventory as they depict the "how" behind the execution of inventoried processes. The key to understanding their relationship lies in recognizing that process models must adhere to the bounded context established in the Process Inventory. This means that each process model should exclusively represent a single process within the Process Inventory.

The creation of process models may occur immediately after developing the Process Inventory, or there might be a time gap between these steps. Regardless of the timing, it's crucial to grasp that the Process Inventory might evolve during the process modeling phase. Teams delving deeper into process understanding might identify the need for updates to the inventory of processes.

In some expansive organizations, the Process Inventory may encompass tens of thousands of processes. It's not feasible to expect every process will be documented with a process model. Prioritization of which processes to document is typically guided by the digital strategy, key use cases, and business demands. Regardless of how priorities are determined, maintaining the integrity between Process Inventory and process models remains paramount.

Construct Process Models

The goal is to achieve consistent documentation and maximize the efficiency of process owner engagement. Therefore, adopting an industrialized approach becomes crucial. This approach encompasses detailed standards, well-defined accountabilities, and multiple review checkpoints to ensure the creation of high-quality process models.

Figure 9-2. The Process Modeling Process

Identify Scope via Process Inventory

As mentioned earlier, this step upholds the integrity of the entire Process Inventory framework. This is crucial for maintaining end-to-end process modeling as there may be handoffs across processes, making the preservation of relationships and connections between events imperative.

However, its significance goes beyond that as it distinctly defines the scope of any process modeling effort. This enables engagement with relevant process owners and provides precision in estimating resource efforts and timeline durations.

Table 9-7. Identify Scope via Process Inventory Activities

Activities	Outcome(s)
• **Match Request to Process Inventory**: Engage with the requestor of the modeling effort to comprehend the processes they intend to have modeled. Correlate the requested processes with those identified in the Process Inventory.	• Identified Process Inventory Processes • Resource and Timeline Estimates • Agreed Upon Plan
• **Estimate Process Modeling Effort**: The process modeling team should maintain an estimation tool. The scope of processes serves as input criteria that determine the total hours required from each involved resource, along with the estimated timeline. An in-depth plan should be the outcome of this step.	
• **Identify Process Owners' Availability**: Assess resource schedules and pinpoint the suitable timeframe for process modeling workshops.	
• **Gain Acceptance on the Plan**: Convene with the requestor and other key stakeholders to review the plan and gain buy-in for the effort.	

Best Practices

- **Maintain Process Modeling Estimation Model**: The key to an industrialized process modeling capability is maintaining an estimation model which takes the details set of steps in the process and determines which resources are required and how many hours are needed for each. When applying the total process count in any scope, this will produce a total amount of hours. This model should be continuously analyzed and improved as the team learns from previous efforts.

Conduct Process Modeling Workshops

Process modeling workshops can be conducted to document either the current process or design a future state process as part of an initiative. Each scenario is distinct: current state workshops center on the identified process owner detailing the existing process, while future state process models may involve a broader set of stakeholders envisioning the path ahead. Irrespective of the context, the outcome of these sessions is to document the process, capturing the sequence of activities and the resources leveraged in execution.

Table 9-8. Conduct Process Modeling Workshops Activities

Activities	Outcome(s)
• **Review Process Inventory**: Validate with the process owner and additional stakeholders that the Process Inventory and the definitions of the processes in scope are accurate and up-to-date.	• Validated Process Inventory • Drafted Process Model • Identified and Mapped Metadata
• **Walk Through the Process**: Ask the process owner to explain the sequence of activities, starting from the initial event(s) and progressing to the ending event(s).	
• **Document the Process**: While the process owner is explaining the process, the process modeler should simultaneously model it during the session.	
• **Identify and Map Metadata**: This step involves documenting the specific technical systems that facilitate activities, data utilization, organizational and third-party actors, customer touchpoints, risks, controls, and more. Collaboration with additional functional stakeholders may be required to ensure alignment.	

Best Practices

- **Start with Process Boundaries**: Initiate the process by confirming the starting and ending events. This approach establishes the process's scope and directs the discussion toward the activities within that defined boundary.

- **Create Process Models in the Workshop**: Develop the process models directly during the workshop using the process modeling tool. This method is highly efficient, allowing the process owner to provide real-time feedback and eliminating the need to input the model into the tool at a later stage.

- **Invite Subject Matter Experts**: Extend invitations to experts in functional areas like technology, data, and risk. Their specialized insights can provide a deeper understanding of certain aspects that the process owner might not be familiar with.

- **Current State and Future State**: Recognize that both current state and future state processes may coexist for a particular process, especially in initiatives where a future deployment will alter the current process. If the current state process has already been documented, it serves as a valuable starting point for future state discussions.

Standards

Adhering to process modeling standards is crucial for documenting clear and consistent processes across the enterprise. Organizations need to document and maintain standards that are appropriate for their context. These standards should be distributed to all process modelers in the form of a checklist to ensure transparency and guide them in creating models that align with these rules. The standards listed in the following are not exhaustive but represent the types of rules to enforce:

- **Adherence to BPMN 2.0 Modeling Standards**: The BPMN 2.0 process modeling standard, created by the Object Management Group, maintains specifications. Many standards for creating good process models should be derived from this specification.

- **Is the Process Clear?** Process models shouldn't read like inside jokes. The test is, can someone unfamiliar with the domain read and understand the activities in the process model? If not, further edits are required to clarify it.

- **Alignment to Process Inventory**: The process model needs to maintain the integrity of the relationship with the Process Inventory. This means that it should fit within a single process and align with the definition given. Process Inventory may need updates, but that integrity must be maintained.

- **Event Naming**: I've seen many process models that start with an event named "start" and end with an event named "end," which is of negligible value. Event names need to be descriptive of the event with a noun plus a past tense verb as the naming standard.

- **Activities Documented with Verb + Noun Convention**: As each activity in a process can be detailed with a subprocess, then every activity needs to maintain the verb + noun naming standard. This also provides clarity to anyone reading the model.

- **No More Than 15 Activities**: To maintain readability, process models should not exceed 15 activities and should be printable on a standard sheet of paper. If more details are necessary than can be accommodated by this standard, subprocesses should be developed to offer additional levels of detail.

Validate and Publish

Process models, especially for critical processes, need to maintain a high level of quality to maximize the benefits for the organization. This phase is an important step to validate that a high level of quality is achieved.

Table 9-9. Validate and Publish Activities

Activities	Outcome(s)
• **Conduct Peer Review**: This is performed by a member of the process modeling team who wasn't part of this specific effort. The quality checklist is leveraged to ensure the model complies with all standards.	• Process model(s) which complies with standards • Process Owner attestation
• **Conduct Final Quality Review**: A member of the Process COE control tower team will perform a second-level review to catch issues not found in the peer review.	
• **Review with Process Owners**: Conduct a review with process owners to validate the accuracy of the complete product.	
• **Obtain Process Owner Attestation**: Request process owners to provide formal attestation to validate the accuracy and completeness of the work product.	

Best Practice

- **Perform Internal Review Prior to Process Owner Attestation**: The process model presented to the process owner should comply with all standards. This will avoid having to ask the process owner to attest additional times if quality issues are found. This will save time and frustration for the process owner.

Key Takeaways

- **Modeling the environment** through Process Inventory and process models is the key to maximizing digital technologies, achieving operational excellence, and delivering competitive business value.

- **Guiding principles** are essential to ensure that your models offer optimal value to the organization by adhering to standards of quality, clarity, and consistency.

- **An industrialized approach** is required to create high-quality modeling, which adheres to consistent standards and makes efficient use of stakeholders' time.

- **Maintaining the relationship** between Process Inventory and process models is critical for delivering on the potential of this framework.

- **Delivering quality models** requires detailed standards and a rigorous review approach.

In the next chapter, we will explore commercially available Business Process Analysis tools and their essential features required to support the modeling of the process environment, as well as the management of metadata.

Modeling Platform and Data Infrastructure

In this chapter, we will explore the importance of Business Process Analysis platforms in managing the Process Inventory framework, associated models, and supporting metadata. You will gain an appreciation for its role in providing alignment across the organization to deliver digital transformation and operational excellence goals.

We will cover a select set of platforms available in the marketplace. We will delve into key features and considerations for implementing and gaining value from Business Process Analysis platforms.

Lastly, we will cover a methodical approach for selecting the right tool for an organization and performing the initial setup.

© Michael Schank 2023
M. Schank, *Digital Transformation Success*,
https://doi.org/10.1007/978-1-4842-9816-9_10

FedEx Dataworks: Leveraging Operational Data for Business Performance

In the fast-paced world of business, operational data has emerged as a potent catalyst for driving enhanced performance. FedEx demonstrates the profound impact of leveraging operational data to fuel business success. By harnessing the power of analytics, artificial intelligence (AI), and machine learning, FedEx has elevated its processes, redefined operational excellence, helped its customers absorb shocks to markets and the supply chain, and gained a significant competitive advantage.

A pivotal philosophy ingrained in FedEx's DNA is the vision that the company's founder, Fred Smith, recognized: the idea that information about a package is just as vital as the package itself [1]. This belief laid the foundation for FedEx's strategic approach to data-driven decision-making. At the heart of this is the ability to transform a staggering 18 million daily shipments across 220 countries into actionable insights.

To further this philosophy, the company built the Dataworks platform, which seamlessly integrates the company's physical and digital networks. This platform is a centralized hub that provides connective tissue to integrate all available data sources within FedEx's global network. They leverage this to track every aspect of a package's movements, including real-time data such as delivery route, environmental conditions, weather, customer delivery locations, and delivery date. This enhances supply chain visibility, enables the identification of deviations from planned paths, improves predictability, and facilitates data-driven decision-making, benefiting high-value and time-sensitive shipments.

This insight has led them to offer FedEx Surround to their customers. Surround is designed for businesses to digitize their supply chains by leveraging data to drive breakthrough real-time inventory tracking and logistics management, which is a digital representation of the physical world [3]. This solution integrates IoT data through SenseAware ID [4], a small Bluetooth tracking sensor that can be placed on a package. This enables FedEx to intervene if a package is at risk of not arriving on time. For example, a team can scoop up the package at a sorting center and place it in a van to leave immediately. From origin to destination, there are multiple intervention points.

To be successful, they designed this platform to be free of operational silos, where data, models, and digital capabilities could be reused across multiple use cases. This reinforces core capabilities, drives innovation in processes and features, accelerates time to market, and ensures accurate decision-making. This centralized hub fosters cross-functional collaborations and the seamless exchange of data.

As organizations navigate the intricacies of modern business, the FedEx Dataworks journey serves as an illustration, highlighting the power of managing and exploiting operational data in shaping a new era of innovation and driving differentiated business performance.

Business Process Analysis Platform Market

It cannot be overstated that to realize the potential of the Process Inventory framework to drive digital transformation and achieve operational excellence, a platform is crucial for modeling the process environment and effectively managing all associated operational metadata in a scalable and sustainable manner. To effectively support the digital strategy, this platform must encompass extensive modeling capabilities, facilitate data integration across numerous authoritative sources of truth, offer capabilities to analyze data to optimize processes or address critical issues, and support accountability through an ownership model, among other essential features.

Fortunately, a mature vendor market of platforms, known as Business Process Analysis (BPA), that provides the necessary capabilities exists. These platforms can successfully implement the Process Inventory framework and harness the benefits of alignment.

In the following, I will present a select set of companies and products within this market, accompanied by a brief description of how each vendor defines their platform. While this list is not exhaustive, it represents vendors and products with which I have some familiarity. I encourage each organization to conduct its own due diligence based on its specific needs and context.

Having worked with several of these platforms in large programs, I can attest that many of their capabilities are impressive, continue to evolve rapidly, and align well with the requirements of implementing the Process Inventory framework.

Table 10-1. Select Vendors and Vendor Platforms in the Business Process Analysis Market

Vendor/Platform	Vendor's Description
Avolution—Abacus [5]	Connect your IT, business processes, and business strategy. Cloud-based data, dashboards, and diagrams support teamwork across locations and departments.
Bizzdesign Horizzon [6]	The business and change platform to design an agile Enterprise Architecture
iGrafx Process360 [7]	The products and capabilities of Process360 Live combine next-generation operational intelligence, automation, and process design to transform your business.
MEGA HOPEX [8]	Build a digital representation of your enterprise by connecting business, IT, data, and risk perspectives in a single platform to share a single source of truth. Derive actionable insights and collaborate with stakeholders to align your company's business objectives and demonstrate the immediate business value of your projects. Seamlessly integrate the HOPEX Platform into your digital ecosystem for faster time to value.
Orbus OrbusInfinity [9]	Our business-centric platform creates a holistic view of your applications, systems, and data, so you can accelerate decision-making, reduce spend, mitigate risks, and stay resilient in the face of disruption.
SAP Signavio Process Transformation Suite [10]	With our SAP Signavio Process Transformation Suite, organizations can understand, proactively manage, and optimize their business processes to achieve the agility needed for successful change.
Software AG ARIS [11]	ARIS improves efficiency, saves time and money, and makes processes more sustainable. It offers true business process transformation via tightly managed and controlled change. With ARIS, you can create, manage, and analyze your end-to-end business processes—the key to operational excellence that gives stakeholders the tools and insights they need to make better decisions every day.

Key Business Process Analysis Features

When evaluating and implementing a Business Process Analysis platform, it's important to develop requirements that align with the context of your organization. This alignment should extend from both the digital strategy and the Process Inventory strategy, ensuring that the platform can robustly support these overarching visions. Implementing a platform requires a significant commitment of effort and resources, making it essential to weigh short-term goals as well as long-term needs.

In this section, I will delve into some of the key features of this platform and highlight their critical role in supporting the Process Inventory vision.

Modeling Capabilities

The most crucial features of these platforms are their ability to create and maintain models that comprehensively represent the organization from diverse perspectives, integrating them to support analysis from multiple viewpoints. Additionally, these platforms must construct models in a manner that facilitates value extraction through analysis.

General Modeling Capabilities

- **Object Orientation**: Real-world concepts or entities, such as processes, systems, and events, are represented as objects. These objects are self-contained units that encapsulate attribute data and behaviors. These objects are reused across models, enabling analysis and reporting on the use of these concepts or entities.

- **Support Multiple Viewpoints**: These platforms need to serve the needs of a diverse set of stakeholders such as leadership, business, technology, data, and risk. By providing customizable views tailored to specific roles, such as strategy, process, technology, and data, the platform ensures that each stakeholder can focus on the information most relevant to their responsibilities. This capability enhances collaboration while anchoring these views to the common language of Process Inventory.

- **Integration Across Model Types**: Linkages across various types of models, anchored to Process Inventory, are important for viewing the business from multiple angles and identifying impacts at various levels of granularity. This ensures consistency and alignment and maintains a comprehensive view of the organization. Integrated models facilitate the identification of dependencies and potential impacts, supporting holistic process optimization.

- **Version Control**: This capability enables organizations to maintain a historical record of changes made to models, ensuring traceability and accountability. Stakeholders can create, compare, and revert to different versions of process models. This is also important for maintaining the current state as well as one or more future states when the organization is implementing change. This feature safeguards against unintended modifications, supports regulatory compliance, and enables teams to analyze the impact of changes before implementation.

- **Import Existing Models**: Organizations often have existing repositories of models created in various tools such as Microsoft Visio. This feature allows seamless migration and integration of these models into the chosen platform, avoiding the need to recreate them from scratch. By preserving existing investments, organizations can save significant time and effort in modeling the organization comprehensively.

- **Collaboration**: The platform should facilitate real-time collaboration among multiple stakeholders, allowing them to co-create, review, and edit process models simultaneously. Collaborative tools, such as commenting, annotation, and discussion threads, enable stakeholders to provide feedback and contribute insights directly within the models. This feature enhances cross-functional collaboration, reduces silos, and ensures that process analysis benefits from the collective knowledge and expertise of the entire team.

- **Customization**: These platforms typically support many modeling standards and will have numerous preloaded frameworks. They should also include the ability to customize the platform to an organization's specific needs. This includes the ability to create user-defined model types or elements which is crucial if an organization has unique characteristics.

Model Types Supported

- **Strategy Model**: These models capture the high-level strategic goals and objectives of the organization. They outline the long-term vision and the path to achieve it, serving as a guiding framework for decision-making. Strategy models can be mapped to processes and capabilities to aid in prioritization and ensure that initiatives are aligned with the organization's overarching strategy. The platform should enable the visualization, analysis, and communication of strategy models to facilitate informed decision-making and ensure alignment across the organization.

- **Customer Journeys**: Customer journeys play a pivotal role in understanding and enhancing the customer experience. The platform should enable teams to create customer personas and map out the journey and the various touchpoints and interactions that customers have with the business as they leverage a product or a service. These models illustrate the end-to-end customer experience, helping organizations identify pain points, opportunities for improvement, and areas to enhance customer satisfaction.

- **Value Streams**: Value streams demonstrate the set of end-to-end actions that take place to add value to the customer from the initial request through the realization of value by the customer. The platform should enable teams to define and map value streams, encompassing all the activities, processes, and interactions involved in these end-to-end processes.

- **Process Inventory**: The backbone of this framework is the Process Inventory taxonomy. The platform should offer the capability to create, manage, and maintain this taxonomy for the current state and for future state changes. This model serves as the storage structure for all process models within the organization, facilitating process documentation, analysis, and optimization. The platform should support the construction of this at multiple levels of granularity and capture the aligned process owners.

- **Capability Model**: Capability models represent high-level views of a business from the perspective of the capabilities they perform. These models are largely independent of organizational structure. When paired with the organizational structure-aligned Process Inventory, they provide business leaders with different viewpoints from which to analyze their business. When used for planning purposes, these models depict the critical capabilities that enable the organization to deliver value to its stakeholders and achieve its goals. This enables leaders to make informed choices about where to focus investments, streamline operations, and drive innovation across organizational boundaries.

- **Business Process Model**: Business process models offer a comprehensive depiction of "how" individual processes are performed, illustrating the sequence of activities, roles, and interactions involved. Business Process Analysis platforms should provide a range of tools to facilitate the creation, visualization, and analysis of business process models, typically adhering to standard modeling notations like BPMN 2.0. It's noteworthy that in certain scenarios, BPMN 2.0 diagrams can be seamlessly imported into workflow tools, which then play a crucial role in generating workflow code needed in the execution of long-running processes.

- **Business Rule Modeling**: Business rules play a pivotal role in maintaining consistency, compliance, and informed decision-making across an organization. A proficient Business Process Analysis platform should offer robust support for Business Rule Modeling, utilizing the widely adopted Decision Model and Notation (DMN) standard. DMN is a standardized approach for defining and modeling repeatable decisions, with the advantage of being easily comprehensible by both business and IT stakeholders. Typically integrated into BPMN processes, DMN enables the creation of decision logic, rule tables, and decision diagrams, effectively aligning business rules with the overall process flow and enhancing the transparency and efficiency of decision-making processes.

- **System Sequence Diagram**: As discussed in Chapter 6, system sequence diagrams illustrate the information flow and interactions among systems. When integrated with business process models, they provide a comprehensive view of the systems that support process activities. By linking system sequence diagrams to business process diagrams, organizations can pinpoint integration nodes, detect possible failure points, and uncover opportunities to enhance system performance. While this feature is present in select Business Process Analysis platforms, it may also necessitate integration with an Enterprise Architecture tool.

Process Mining

Many Business Process Analysis platforms have integrated process mining capabilities, which are instrumental in leveraging available system data to gain insights into the execution of processes and identifying opportunities for improvement. While there are stand-alone process mining platforms, the insights derived become more valuable when aligned with the organization's models. These capabilities encompass several key features:

- **Process Discovery**: By analyzing event data from system logs, this functionality creates process models that illustrate the sequence of activities, decisions, and interactions. It enables organizations to validate processes documented from stakeholder interviews with real-world data. This can help identify potential variations, inefficiencies, and bottlenecks, paving the way for targeted improvements and optimizations. As mentioned in Chapter 2, to maximize the effectiveness of this feature, the output should be harmonized with the Process Inventory, allowing for the alignment of metadata and benefits beyond process optimization.

- **Conformance Checking**: Conformance checking is a critical feature that focuses on comparing discovered or actual process instances with predefined or expected process models. By doing so, organizations can assess the level of alignment between designed processes and their real-world execution. This process highlights discrepancies, deviations, or noncompliance instances, which could indicate process inefficiencies or unacceptable risks.

- **Performance Analysis**: This functionality enables organizations to quantify the performance of processes by analyzing metrics such as process cycle time, throughput, bottlenecks, and resource utilization. By assessing these performance indicators, stakeholders gain insights into the efficiency and effectiveness of their processes, which points them to specific opportunities for process optimization. This data-driven approach enables organizations to make informed decisions about process enhancements, resource allocation, and change strategies.

Data Management Capabilities

The Business Process Analysis platform, especially when equipped with extensive process models and metadata, serves as a pivotal authoritative source of data that describes an organization's entire operational landscape. Given this significance, I referred to it as the Integrated Operational Repository. The implications of this status necessitate an organization's commitment to maintaining the quality and accuracy of this data with rigor to lock its potential benefits. As a result, the Business Process Analysis platform requires sophisticated functionality to effectively manage this data, ensuring alignment with organizational goals and driving insightful decision-making:

- **Import Metadata**: The platform will need to import data from key authoritative sources of information to integrate with the models built on the platform. The data to import should be aligned to the use cases and benefits that are defined in the Process Inventory strategy. The information imported should be limited to the data required for modeling, analysis, and reporting on this platform. This typically includes ID information along with a few more descriptive fields. Additional details can be retrieved from the source when needed. There will be an initial load of data and periodic refreshes as the original source undergoes changes. During subsequent imports, conflicts will inevitably occur, requiring workflow and manual work to address these conflicts. Figure 10-1 depicts the importing of data in a conceptual architecture diagram.

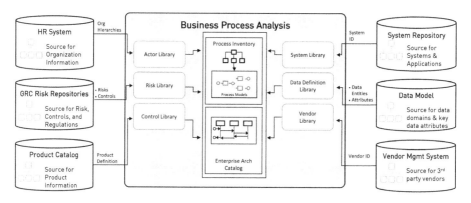

Figure 10-1. Conceptual BPA Architecture

- **Manage Data Libraries**: The platform will have to include the ability to establish libraries with this imported data and other modeled data, such as capability models. Teams creating models will need access to this metadata to integrate into their models. This establishes the relationship from the appropriate points in the digital models that represent the real world to data in disparate authoritative sources of data, which is so critical for alignment.

- **Export Data**: As this platform becomes the authoritative source for an organization's operating information and establishes a common language for alignment, other platforms across the organization will require this data. Figure 10-2 depicts this sharing of data. The most prominent requirement will be exporting Process Inventory data to platforms that generate data, such as transaction processing systems, and issue management, to ensure accurate categorization at the source. External business intelligence tools can also serve as another destination for performing additional reporting and analysis on this data.

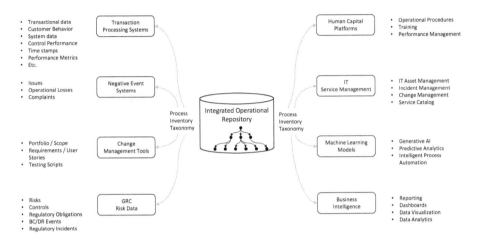

Figure 10-2. Publishing Process Inventory Taxonomy

- **Manage Data Quality**: Recognizing the pivotal role of data in driving accurate insights and informed decision-making, the platform should incorporate robust function-alities for effective data quality management. Central to this capability is the provision of visualizations, metrics, and reports that vividly portray the current state of data quality. These tools empower administrators to enforce data quality rules that align with organizational standards. This includes identifying and rectifying inconsistencies, anomalies, missing values, and potential quality issues present within the data. Moreover, the platform should empower administrators with tools to address inaccuracies, rectify duplicates, and resolve inconsistencies, thereby facilitating the sustained improvement of data accuracy and reliability.

Process Analysis

The comprehensiveness of the operational data this platform will store means that there are a tremendous number of insights to be mined which can be leveraged for continuous improvement, optimization of processes, and driving greater business performance. To capture this benefit, the Business Process Analysis platforms need to offer a suite of comprehensive process analysis features. In this section, we delve into the essential analytical functionalities that a robust BPA platform should provide:

- **Dashboards and Visualization**: Dashboard and visualization capabilities allow users to create interactive and customizable dashboards that display key process performance metrics and KPIs. These dashboards provide an overview of process health, trends, and patterns with ease. The tool should offer drill-down capabilities, enabling users to explore data at different levels of granularity and gain deeper insights into process performance.

- **Heatmaps**: This functionality enables users to visualize the status of various topics relative to the process environment using color-coded representations. Examples of heatmaps applied to process areas include strategic importance, performance, risk management, application redundancy, and more. These views focus leaders on important areas to focus on and outliers to address, facilitating data-driven decision-making and ensuring resources are allocated appropriately.

- **Impact Analysis**: This powerful feature enables users to explore the relationships between entities in the environment and assess the potential consequences of changes, issues, risks, regulations, and more. Users can model different scenarios and simulate changes to understand how they will affect other processes, systems, and stakeholders. Focusing on change management, this enables program managers to identify each resource impacted by a change initiative, resulting in comprehensive requirements, better engagement of resources, and more accurate estimates of cost and timeline. This helps organizations make decisions with comprehensive information and avoid unintended consequences.

- **Process Simulation**: Process simulation capabilities enable users to create and analyze various process scenarios with different variables, resources, and conditions to understand how they influence process performance. By running simulations, users can identify opportunities for improvement, optimize resource allocation, and predict the outcomes of process changes. The platform should offer user-friendly modeling interfaces and provide detailed simulation results to guide decision-making.

- **Process Intelligence**: Process intelligence enables users to conduct in-depth analysis of process data. This includes identifying patterns, trends, and hidden opportunities for optimization. This feature leverages advanced analytics capabilities, such as process mining, text mining, and machine learning, to extract valuable insights from process data.

- **Root Cause Analysis**: When an issue occurs in the production or test environment, coordinating analysis across a group of stakeholders to identify the root cause can be challenging. The information within the Business Process Analysis platform, combined with root cause analysis features, allows users to analyze event logs and identify underlying causes of defects and inefficiencies.

- **Process Optimization**: Process optimization features provide recommendations for improving process efficiency and effectiveness. By analyzing process data, the tool can suggest changes, such as reordering tasks, optimizing resource allocation, or eliminating redundant steps. Users can explore optimization scenarios and assess the potential impact of changes before implementation, ensuring that process improvements align with organizational goals and strategic objectives.

Reporting

Robust reporting capabilities are essential to provide stakeholders with valuable insights into the process environment and identify trends and key metrics. These capabilities empower leaders and other stakeholders with valuable insights:

- **Out-of-the-Box Reporting**: These platforms should offer a selection of out-of-the-box reporting options that provide immediate insights into process performance and operational trends. These predefined reports are designed to address common reporting needs and offer a quick overview of processes without requiring extensive customization.

- **Custom Reports**: In addition to out-of-the-box reporting, users need the ability to create custom reports tailored to their specific requirements. This feature allows users to design reports that highlight specific key performance indicators (KPIs), performance metrics, or process aspects that align with their unique use cases and business objectives to drive informed decisions.

Governance

Just as data management capabilities are critical for ensuring the quality of data in the Business Process Analysis platform, robust governance is needed to maintain the accuracy, consistency, and compliance of the models, especially the Process Inventory and process models, and associated metadata. These features are key to effective model management, providing the tools and mechanisms needed to rigorously maintain a controlled environment:

- **Quality Assurance**: Quality assurance is a crucial governance feature that ensures the accuracy, consistency, and reliability of models by performing automated checks to validate and verify that models conform to defined standards and best practices. These automated quality checks should occur in conjunction with human reviews.

- **Administration, Roles, and Entitlements**: Effective administration, role management, and entitlements are integral to maintaining a controlled and secure environment for the assets stored in this platform. At a minimum, there should be three distinct roles: viewer, contributor, and administrator. Viewers have read-only access and are typically granted to those who consume models, such as business and other functional stakeholders. Contributors are the teams responsible for creating, updating, and managing models. Administrators, typically part of the core Process Center of Excellence (COE) organization, oversee and maintain the platform. The platform should allow roles and permissions to be tailored to different deployment environments. Administrators can define user access levels, privileges, and responsibilities that align with their specific needs. This ensures that the right individuals have the appropriate access to support collaboration, data integrity, and compliance.

- **Environment Management**: Environment management involves orchestrating and overseeing various deployment environments, each serving distinct purposes within the process life cycle. These environments, which include sandbox, development, test, and production stages, are crucial for validating, refining, and executing processes before they are fully deployed. The specific objectives of each environment and the criteria for transitioning between them should be clearly defined. For instance, the sandbox environment should be relatively open for modelers to explore concepts, while the production environment should be reserved for models that have undergone thorough quality reviews and attestations and accurately represent the current operational state. Models for future state processes, created through a change initiative, should only be promoted to the main production environment once the change has been implemented. Effective environment management ensures that stakeholders have an environment to leverage that accurately reflects the real world and adheres to high-quality standards. This approach not only safeguards operational integrity but also supports the separation of duties and minimizes disruptions during the testing and optimization phases.

- **Workflow Management**: Workflow management is a governance feature that facilitates the coordination and monitoring of tasks and activities within quality assurance and attestation processes, which often entail multiple steps and involve numerous stakeholders. This feature encompasses automated email notifications sent to process participants and dashboards that offer leaders real-time visibility into the status of approval requests.

- **Audit Trail**: These platforms need to maintain an audit trail which captures changes to models across different environments but also a detailed list of quality approvers and owner attestations. This is critical in maintaining accountability and tracing approvals if quality issues are raised that must be traced to the source to perform root cause analysis.

- **Risk Management**: Some Business Process Analysis platforms integrate governance, risk management, and compliance (GRC) functionality, which enables organizations to track their risks and regulatory obligations and ensures the presence of effective controls. While integration with an external GRC tool can suffice, this feature can be valuable if your organization lacks or requires an upgrade to this risk management functionality.

User Experience

The experience these platforms provide to your users cannot be overlooked. If a platform offers superior functionality, but users struggle to use it, then broad adoption will suffer:

- **Persona-Centric User Experiences**: The requirements for using the platform will vary greatly across the roles of viewer, contributor, and administrator. The population of contributors and administrators will be relatively low, and their needs will be robust, necessitating a more technical experience that should be adequately supported by training. The population of viewers will be larger, encompassing numerous stakeholders within the organization who will access the model. Therefore, extensive training isn't feasible, making it crucial to provide a streamlined experience tailored to their specific needs. In my experience, I've observed one organization switch their platform to another vendor primarily due to the perceived subpar experience.

- **Mobile Access**: In today's dynamic business environment, enabling mobile access is imperative for maintaining productivity and connectivity on the go. Mobile access allows users to view models and data using their smartphones and tablets to review process documentation, participate in approval workflows, or access key insights.

- **User Training**: To ensure that users can effectively leverage the capabilities of the platform, integrated user training modules are critical. User training should provide guided tutorials, documentation, and best practice guidelines to familiarize users with the tool's functionalities. By offering resources within the platform, users can quickly learn how to navigate, create, and analyze process models, ultimately enhancing their proficiency and confidence.

Business Process Analysis Platform Selection and Setup

Selecting and implementing the right Business Process Analysis platform is a significant activity especially if they are committed to pursuing a Process Inventory strategy to achieve an ambitious digital and business vision. Leveraging a methodical approach to documenting the organization's short-term and long-term needs and performing a rigorous platform evaluation is crucial in selecting the right tool that will set up the program for success. Figure 10-3 illustrates a high-level approach, which I'll delve into to highlight key steps, best practices, and considerations needed to succeed.

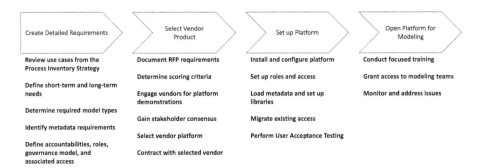

Figure 10-3. Platform Selection and Setup

Create Details Requirements

Creating detailed requirements for the chosen Business Process Analysis platform is a pivotal phase in ensuring alignment with the organization's digital strategy and the value-generating use cases identified through the Process Inventory strategy. This comprehensive set of requirements must encompass both immediate short-term objectives and a forward-looking vision for the platform's future needs. While my previous discussions have primarily focused on functional features, it's essential to recognize that technical considerations such as hosting options (vendor hosted cloud, internally hosted cloud, on-premises, etc.), data integration, and security also play a vital role in shaping these requirements.

The formulation of use cases, which articulate how the platform and models will contribute tangible business value, holds the key to determining the required model types and their structure. It even influences the specific data elements to be incorporated within the models. Use case requirements in the platform must be harmonized with the modeling standards and checklists crafted by the Process COE team to ensure a cohesive approach.

The process of defining metadata requirements involves active dialogue with the custodians of authoritative data sources. This interaction helps in comprehending the available data elements and gauging their quality. When encountering data of subpar quality, a critical decision must be made whether to omit such metadata even if use cases suggest their necessity. Such exclusions can be justified by the potential to maintain platform integrity and quality perceptions. Additionally, the collection of technical specifics is essential to shape data integration processes and routines for data quality validation.

Ultimately, the creation of an operating model design is important to outline the individuals responsible for model creation, utilization, and platform administration. This delineation significantly contributes to shaping access roles, entitlements, and privileges, thus establishing a robust governance framework. Through these meticulous steps, a well-defined set of requirements is forged, serving as the cornerstone for selecting and implementing the most suitable platform.

Select Vendor Product

Selecting the ideal vendor platform that aligns with your organization's unique needs requires engaging potential vendors to delve into their capabilities and future product vision. To initiate this process, crafting a well-defined request for proposal (RFP) is imperative. The RFP serves as the blueprint for your requirements, which is then distributed to potential vendors. This document guides vendors to showcase how their features fit with your needs.

Inviting vendors to present their platforms through product demonstrations is the subsequent step. This allows the evaluation team the opportunity to assess platform capabilities, gauge user experience, and seek clarifications directly from the vendors. A recommended practice is to provide vendors with high-priority use cases, which provide insights into the platform's functionality within scenarios integral to the organization's goals.

The evaluation process should be underpinned by well-documented selection criteria and a scoring mechanism. This ensures an objective assessment, enabling the identification of the best-fitting platform for your organization's needs. Given that this platform will serve various user groups, it's crucial to review recommendations with key stakeholder groups to address any concerns and gain consensus before proceeding with a selection.

While prioritizing features aligned with the Process Inventory strategy is vital, it's crucial to consider additional factors such as cost, vendor viability, and support during the selection process. Additionally, most vendors extend professional services to aid in platform installation and setup, a valuable resource particularly when the implementation team lacks detailed experience with the platform.

Setup Platform

Setting up the platform requires close collaboration with IT infrastructure teams for the installation and technical configurations. The administrator should oversee configurations that support the required model types and metadata libraries. The process includes loading libraries from their respective authoritative sources and importing existing models from previous tools to populate the platform with content.

Lastly, it's crucial to identify a subset of users who can test functionalities such as model creation, analysis, and report generation. This testing phase allows for the identification and resolution of any issues before deploying the platform to a broader user base.

Open Platform for Modeling

Before the full release, arrange training sessions that focus on key features and functionalities for a selected group of initial users and stakeholders. Once access is granted, administrators should be prepared to offer ongoing support to assist users in addressing issues and navigating their tasks.

Key Takeaways

- **Business Process Analysis platforms are critical** to manage the Process Inventory framework, associated models, and supporting metadata to deliver digital transformation and operational excellence goals.

- **An established market exists** that contains vendor platforms that have mature features that can enable success with the Process Inventory framework.

- **A methodical approach** is needed to select the right platform, involving documenting requirements, evaluating platform capabilities, and setting up the platform for modeling.

R

References

Chapter 1—The Key to Digital Transformation Success

1. Nokia Wikipedia https://en.wikipedia.org/wiki/Nokia

2. Why did Nokia fail and what can you learn from it? https://medium.com/multiplier-magazine/why-did-nokia-fail-81110d981787

3. Distributed Attention and Shared Emotions in the Innovation Process: How Nokia Lost the Smartphone Battle https://mycourses.aalto.fi/pluginfile.php/898294/mod_folder/content/0/VuoriHuy.pdf

4. Creative Destruction https://en.wikipedia.org/wiki/Creative_destruction

5. Creative Destruction vs Disruptive Innovation www.the-waves.org/2020/06/27/creative-destruction-vs-disruptive-innovation/

6. Digital Transformation https://en.wikipedia.org/wiki/Digital_transformation

7. The Essential Components of Digital Transformation https://hbr.org/2021/11/the-essential-components-of-digital-transformation

© Michael Schank 2023
M. Schank, *Digital Transformation Success*,
https://doi.org/10.1007/978-1-4842-9816-9

8. Flipping the Odds of Digital Transformation Success `www.bcg.com/publications/2020/increasing-odds-of-success-in-digital-transformation`

9. Digital Transformation Market by Offering (Solutions & Services), Technology (Cloud Computing, Big Data & Analytics, Blockchain, Cybersecurity, AI), Business Function (Accounting & Finance, IT, HR), Vertical,& Region - Global Forecast to 2030 `www.researchandmarkets.com/reports/5136097/digital-transformation-market-by-component?utm_source=GNOM&utm_medium=PressRelease&utm_code=j2bzdn&utm_campaign=1426023+-+The+World%27s+Digital+Transformation+Industry+2020-2025%3a+Trends%2c+Opportunities+and+Competitive+Landscape&utm_exec=joca220prd`

10. Forbes 100 Stats On Digital Transformation And Customer Experience `www.forbes.com/sites/blakemorgan/2019/12/16/100-stats-on-digital-transformation-and-customer-experience/?sh=70c8c9bf3bf3`

11. Perspectives on transformation `www.mckinsey.com/capabilities/transformation/our-insights/perspectives-on-transformation`

12. A Simple Way to Test Your Company's Strategic Alignment `https://hbr.org/2016/05/a-simple-way-to-test-your-companys-strategic-alignment?registration=success`

13. How Google Builds Its Maps—and What It Means for the Future of Everything `www.theatlantic.com/technology/archive/2012/09/how-google-builds-its-maps-and-what-it-means-for-the-future-of-everything/261913/`

Chapter 2—Overview of the Process Inventory Framework

1. History of business architecture `https://en.wikipedia.org/wiki/History_of_business_architecture#cite_note-EET_1986-9`

2. Business Capability Model `https://en.wikipedia.org/wiki/Business_capability_model`

3. Ontology https://en.wikipedia.org/wiki/Ontology

4. A Translation Approach to Portable Ontology Specifications https://tomgruber.org/writing/ontolingua-kaj-1993.pdf

5. Shadow IT https://en.wikipedia.org/wiki/Shadow_IT

6. Process Mining https://en.wikipedia.org/wiki/Process_mining#cite_note-4

7. Omnichannel https://en.wikipedia.org/wiki/Omnichannel

8. Business Process and Modeling Notation www.omg.org/spec/BPMN/2.0/PDF

9. Voice of The Employee Can Cure Broken Customer Experiences, But You Need An Effective Program to Mine It www.forrester.com/blogs/15-01-25-voice_of_the_employee_can_cure_broken_customer_experiences_but_you_need_an_effective_program_to_mine_it/

Chapter 3—Defining the Digital Transformation Program

1. John Deere https://en.wikipedia.org/wiki/John_Deere#Finances

2. John Deere unveils fully autonomous 8R tractor www.agriculture.com/news/technology/john-deere-unveils-fully-autonomous-8r-tractor

3. John Deere: Planting the Digital Seeds of Change www.intelligentautomation.network/transformation/articles/john-deere-planting-the-digital-seeds-of-change

4. What do Starbucks, Tesla, and John Deere have in common? They've used A.I. to reinvent their businesses https://fortune.com/2022/04/01/ai-artificial-intelligence-starbucks-tesla-reinvention/

5. Near real-time monitoring headlines John Deere Digital Ecosystem Update www.deere.com.au/en/news/all-news/technology-seeds-logistical-improvements/

6. John Deere to Deploy 5G in Manufacturing Facilities `www.forconstructionpros.com/construction-technology/article/21203330/john-deere-john-deere-to-deploy-5g-in-manufacturing-facilities`

7. Tami Hedgren explains how digital transformation is leading a manufacturing revolution. `www.deere.com/en/stories/featured/tami-hedgren-explains-digital-transformation/`

8. E-Commerce Trends 2022: What The Future Holds `www.forbes.com/sites/forbestechcouncil/2022/03/14/e-commerce-trends-2022-what-the-future-holds/?sh=2aeffb5158da`

9. The Growth Of Subscription Commerce `www.forbes.com/sites/jiawertz/2022/07/15/the-growth-of-subscription-commerce/?sh=291190e3b572`

10. Platform business models: A primer `www.cio.com/article/236399/platform-business-models-a-primer.html`

11. Democratizing Transformation `https://hbr.org/2022/05/democratizing-transformation`

12. Open Innovation: definition and explanation `https://oxford-review.com/oxford-review-encyclopaedia-terms/encyclopaedia-open-innovation-definition-explanation/`

13. Bricks & Code: Open Innovation at LEGO Group `https://d3.harvard.edu/platform-rctom/submission/bricks-code-open-innovation-at-lego-group/`

14. Lego Ideas `https://ideas.lego.com/`

15. The strategy that makes 3M an innovation powerhouse `https://thestrategystory.com/2021/05/27/3m-innovation-strategy/`

16. How the 15% Rule Became a Stepping Stone for 3M's Innovation `https://marketrealist.com/2016/06/15-rule-became-stepping-stone-3ms-innovation/`

17. Why Customer Centricity Is A Key To Long-Term Success `www.forbes.com/sites/forbesbusinesscouncil/2023/07/18/why-customer-centricity-is-a-key-to-long-term-success/?sh=39552d3d7f64`

18. The What, Why & How of the 360-Degree Customer View `https://digitalmarketinginstitute.com/blog/the-what-why-and-how-of-360-degree-customer-view`

19. 10 Customer Experience Lessons From Tesla `www.forbes.com/sites/blakemorgan/2019/02/06/10-customer-experience-lessons-from-tesla/?sh=67436d056347`

20. Lululemon calls its ideal customers "Ocean" and "Duke"—here's everything we know about them `www.businessinsider.com/lululemon-idea-customers-ocean-and-duke-2015-2?op=1`

21. Nike Zones In on Consumer Engagement With Digital Approach: How Mobile Apps Drive Value and Membership Growth `https://consumergoods.com/nike-zones-consumer-engagement-digital-approach-how-mobile-apps-drive-value-and-membership-growth`

22. Nike Annual Profits Soar 196%, Best In Company History `www.forbes.com/sites/shelleykohan/2021/06/24/nike-profits-soar-196-best-in-company-history/?sh=1762f712500e`

23. 54 Predictions About The State Of Data In 2021 `www.forbes.com/sites/gilpress/2021/12/30/54-predictions-about-the-state-of-data-in-2021/?sh=abb6778397d3`

24. AI is embedded everywhere at Walmart `https://venturebeat.com/ai/ai-is-embedded-everywhere-at-walmart/`

25. Data Exhaust Turbocharges Mastercard `www.forbes.com/sites/tomdavenport/2021/01/13/data-exhaust-turbocharges-mastercard/?sh=47ceec8687df`

26. Understanding Digital Strategy `https://hbr.org/podcast/2018/08/understanding-digital-strategy`

27. PESTEL Framework: The 6 Elements of a PESTEL Analysis `www.masterclass.com/articles/pestel-framework`

28. How to Use Porter's Five Forces Analysis to Create a Business Strategy `www.masterclass.com/articles/how-to-use-porters-five-forces-analysis-to-create-a-business-strategy`

29. The Five Rules of Digital Strategy www.bcg.com/publi-cations/2019/five-rules-digital-strategy

30. Digital Strategy Roadmap www.bcg.com/capabilities/digital-technology-data/digital-strat-egy-roadmap

31. The Chief Transformation Officer www.brightline.org/resources/the-chief-transformation-officer/

Chapter 4—Driving Operational Excellence

1. The Toyota Way, Second Edition: 14 Management Principles from the World's Greatest Manufacturer www.amazon.com/Toyota-Way-Second-Management-Manu-facturer-ebook/dp/B088P46Q9P/ref=tmm_kin_swatch_0?_encoding=UTF8&qid=1692974013&sr=8-1

2. Toyota https://en.wikipedia.org/wiki/Toyota

3. The 'law' that explains why you can't get anything done www.bbc.com/worklife/article/20191107-the-law-that-explains-why-you-cant-get-any-thing-done

4. Two-factor theory https://en.wikipedia.org/wiki/Two-factor_theory

5. Lean Six Sigma https://en.wikipedia.org/wiki/Lean_Six_Sigma

6. Lean Six Sigma for Dummies, 4th Edition www.amazon.com/Lean-Six-Sigma-Dummies-4th/dp/B09N9ZZTN3/ref=sr_1_1?crid=JBRA7MST3GE6&keywords=lean+six+sigma+for+dummies&qid=1693247448&sprefix=%2Caps%2C97&sr=8-1

7. The origins of Lean Six Sigma www.quality.org/knowl-edge/origins-lean-six-sigma

8. Diffusion of responsibility https://en.wikipedia.org/wiki/Diffusion_of_responsibility

9. Digital Twin https://en.wikipedia.org/wiki/Digital_twin

Chapter 5—Transform the Change Process

1. How five brands learned from digital transformation failure www.raconteur.net/digital/digital-transformation-failure/

2. BBC Digital Media Initiative Review of the BBC's management of DMI https://downloads.bbc.co.uk/bbc-trust/assets/files/pdf/review_report_research/vfm/dmi/pwc_dmi.pdf

3. Systems development life cycle https://en.wikipedia.org/wiki/Systems_development_life_cycle

4. Waterfall model https://en.wikipedia.org/wiki/Waterfall_model

5. Agile software development https://en.wikipedia.org/wiki/Agile_software_development

6. Organisational Change Management (OCM): What is it and when should we start? www.linkedin.com/pulse/organisational-change-management-ocm-what-when-should-we-/

7. Project management https://en.wikipedia.org/wiki/Project_management

8. Success in Disruptive Times Expanding the Value Delivery Landscape to Address the High Cost of Low Performance www.pmi.org/-/media/pmi/documents/public/pdf/learning/thought-leadership/pulse/pulse-of-the-profession-2018.pdf

9. 14 Common Reasons Software Projects Fail (And How To Avoid Them) www.forbes.com/sites/forbestechcouncil/2020/03/31/14-common-reasons-software-projects-fail-and-how-to-avoid-them/?sh=115b079f798c

10. Strategic planning https://en.wikipedia.org/wiki/Strategic_planning

11. PMI 2021 Pulse of the Profession® Report www.pmi.org/-/media/pmi/documents/public/pdf/learning/thought-leadership/pulse/pmi-pulse-2021-appendix.pdf?v=fef7116b-b3d6-4c8e-a274-4ac5db30c48e

12. What Is the Cost of a Requirement Error? `www.sticky-minds.com/article/what-cost-requirement-error`

13. Do developers benefit from requirements traceability when evolving and maintaining a software system? `https://link.springer.com/article/10.1007/s10664-014-9314-z`

14. The science behind transformations: Sustaining value after implementation `www.mckinsey.com/capabilities/people-and-organizational-performance/our-insights/the-organization-blog/the-science-behind-transformations-sustaining-value-after-implementation`

15. How Southwest Airlines' Culture Fuels its Success `https://topicinsights.com/leadership-management/southwest-airlines-culture/`

16. The High Cost of Low Performance `www.pmi.org/-/media/pmi/documents/public/pdf/learning/thought-leadership/pulse/pulse-of-the-profession-2016`

Chapter 6—The Technology Path to Digitization

1. Netflix, Inc. `https://en.wikipedia.org/wiki/Netflix,_Inc.`

2. This is how Netflix's top-secret recommendation system works `www.wired.co.uk/article/how-do-netflixs-algorithms-work-machine-learning-helps-to-predict-what-viewers-will-like`

3. Understanding design of microservices architecture at Netflix `www.techaheadcorp.com/blog/design-of-microservices-architecture-at-netflix/`

4. Netflix Subscriber and Growth Statistics `https://backlinko.com/netflix-users`

5. The State of Process Automation `https://camunda.com/wp-content/uploads/2020/10/Camunda-State-Of-Process-Automation.pdf`

6. The imperatives for automation success www.mckinsey. com/capabilities/operations/our-insights/the-imperatives-for-automation-success

7. Worldwide intelligent process automation market from 2020 to 2024 www.statista.com/statistics/1231589/ worldwide-intelligent-process-automa-tion-market/

8. Five design principles to help build confidence in RPA implementations www.ey.com/en_us/consulting/ five-design-principles-to-help-build-confi-dence-in-rpa-implement

9. Machine learning https://en.wikipedia.org/wiki/ Machine_learning

10. The economic potential of generative AI: The next pro-ductivity frontier www.mckinsey.com/capabilities/ mckinsey-digital/our-insights/the-economic-potential-of-generative-AI-the-next-produc-tivity-frontier#/

11. How to Scale AI in Your Organization https://hbr. org/2022/03/how-to-scale-ai-in-your-organization

12. Why it's time for 'data-centric artificial intelligence' https://mitsloan.mit.edu/ideas-made-to-matter/ why-its-time-data-centric-artificial-intelligence

13. How ChatGPT and Other LLMs Work—and Where They Could Go Next www.wired.com/story/how-chatgpt-works-large-language-model/

14. A Chat with Andrew on MLOps: From Model-centric to Data-centric AI www.youtube.com/watch?v=06-AZXmwHjo

15. Poor-Quality Data Imposes Costs and Risks on Busi-nesses, Says New Forbes Insights Report www.forbes. com/sites/forbespr/2017/05/31/poor-quality-data-imposes-costs-and-risks-on-businesses-says-new-forbes-insights-report/?sh=65957e5e452b

16. Choose Adaptive Data Governance Over One-Size-Fits-All for Greater Flexibility www.gartner.com/en/articles/choose-adaptive-data-governance-over-one-size-fits-all-for-greater-flexibility?_its=JTdCJTIydmlkJTIyJTNBJTIyY2UyY2JkZmYtMTI0N-SOOYjk1LTlmMjMtZTk0MjZlYzFkZTM1JTIyJTJDJTI-yc3RhdGUlMjIlMOElMjJybHR%2BMTY4ODA3N-TgyM35sYW5kfjJfMTYONjVfc2VvX2YOODBkMTFlNjMwN-WExMzUyYzQ3YzViOTI3OTM2ZjI1JTIyJTJDJTI-yc2loZUlkJTIyJTNBNDAxMzElNOQ%3D

17. The CEO's Guide to the Generative AI Revolution www.bcg.com/publications/2023/ceo-guide-to-ai-revolution

18. Microservices https://aws.amazon.com/microservices/

19. The Story of Netflix and Microservices www.geeksfor-geeks.org/the-story-of-netflix-and-microservices/

20. How Amazon handles a new software deployment every second www.zdnet.com/article/how-amazon-handles-a-new-software-deployment-every-second/

21. New Research Shows 63% of Enterprises Are Adopting Microservices Architectures https://dzone.com/articles/new-research-shows-63-percent-of-enterprises-are-a

22. What is enterprise architecture? A framework for trans-formation www.cio.com/article/222421/what-is-enterprise-architecture-a-framework-for-transformation.html

23. Tech debt: Reclaiming tech equity www.mckinsey.com/capabilities/mckinsey-digital/our-insights/tech-debt-reclaiming-tech-equity

24. The Open Group Architecture Framework https://en.wikipedia.org/wiki/The_Open_Group_Archi-tecture_Framework

Chapter 7—Strengthening Risk Management

1. Deepwater Horizon https://en.wikipedia.org/wiki/ Deepwater_Horizon

2. Ten years after Deepwater disaster, scientists and activists worry no lessons have been learned www.nbcnews. com/science/science-news/ten-years-after- deepwater-disaster-scientists-activists- worry-no-lessons-n1187741

3. Deepwater Horizon oil spill settlements: Where the money went www.noaa.gov/explainers/deepwater- horizon-oil-spill-settlements-where- money-went

4. Deepwater Horizon litigation https://en.wikipedia. org/wiki/Deepwater_Horizon_litigation

5. BP Deepwater Horizon costs balloon to $65 billion www. reuters.com/article/us-bp-deepwaterhorizon- iduskbn1f50nl

6. Deepwater Horizon oil spill www.britannica.com/ event/Deepwater-Horizon-oil-spill

7. Deepwater Horizon Accident Investigation Report www. bp.com/content/dam/bp/business-sites/en/global/ corporate/pdfs/sustainability/issue-briefings/ deepwater-horizon-accident-investigation- report-executive-summary.pdf

8. How Regulations at Every Level Hold Back Small Business www.uschamber.com/small-business/how-regulations- every-level-hold-back-small-business

9. Reimagine risk: Thrive in your evolving ecosystem www2. deloitte.com/us/en/insights/topics/risk- management/cro-risk-management-survey- results.html

10. The Important Work of Boards of Directors www.sec. gov/news/speech/important-work-boards- directors

11. Enterprise risk management https://en.wikipedia. org/wiki/Enterprise_risk_management#cite_ note-COSO_Summary-5

12. 2020 Enterprise Risk Management Benchmark Survey www.tamus.edu/business/wp-content/uploads/sites/20/2021/06/2021-ERM_Benchmark_Survey.pdf

13. The Failure of Risk Management: Why It's Broken and How to Fix It www.amazon.com/Failure-Risk-Management-Why-Broken/dp/111952203X/ref=sr_1_1?crid=VA8QK3KD52A2&keywords=the+failure+of+risk+management&qid=1694529360&sprefix=the+failure+of+risk+%2Caps%2C95&sr=8-1

14. Cadbury Report https://en.wikipedia.org/wiki/Cadbury_Report

15. Turnbull Report https://en.wikipedia.org/wiki/Turnbull_Report

16. EY Global Board Risk Survey www.ey.com/en_us/global-board-risk-survey

17. Wikipedia 2007–2008 financial crisis https://en.wikipedia.org/wiki/2007%E2%80%932008_financial_crisis#cite_note-newcentury-89

18. Poor-Quality Data Imposes Costs and Risks on Businesses, Says New Forbes Insights Report www.forbes.com/sites/forbespr/2017/05/31/poor-quality-data-imposes-costs-and-risks-on-businesses-says-new-forbes-insights-report/?sh=5e22df20452b

19. United States of America Department of the Treasury Office of the Comptroller of the Currency www.occ.gov/static/enforcement-actions/ea2020-056.pdf

20. Deloitte Insights Global Risk Management Survey, 12th Edition www2.deloitte.com/content/dam/insights/articles/US103959_Global-risk-management-survey-12ed/DI_Global-risk-management-survey-12ed.pdf

21. Enterprise Governance, Risk And Compliance Market Worth $134.86 Billion By 2030 www.grandviewresearch.com/press-release/global-enterprise-governance-risk-compliance-egrc-market

22. The London Whale: what can we learn from JP Morgan's $6bn loss? https://flowandebb.com/insights/learning-from-the-london-whale/

23. Sound Practices for the Management and Supervision of Operational Risk www.bis.org/publ/bcbs96.pdf

24. The Orange Book Management of Risk – Principles and Concepts https://assets.publishing.service.gov.uk/government/uploads/system/uploads/attachment_data/file/1154709/HMT_Orange_Book_May_2023.pdf

25. The roles of the board and chief risk officer in risk governance www2.deloitte.com/us/en/pages/advisory/articles/board-and-chief-risk-officer-reimagine-risk-governance.html

26. Why it's time for 'data-centric artificial intelligence' https://mitsloan.mit.edu/ideas-made-to-matter/why-its-time-data-centric-artificial-intelligence

27. Risk Intelligence: Learning to Manage What We Don't Know www.amazon.com/Risk-Intelligence-Learning-Manage-What-ebook/dp/B002BDU1JY/ref=tmm_kin_swatch_0?_encoding=UTF8&qid=&sr=

28. Dynamic, Integrated Risk Assessments for a New Era https://deloitte.wsj.com/articles/dynamic-integrated-risk-assessments-for-a-new-era-01646690239

29. 2021 Texas power crisis https://en.wikipedia.org/wiki/2021_Texas_power_crisis

30. Report: More than 456.5K Claims Filed in Texas After Winter Storm www.insurancejournal.com/news/southcentral/2021/09/24/633569.htm

Chapter 8—The Process Inventory Accountability Model

1. Spotify https://en.wikipedia.org/wiki/Spotify

2. Spotify's Organizational Culture & Strategic Considerations www.rancord.org/spotify-organizational-culture-strategic-cultural-characteristics

3. America's Most Loved Workplaces 2021 www.newsweek.com/americas-most-loved-workplaces-2021

4. Here at Spotify, we like to think of ourselves as a band `www.lifeatspotify.com/being-here/the-band-manifesto`

5. How Spotify Balances Employee Autonomy and Accountability `https://hbr.org/2017/02/how-spotify-balances-employee-autonomy-and-accountability`

6. Re-Engineering Performance Management `www.gallup.com/workplace/238064/re-engineering-performance-management.aspx?thank-you-report-form=1`

7. Data steward `https://en.wikipedia.org/wiki/Data_steward`

8. How the operating model can unlock the full power of customer experience `www.mckinsey.com/capabilities/growth-marketing-and-sales/our-insights/how-the-operating-model-can-unlock-the-full-power-of-customer-experience`

Chapter 9—Process Methods and Modeling Rules

1. Digital Supply Chain and Innovation at Unilever `www.cxotalk.com/episode/digital-supply-chain-innovation-unilever`

2. Unilever's 'Groundbreaking' Supply Chain Investments Lean Into AI and Geolocation `https://consumergoods.com/unilevers-groundbreaking-supply-chain-investments-lean-ai-and-geolocation`

3. Now it's personal: Unilever's digital journey leads to real results for consumers and employees `https://news.microsoft.com/source/features/digital-transformation/now-its-personal-unilevers-digital-journey-leads-to-real-results-for-consumers-and-employees/`

4. Unilever Uses Virtual Factories to Tune Up Its Supply Chain `www.wsj.com/articles/unilever-uses-virtual-factories-to-tune-up-its-supply-chain-11563206402`

Chapter 10—Modeling Platform and Data Infrastructure

1. How FedEx Dataworks is using analytics, AI to fortify supply chains https://venturebeat.com/enterprise-analytics/how-fedex-dataworks-is-using-ana-lytics-ai-to-fortify-supply-chains/

2. FedEx Works To Monetize Their Big Data www.forbes.com/sites/stevebanker/2022/01/20/fedex-works-to-monetize-their-big-data/?sh=6c069307277d

3. FedEx Surround: a platform to digitize supply chain data https://trans.info/fedex-surround-a-platform-to-digitize-supply-chain-data-186688

4. Real-time tracking with FedEx SenseAware www.fedex.com/en-us/senseaware.html

5. Avolution ABACUS www.avolutionsoftware.com/abacus/

6. Bizzdesign Horizzon https://bizzdesign.com/plat-form/platform-overview/

7. iGrafx www.igrafx.com/products/

8. MEGA HOPEX Platform www.mega.com/hopex-platform

9. ORBUS www.orbussoftware.com/solutions

10. SAP Signavio Process Transformation Suite www.sig-navio.com/products/process-transforma-tion-suite/

11. Software AG www.softwareag.com/en_corporate/platform/aris.html

I

Index

© Michael Schank 2023
M. Schank, *Digital Transformation Success*,
https://doi.org/10.1007/978-1-4842-9816-9